MW01003069

Religion and culture

Religion and culture
Michel Foucault

selected and edited by Jeremy R. Carrette

Routledge

New York

Copyright © Jeremy R. Carrette 1999

While copyright of the volume as a whole and of all editorial matter is vested in Jeremy Carrette, copyright of all other material belongs to the respective authors, translators and institutions as acknowledged, and no editorial or documentary material may be reproduced wholly or in part without the express permission in writing of both author and publisher.

All rights reserved

First published in the USA in 1999 by
Routledge Inc
29 West 35th Street, New York
NY 10001-2299, USA
www.routledge-ny.com

Routledge edition published by special arrangement with
Manchester University Press
Oxford Road, Manchester M13 9NR, UK

Library of Congress Cataloging-in-Publication Data
Foucault, Michel
     Religion and culture / by Michel Foucault : selected and edited by
  Jeremy R. Carrette
        p.   cm.
     Includes bibliographical references and index.
     ISBN 0-415-92361-1 — ISBN 0-415-92362-X (pbk.)
     1. Religion and culture. I. Carrette, Jeremy R. II. Title.
  BL65.C8F69   1999
  291.17—dc21   99-30803

ISBN 0 415 92361 1 *hardback*
     0 415 92362 X *paperback*

Typeset in Joanna with Frutiger Light Display
by Koinonia, Manchester

Printed in Great Britain
by Biddles Ltd, Guildford and King's Lynn

Gather up the fragments that remain, so that nothing be lost.

JOHN 6:12

CONTENTS

It is not that religion is delusional by nature, nor that the individual, beyond present-day religion, rediscovers his most suspect psychological origins. But religious delusion is a function of the secularization of culture: religion may be the object of delusional belief insofar as the culture of a group no longer permits the assimilation of religious or mystical beliefs in the present context of experience.

Michel Foucault [1962], *Mental Illness and Psychology*,
University of California Press, Berkeley, 1976, p. 81

Cry of spirit

James Bernauer SJ

When Michel Foucault died, I mourned the silencing of a voice which had articulated such intense and necessary questions for me, first in his texts, then in his lectures and finally in several personal exchanges. What I had not anticipated on that sad June day in 1984 was the eloquent survival of that voice in the community of those many who have been drawn into dialogue as a result of dealing with Foucault's questions. For me it has been a personal as well as an intellectual pleasure to be in conversation with other readers of Foucault, men and women, in and outside of academic institutions. Jeremy Carrette is an exciting new interlocutor in those Foucauldian circles, as his essay at the beginning of this book makes very clear. While I was honoured by the invitation to write a foreword to his selection of Foucault's texts, I was reminded once again of how students of Foucault so often challenge one another to risk the exploration of new terrain rather than just report their knowledge of the already mapped. Certainly, Dr Carrette's request has directed me to a place which, I recognise now, desired more scrutiny.

His theme of Foucault's relationship to religion has jolted me back into a discarded personal moment which joined satisfaction and stress in equal measure. While I was writing the conclusion to my book *Michel Foucault's Force of Flight: Toward an Ethics for Thought*, after almost a decade of study, I found myself typing these final sentences:

Perhaps, as has been charged, his thought is 'not a shout of joy'. But, it should be asked, when did that become the standard for evaluating a thinker? As far as Foucault's work is concerned, we will have to be satisfied with hearing a voice that suffered with some of the victims, not only those of obvious captivities but also of modern liberties and their programs. It was a thought that struggled impatiently for new practices of freedom. Ultimately, it was a cry of spirit.[1]

That last sentence had not been in any of the drafts from which I worked and seemed to come out of nowhere; it sounded inappropriate in the context and, to my ear, did not echo the Foucauldian ethical accent which my book had tried to capture. I had taken pride in trying to do a reading of Foucault's works which aimed at accurate rendition over imaginative interpretation. What is this 'cry of spirit'? I wanted to eliminate the sentence and perhaps even the 'shout of joy' to which 'cry' rhetorically

---

[1] J. Bernauer, *Michel Foucault's Force of Flight: Toward an Ethics for Thought*, Humanities Press, Atlantic Highlands, New Jersey, 1990, p. 184.

responded and end the book with the very Foucauldian 'new practices of freedom'. But 'spirit' said something I wanted to say even if I could not have told you why. I had the feeling that there was something deeply accurate in the phrase and so it stayed and I hoped that no reviewer would make too much of a fuss over it. Dr Carrette's invitation has led me back to my affirmation that Foucault's thought was ultimately a cry of spirit and I must thank him for doing so. I hope that I will not weary the reader in indicating here why I believe it to be appropriate then and now.

Certainly I was acknowledging a personal sense of Foucault's fullness of presence. I had first encountered Foucault in a reading of *Madness and Civilization* while I was on a long train trip to New York City. By the time of arrival I knew I was caught, intrigued by a mind, perhaps even hooked by a problematic. That led me to a lengthy stay in Paris where I was able to follow his courses in 1979 and 1980 and, later, his 1982 summer course in Toronto. Because of his characteristic solicitude for students, I also had the opportunity for several conversations with him. As a consequence, well before his biographies appeared, I did not need to 'hallucinate' Foucault, to use the word of a recent novel which integrated him into its plot. I felt privileged to have encountered a full spiritual presence: yes, the intellectual power which could intimidate at times, but also the emotional presence, a sense of humour, an interest in others, and a deep compassion for people especially those whom life turns into victims. That compassion may be touched in his books and interviews but it was also in his conversations. For example, I recall his intense concern with Poland's Solidarity movement but also his special curiosity about an undergraduate programme in which I teach that has students make a very strenuous commitment to some form of social service (working in a homeless shelter, or a prison, or a hospice for the dying among others) while working through their philosophy and theology readings. He was keen to know about the course's structure, and seemed pleased that it was not the social sciences which would provide the integrating perspective for the students' experience. For me, 'cry of spirit' alluded to that legendary compassion and the unity of his philosophical life with the worldly experiences out of which his wisdom came, so different from mere academic brilliance.

As a Jesuit priest, I have often been met by surprise, occasionally hostility, when it is discovered that I am a respectful student of Foucault's philosophy. 'Why should a priest be concerned with that style of thought?' 'Wouldn't it be more fruitful to be involved with a thinker engaged with, or at least open to, the religious rather than one identified with themes of madness, imprisonment and sexuality?' I am sure that 'cry of spirit' was in part a reply to that narrow-mindedness which my area of research sometimes forced me to confront. Fortunately, I had many teachers through the years who had shown that philosophers who are also priests were stimulated, by that very commitment, to become adventuresome in thinking rather than assume guard duty for some ancient treasure. Less personally, my book's final sentence indicated the importance which I attached to the experience of flight or escape in his work. That theme gave the title to the book and structured Foucault's diverse investigations for me: first, an intellectual release from his earliest commitment to psychology as a human science; then his cathartic flight from the anthropological foundations for the modern human sciences; third, his effort to place before the mind a constantly sounding dissonance, disruptive of our passion for historical harmony and continuity; next the dissident thinking he embraced as a way of freeing himself from the political programmes and creeds of both Marxism and liberalism; finally, his ecstatic thinking which witnesses to an ethical liberation from the project of modern humanism. While I am encouraged in my interpretation of Foucault by Dr Carrette's support for my description of Foucault's escapes as a form of negative theology, I believe that even the most a-theological of Foucault's readers would find it impossible not to see how distinctive was his effort to escape identities. He claimed he wrote in order to have no face, and certainly his readers will not forget their reaction to a special, strange ambition which expressed itself in lines such as these: 'Do not ask who I am and do not ask me to remain the same: leave it to our bureaucrats and our police to see that our papers are in order. At least spare us their morality when we write.'[2]

Certainly, Foucault is denouncing a type of academic morality but he is also, I now see, forging a spirituality. He once spoke of a 'world without a spirit', and I have come to understand how extensive that 'world without a spirit' was for him. I am tempted to claim that the single most important phrase in Foucault's writing is 'l'âme, prison du corps', 'the soul is the prison of the body'.[3] If the principal streams of both Western and Eastern spiritualities have been to see a dualism between body and soul and to put forward an asceticism for liberating the soul from the body, Foucault envisions a dramatically different task: creating an alienation from one's soul, from how one's interior state and meaningful story have been constructed. Through his eyes, the very process of that soul taking on positive content in the human sciences turned it into something lifeless, ghostly and relating to it as one's centre established a phantom life and, thus, the greatest of human losses: not of one's world, but of one's spirit. Foucault presents a necessary spiritual art, a duty of self-relation, of going beyond how we have been created to experience ourselves as animated. He looked widely for anticipations of and traditional insights into this art. Biographers have told of how Foucault's examination of ancient and Christian texts as well as his dissatisfaction with the working conditions at the Bibliothèque Nationale led him to occupy the quiet reading room of the Dominican library of Saulchoir in Paris. At one point, however, he did take a look at the Jesuit Library of Centre Sèvres, to which I escorted him one afternoon. I remember that when we came to the first section of books, which a sign announced as 'dogmatic theology', he joked that this was not his place and rushed towards the section farther down the long room as his goal: moral theology. I mention the incident because this volume's texts show once again the depth of Foucault's interest in the practices rather than the theories of the moral and spiritual life. While his studies on Greek, Roman and Christian practices of the self exhibit the scholarly concerns of his last years, interviews such as the one on Zen included in this volume testify to his personal engagement.

[2] Michel Foucault, *The Archaeology of Knowledge*, Harper Colophon, New York, 1976, p. 17 (British edition: Routledge, London, 1989).

[3] Michel Foucault, *Surveiller et punir: naissance de la prison*, Gallimard, Paris, 1975, p. 34; *Discipline and Punish*, Pantheon, New York, 1977, p. 30 (British edition: Penguin, London, 1991).

I would argue that Foucault's own intellectual practice at this final stage is closer to the specific style of early Christian practice of the self than it is to the pagan. The ambition of his practice was not to strengthen the soul or confirm it in its truth but rather to renounce it, to transgress its borders, to reinvent one's relationship to it. His friend and patron Georges Dumézil emphasised in his posthumous tribute this most distinctive feature in Foucault's intellectual style: 'Foucault's intelligence literally knew no bounds, even sophisticated ones. He set up his observatory on the regions of living being where the traditional distinctions between body and soul, between instinct and idea, seem absurd: madness, sexuality, and crime.'[4] These transgressions of traditional boundaries should be taken literally as, for example, when Foucault, in speaking about Zen, talks about the 'new relationships which can exist between the mind and the body'.[5] For a modern culture, sustained as well as imprisoned by psychology and anthropology, Foucault came to esteem and utilise a Christian style of liberty which combined a care of the self with a sacrifice and mortification of that self. I knew, from his 1980 course at the Collège de France, 'The governance of the living', and even more clearly from his 1982 summer course, 'The discourse of self-disclosure', that Foucault was fascinated with Christianity's earliest form of penance: the public manifestation to a congregation of oneself as sinner and the dramatic renunciation of that dead soul. He was drawn to the paradox of a self-revelation that was also a self-destruction. His regard for that paradox increased even more his distance from the modern obligation to identify with that self which was fashioned by positive truths of self-knowledge. His cry of spirit is precisely an effective resistance to the prison for the human spirit today, not the body but the soul as fundamental personal truth and ground for self-relation. Self-possession is abandoned to a breath of life, a spirit in a spiritless, soul-filled world. His cry of spirit was commitment to passionate redefining of our relationship to the fruits of human intellect and discipline.

This Foucauldian spirituality of critical enlightenment had several stages in its evolution but I do think that it was his original project of a history of sexuality which fully opened this domain to him. Already in 1962 Foucault sensed that 'never did sexuality enjoy a more immediately natural understanding and never did it know a greater "felicity of expression" than in the Christian world of fallen bodies and of sin'.[6] This region of spirit–soul struggles must have presented itself much more sharply as Foucault worked on the projected second volume of his series, which was to be entitled *Flesh and Body* (*La chair et le corps*) and was to have contrasted the modern biological concept of the body with the traditional Christian notion of the flesh. Although that volume was abandoned, I believe that we are able to appreciate the legacy of its research in the accents of Foucault's grasp of spiritual struggle and its vision of philosophical life. In exploring flesh, he would have come face to face with

---

[4] 'Un homme heureux', *Le Nouvel Observateur*, 29 June 1984. Cited in Didier Eribon, *Michel Foucault*, Harvard University Press, Cambridge, Massachusetts, 1991, p. 329 (British edition: Faber & Faber, London, 1992).

[5] 'Michel Foucault et le zen: un séjour dans un temple zen' in *Michel Foucault, Dits et écrits, 1954–1988*, vol. III, Gallimard, Paris, 1994, p. 621; 'Michel Foucault and Zen: a stay in a Zen temple', in this volume, p. 112.

[6] Michel Foucault, 'A preface to transgression' in this volume, p. 57.

an arena for self-relationship very different from the body–soul dichotomy. The Pauline flesh was not a body but rather an entire way of existing, an embrace of the carceral and slavish in contrast to that freedom of spirit discovered in living as children of God. Foucault's reading of Ambrose, Augustine and Jerome would have brought him into the combat of lives lived according to the flesh or the spirit. We might imagine Foucault nodding assent to Peter Brown's judgement about the historical significance of the struggle as Paul had formulated it: 'Paul crammed into the notion of the flesh a superabundance of overlapping notions. The charged opacity of his language faced all later ages like a Rohrschach test: it is possible to measure, in the repeated exegesis of a mere hundred words of Paul's letters, the future course of Christian thought on the human person.'[7] That conflict was to become associated with the dualism of body and soul in some of the Patristic writings but that theme is beyond my concern here. I do think it is difficult not to see traces of the spirit–flesh model of struggle in the key focus Foucault places on the relationship of one's self to the self or in some of the formulations of central directions for his life which he arrived at in the shadow of his death. For example there is his description of the motivation for changing the history of sexuality investigations: 'As for what motivated me, it is quite simple; I would hope that in the eyes of some people it might be sufficient in itself. It was curiosity – the only kind of curiosity, in any case, that is worth acting upon with a degree of obstinacy: not the curiosity that seeks to assimilate what it is proper for one to know, but that which enables one to get free of oneself.'[8]

Getting free of oneself. As ascetics and religious mystics have recognised through the ages, this getting free of oneself, of leaving the prison of one's soul need not guarantee passage to tranquil seas. If many choose a spirituality which despises the world and provides a shelter from it, Foucault was among those others who seek a spiritual existence which will expose them to the contingent mysteries of themselves and others. Such a spirituality might be thought of as that of the parrhesiast. Is not Foucault's delineation of the parrhesiast in his very last courses the description of a truth-teller dealing with spiritual discernments rather than the experience of truth attached to the roles of prophet, sage, or teacher? This is one of his formulations: parrhesia

is a verbal activity in which a speaker expresses his personal relationship to truth, and risks his life because he recognises truth-telling as a duty to improve or help other people (as well as himself). In parrhesia, the speaker uses his freedom and chooses frankness instead of persuasion, truth instead of falsehood or silence, the risk of death instead of life and security, criticism instead of flattery, and moral duty instead of self-interest and moral apathy.[9]

Although his treatment of the practice of parrhesia was worked out in relation to Greek culture, careful textual review of his sources shows a definite dependence on

---

[7] Peter Brown, The Body and Society: Men, Women, and Sexual Renunciation in Early Christianity, Columbia University Press, New York, 1988, p. 48.

[8] Michel Foucault, The Use of Pleasure: The History of Sexuality Volume Two, Pantheon, New York, 1985, p. 8 (British edition: Penguin, London, 1992).

[9] Michel Foucault, 'Discourse and truth: the problematization of Parrhesia' (Notes to the Seminar given by Foucault at the University of California, Berkeley, 1983). Edited by Joseph Pearson. Foucault Archive, Paris, Unpublished Document D213*, p. 8.

Christian understandings of *parrhesia* as well. While the frank speaking of confessional practice is the most evident of these sources, Foucault certainly knew how *parrhesia* took on a unique dimension in Christianity: not the political and moral virtues of the ancient world but the special power of courageous openness to the experiences of mystery. This strength was linked to Jesus of Nazareth's full revelation of God and to the person of prayer's openness to the divine realm. For the religious person, this *parrhesia*, this availability for spiritual transformation was a grace and the source of both hope and love.[10]

Foucauldian spirituality exhibits these two forces. Foucault possessed a non-ideological hope, a confidence that effective resistance could take place, even against the most entrenched of political or moral systems. Suspicion was an ally of his hope and its protector from ideological fiction and revolutionary excess. This is how he expressed his view in an unpublished part of a discussion with several Americans at Berkeley:

Despair and hopelessness are one thing; suspicion is another. And if you are suspicious, it is because, of course, you have a certain hope. The problem is to know which kind of hope you have, and which kind of hope it is reasonable to have in order to avoid what I would call not the 'pessimistic circle' you speak of, but the political circle which reintroduces in your hopes, and through your hopes, the things you want to avoid by these hopes.

When one of his discussants noted that his comment seemed 'very Christian', Foucault replied: 'Yes, I have a very strong Christian, Catholic background, and I am not ashamed.'[11] His hope is not built on a sense of sin, but who would deny that it reflects a Christian realism about human imperfection? It was Foucault's capacity for love and friendship, however, that was even more remarkable, as was shown in the extraordinary grief that met the news of his sudden death. He cared for many and communicated that care to friends, acquaintances, students and readers. His first biographer, Didier Eribon, indicated his gift for friendship in confessing a difficulty he met regularly in doing his research on Foucault's life: 'Many people found their relationship with Michel Foucault enormously important. But because I was writing a biography of Foucault, I had to focus on those who mattered to him, rather than on those for whom he mattered.'[12] Foucault's companion, Daniel Defert, made me think of this special gift for friendship when he wrote: 'Michel always gave each one the liberty to love him according [to] one's own way'.[13]

If I have placed my emphasis on a personal Foucauldian spirituality in this foreword, it is in large measure rooted in my respect for Dr Carrette's excellent treatment of the broader issues involved in Foucault's relationship to religion. We are in Dr Carrette's debt for establishing the basis of a new dialogue between Foucault's work and the searches of theologians and philosophers of religion. While I look forward to

---

[10] For a brief study of the Christian notion and its treatment in scholarship, see Stanley Marrow, '*Parrhesia* and the New Testament', *The Catholic Biblical Quarterly*, vol. 44, July 1982, pp. 431–46.

[11] Document D250 (7) of the Foucault Archive, Paris, 21 April 1983 discussion between M. Foucault and P. Rabinow, B. Dreyfus, C. Taylor, R. Bellah, M. Jay and L. Lowenthal, 32 pages, p. 11.

[12] *Michel Foucault*, p. xii.

[13] Note to J. Bernauer of 31 July 1984.

the energy and excitement of that conversation, I must conclude my thoughts here on a sad note.

Dr Carrette writes in his introduction about a discussion which, at Foucault's request, I arranged between him and several theologians. It took place on 6 May 1980 at the Jesuit community in Paris where I lived at the time. His desire for the discussion was motivated by his research in Christian authors and practices and he asked me to invite a few people who would be able to deal with some of his questions. Knowing the wide range of Foucault's interests and being uncertain as to where his work on Christianity was moving, I chose the discussants on the basis of their representation of very broad competencies and concerns. Among the invited was a Jesuit from Colombia, Mario Calderon, who I knew had been attending Foucault's lectures and who had a reputation for good understanding of Christianity's role in contemporary movements for social change. Calderon was later to leave the priesthood but he and his wife worked for a Jesuit-sponsored, Bogota-based social research institute which is deeply involved in the struggle for justice and human rights in Colombia, the Centre for Popular Investigation and Education. While I was in the process of planning this essay, I received the news that Mario and his wife, Elsa Alvarado, were murdered on 19 May 1997 by five assassins who carried identification as government agents. Although the killers have not been apprehended, there is firm belief that they were right-wing opponents of Mario and Elsa's work for justice. More than five thousand human rights activists marched through Bogota on the day after the killings to protest at the murders. I would like to dedicate this essay to the memory of Mario and Elsa.

This book arose from my wider research on Foucault and religion.[1] It has been made possible by the generosity and friendship of the many people whom I encountered during the years of work. It was conceived somewhat unexpectedly over Guinness and the music of the melodion when my friend and French expert Richard Townsend offered to translate a number of texts. This work reflects to some extent a series of rewarding conversations on Friday afternoons in west London. It then took life through the encouragement of my friend and historian of psychology Sonu Shamdasani – he has always encouraged me to keep believing in myself and my project. In subsequent years I had the privilege of meeting and developing friendships with both David Macey and James Bernauer, who opened up ideas and gave me access to documents that any Foucault researcher dreams of reading. I am indebted to James Bernauer on many counts, not least for agreeing to write the foreword for this book, but also for inviting me to lecture at Boston College and for meetings in, through and beyond this work. The book formally took life through discussions with Grace Jantzen at Manchester University. The journey of our work together from King's College, London to Manchester University is one of many unexpected turns which have brought our paths to meet in extraordinary ways. I am indebted to Grace for all her support and encouragement – which has been immense – and for agreeing to include this work in the Manchester series on Religion, Culture and Gender for the UK publication. Without the support of these friends and colleagues this book would never have developed.

The book was further shaped by many fortuitous meetings and events which show the interdependence of all lives and ideas. I am grateful to Peter Selby, who has listened to many aspects of the development of this book, and to Mark Vernon, for offering to write the postscript and for sharing visits to the Foucault archive. These friendships were invaluable parts of my journey through my work in London, Manchester and Stirling and have enriched me enormously. In its final stages I have been grateful to Lucille Cairns and Elizabeth Ezra, from the French department at Stirling University, both of whom have provided enormous help in working through Foucault's texts. I would particularly like to thank Lucille for all her time, support and help in the final weeks completing this book – without her the final editing would have been much more difficult. I am very grateful to all those who have worked on the translations and to David Macey in particular for some helpful clarifications on some of the texts. My thanks also to Richard Lynch for his useful comments and continual updating on the Foucault archive. I owe a special thanks to David Halperin for extending the horizons of my thought, for his many useful insights and clarifications, and above all for his support and friendship.

Vanessa Graham at Manchester University Press has guided this project through the long and complex process of chasing copyright from Paris, New York, London and back to Paris. She anchored the whole project and with Adrian Driscoll and William Germano made the American Routledge publication possible. In addition I am grateful to John Banks and the production team at Manchester University Press for their helpful suggestions and comments. I would also like to thank my colleagues in the department of Religious Studies at Stirling University for their support and for granting me additional research time to finish this project. Many other friends and colleagues have shaped the outer contours of this work in ways only each individual is aware. I would like to thank in this respect the late Tony Dyson, Roy Findlayson, Otto and Jean Wangermann, Warren Colman, Anita Phillips, Hugh Pyper, Bridget Hinkley, Darrian Gay and Rob Tarling. Thanks also to Matthew Harrison for accommodation and company while in Paris.

I would like to thank the following publishers for permission to reproduce the texts in this book: Blackwell Publishers, Cornell University Press, Editions Bernard Grasset, Editions Gallimard, Eridanos Press, the London Review of Books, New Press, Penguin Books, Sage Publications and also Thomas Keenan.

---

[1] See J. R. Carrette, *Foucault and Religion*, Routledge, London and New York 2000.

Acknowledgements

Without doubt one of my greatest debts is to my friend and colleague at Stirling University Richard King. He has followed many of the steps of this project and many years ago in a bookshop picked out a copy of Foucault's work – neither he nor I could have imagined what would have emerged from such a moment. Richard has become a true intellectual companion. I am deeply indebted to Richard King and Juli Stewart for their support – they have given me more than anyone could wish from friendship.

Finally, this book would not be complete without acknowledging my family for all their love and support through the years of this work. Research creates many debts and without the support of my mother, Susan Carrette, much of this dream would not have been realised. She died before this book went to print, and sadly she did not see one aspect of what her generosity and love made possible. Tim, Ruth and Simon have all in very different ways provided much support and encouragement. I am particularly grateful to my brother Tim for all his insight and understanding. Above all I am indebted to my father the Rev. Canon David Alan Carrette for all his loving engagement with me before he died. My father's death and the death of Foucault were the points from which this work began. This work rescues something of Foucault's unfinished works on religion and carries forward the spirit of my father's unpublished vision of pastoral ministry as inclusion rather than exclusion – to him I owe so much.

One of the problems of Foucault scholarship is dealing with the many tapes, transcripts and interviews of Foucault's work. In certain cases this involves the complex process of working with texts that have been translated from Italian to French, oral transmissions that have been turned into written documents, and working with different versions of the same lecture or interview. There are inevitable difficulties involved in this process, and the editor and translators have attempted to deal with these textual irregularities in the most coherent and effective way possible.

There are also a number of problems with gender-exclusive language in Foucault's texts, both in existing translations and in Foucault's own work. This language has been retained in order to mark out clearly the gender-blind analysis of Foucault's work. This issue is discussed in my own essay at the beginning of this work.

Footnotes supplied by the present translators or editors are in square brackets.

Prologue to a confession of the flesh

Jeremy R. Carrette

By spirituality, I understand – but I am sure that it is a definition which we cannot hold for very long – that which precisely refers to a subject acceding to certain mode of being and to the transformations which the subject must make of himself in order to accede to this mode of being. I believe that, in ancient spirituality, there was identity or almost so between spirituality and philosophy. (Foucault, 'Interview', 20 January 1984)

In March 1980, at the end of a private discussion with the Jesuit doctoral student James Bernauer, Foucault suggested setting up a meeting with a group of theologians. After a short correspondence between Bernauer and Foucault on the matter, the meeting took place on 6 May 1980 at the Jesuit community, 42 rue de Grenelle, Paris.[1] This meeting began by Foucault asking the assembled theologians where the idea of 'debitum', in the context of marital debt, originated. The room was soon silenced by Foucault's astonishing erudition on the matter. The philosopher-historian was courting the theologians.

Foucault's engagement with theology in the 1980s had been augmented by the various fragmented avenues of his multi-volume *History of Sexuality*. In the first volume in 1976 he saw Christianity as playing a fundamental role in shaping the discourse of sexuality in the West and some years later he examined Christianity according to a particular 'technology of self' based on the analytics of confession and salvation.[2] The transition from Christian themes of sexuality to the technologies of self in 1980 occurred through a series of intermediary concerns with 'governmentality' – both of the self and of the nation state. Foucault had considered the theme of 'governmentality' in his lectures at the Collège de France from 1978. It was this analysis which led Foucault to consider 'the government of souls and lives' and 'how one must

---

[1] Private interview with James Bernauer, October 1995; Bernauer–Foucault correspondence, letters 2 April; 18 April; 24 April 1980.

[2] See Foucault [1976], *The History of Sexuality Volume One: An Introduction*, Penguin, London, 1990 (American edition: Pantheon, New York, 1978); Foucault [1980], 'About the beginnings of the hermeneutics of the self' in this volume; [1982], 'Technologies of the self' in *Technologies of the Self*, ed. L. H. Martin, H. Gutman and P. H. Hutton, Tavistock, London, 1988, pp. 16–49 (American edition: University of Massachusetts Press, Amhurst, 1988).

be spiritually ruled and led on this earth in order to achieve eternal salvation'.[3] These studies considered the issue of pastoral power and eventually led Foucault to become somewhat controversially interested in the question of a 'political spirituality' in the Iranian Revolution.[4] In his lecture series from 1979 to 1980 Foucault extended his analysis of government to its 'wider sense of techniques and procedures designed to direct the behaviour of men', which involved a new consideration of the 'examination of conscience' and confession in early Christian literature.[5] These themes of early Christian literature seemed to dominate Foucault's work, alongside his study of Greek and Roman literature, until the end of his life. However, Foucault's death from AIDS left the work incomplete, and the planned fourth volume of his *History of Sexuality* on Christianity was never published.[6]

The theological themes that Foucault introduced into his 1980 lecture series were – as Bernauer indicated in a private paper to the theologians who were to meet Foucault – striking in the context of his wider work to date: 'For many in his audience, the lectures Foucault presented this year, from January through March, must have seemed as though they were written by someone else. Certainly the cast was new: Philon d'Alexandrie, Hermes, Justin, Tertullian, Hippolyte, Cyprien, Origene, Jerome, Cassien.' As Bernauer continued: 'These were not figures with whom Foucault has been identified ... thought and praxis were continually introduced into his course and his interrogation of them reflects his current concern with theology in general and pastoral theology in particular.'[7]

The extension of Foucault's work into the theological documentation of the early church was perhaps surprising; but what is often neglected is the extent of Foucault's fascination with issues of Christianity and religion. It was neither restricted to his later work or merely a series of passing historical glosses. The 'explicit focus' on Christian experience may have occurred in the later works but, as Bernauer points out in his own study, there are 'scattered remarks' throughout his work to Christianity.[8] There is in Foucault's work an important theological and religious sub-text which remains

---

[3] Foucault [1978], 'Governmentality' in *The Foucault Effect: Studies in Governmentability*, ed. G. Burchell, C. Gordon and P. Miller, Harvester Wheatsheaf, Hemel Hempstead, 1991, pp. 87–8.

[4] Foucault [1979], 'The spirit of the world without spirit' in *Politics, Philosophy, Culture: Interview and Other Writings*, ed. L. D. Krizman, Routledge, London, 1988 (American edition: Pantheon, New York, 1980); Foucault [1979], 'Is it useless to revolt?' in this volume. For a discussion of the Iranian question see G. Stauth [1991], 'Revolution in spiritless times: an essay on Michel Foucault's enquiries into the Iranian Revolution' in *Michel Foucault: Critical Assessments*, ed. B. Smart, vol. III, Routledge, London, 1994, pp. 379–401, and C. Jambet [1989], 'The constitution of the subject and spiritual practice' in *Michel Foucault: Philosopher*, ed. T. J. Armstrong, Harvester Wheatsheaf, London, 1992, pp. 233–47.

[5] See Foucault [1980], 'On the government of living', and Foucault, 'About the beginning of the hermeneutics of the self', both in this volume.

[6] The fourth volume was to be entitled *Les aveux de la chair* (*Confessions of the Flesh*). The volume was almost complete before Foucault's death and a copy of it is privately held in the Foucault archive. It cannot be published under the restrictions of the Foucault's estate. See Part 3 below for material which would have contributed to the final volume.

[7] Bernauer, private paper introducing Foucault to theologians, 28 April 1980. Those present at the meeting included Alfonso Alfaro, Mario Calderon SJ, Charles Kannengiesser SJ, Gustave Martelet SJ and William Richardson SJ. This meeting is unfortunately not discussed in any of the biographies.

[8] J. Bernauer, *Michel Foucault's Force of Flight: Toward an Ethics for Thought*, Humanities Press, Atlantic Highlands, New Jersey, 1990, p. 161.

unexamined and neglected. It is the aim of this volume of texts to bring together for the first time Foucault's engagement with religious themes outside the main corpus of his writing.

Foucault's work in many ways, to use one of his dramatic phrases in a different context, 'prowls the borderlands of Christianity'.[9] He is a writer who engages with the historical and political formations of Western culture, of which religion is a formative stratum. Foucault's work is also informed by the residue of his French Catholic background and more importantly by the avant-garde fascination with religious ideas, particularly in the works of Georges Bataille. Foucault may come from the intellectual left wing with its fundamentally atheist values but he is not immune to religious images and ideas. His work, alongside many so-called post-structuralist writers, engages with many theological themes with fresh historical and analytical critique, reappraising the sources of Western culture.

What Foucault does is to open new frontiers on the boundaries of sexuality, religion and politics, extending the platform of religious discourse by bringing it back into the historical process, not in an Hegelian sense, but by dislocating the subject and object of religious meaning through an analysis of truth, power and the body. The theological and religious ideas become invested with a new currency which is often difficult to isolate and locate when the epistemological categories are redrawn. There is in Foucault, as in much of contemporary continental philosophy, a re-mapping of religious ideas. It is the need to understand this new positioning that makes Foucault's work even more significant to theologians and philosophers of religion.

Theological invitations

It is a tragedy that Foucault's death will not allow him to show how his last theme of care of the self would have provided a home for those voices of transcendence which his works encouraged his readers to hear, often for the first time. That unfinished business is an invitation to others. (James Bernauer, 'The prisons of man', *International Philosophical Quarterly*, vol. 27, no. 4, p. 36)

The dialogue between Foucault and religion has to a large extent been ignored and subsumed under the more prominent disciplinary concerns of philosophy and social science. There is however a growing body of literature within religious studies and theology which has utilised Foucault's methodological framework to explore certain religious and theological themes.[10] These studies are concerned with the application

---

[9] Foucault [1966], 'Maurice Blanchot: the thought from the outside' in *Foucault/Blanchot*, Zone Books, New York, 1987, p. 16.

[10] The literature applying Foucault to religious themes is varied and constantly expanding, see for example: B. Turner [1983], *Religion and Social Theory*, Sage, London, 1991; S. Welch [1985], 'The truth of liberation theology' in *Feminism and Foucault: Reflections on Resistance*, ed. I. Diamond and L. Quinby, Northeastern University Press, Boston, 1988, pp. 207–28; D. Chidester, 'Michel Foucault and the study of religion', *Religious Studies Review*, vol. 12, no. 1, 1986, pp. 1–9; S. A. Ray, *The Modern Soul: Michel Foucault and the Theological Discourse of Gordon Kaufman and David Tracey*, Fortress, Philadelphia, 1987; M. P. Lalonde, 'Power/knowledge and liberation: Foucault as parabolic thinker', *Journal of the American Academy of Religion*, vol. 16, no. 1, 1993, pp. 81–100; S. D. Moore, *Mark and Luke in Post-structuralist Perspective: Jesus Begins to Write*, Yale

of Foucault's work, rather than attempting to ascertain the nature of Foucault's own theological and religious concerns. The absence of theological and religious engagement with Foucault's work results predominantly from a lack of awareness of his more peripheral articles and interviews and the specific 'strategic' use by Foucault of religious concepts and history. There is no specific discussion of religion or any clear outline of his theological views. They remain components of wider social and political issues. One other problem is the reluctance of the wider theological community to explore ideas in contemporary continental philosophy because of the principal alliance of theology with analytical certainties and the resulting anxiety about 'truth' created by post-structuralist thinkers such as Foucault.[11] Foucault's religious and theological ideas have become neglected because of the closure of religious discourse in Foucault studies and the closure of Foucault studies inside theology and the philosophy of religion. It is only with the emergence in the 1990s of critical theory and cultural studies inside religious studies that Foucault is finding a new audience in religion and theology – as disciplinary boundaries are redefined Foucault's work finds new possibilities.

There are however a few works which consider the theological and religious views contained in Foucault's work, the most significant of which comes from James Bernauer, who, as I have already indicated, was one of the first to engage personally in a theological dialogue with Foucault.[12] Bernauer picked up the weight and relevance of Foucault's work theologically, providing the first detailed outline of Foucault's later work on Christianity.[13] Bernauer carefully unfolds the later interest in Christianity from the study of confession (which Foucault told him was originally suggested by Ivan Illich) to the examination of the work of John Cassian and the Christian technology of self. Despite his presenting these theological and religious perspectives, few have taken up the challenge to grapple with the intricacies of Foucault's writings on religious themes.

University Press, New Haven, 1992; E. Castelli, 'Interpretations of power in 1 Corinthians', *Semeia* 54, 1992, pp. 199–222; J. Behr, 'Shifting sands: Foucault, Brown and the framework of Christian asceticism', *The Heythrop Journal*, vol. 34, no. 1, January 1993, pp. 1–21; J. D. Caputo, 'On not knowing who we are: madness, hermeneutics, and the night of truth in Foucault' in *Foucault and the Critique of Institutions*, ed. J. D. Caputo and M. Yount, Pennsylvania State University Press, Pennsylvania, 1993, pp. 233–62; G. Jantzen, *Power, Gender and Christian Mysticism*, Cambridge University Press, Cambridge, 1995; and I. Strenski, 'Religion, power, and final Foucault', *Journal of the American Academy of Religion*, vol. 66, no. 2, summer 1998, pp. 345–67.

[11] For a discussion of the relationship between Foucault and analytical philosophy see C. G. Prado, *Descartes and Foucault: A Contrastive Introduction to Philosophy*, University of Ottawa Press, Ottawa, 1992, and C. G. Prado, *Starting with Foucault: An Introduction to Genealogy*, Westview, Boulder, Colorado, 1995. There is a fundamental difference in the construction of 'religion' in Continental and analytical philosophy. In Continental philosophy religion equates with the unconscious, the Other and the symbolic, while in traditional analytical thinking it is seen within dualistic categories and separate from the world.

[12] As stated earlier in the text, Bernauer had a private discussion with Foucault in 1980 and organised a meeting for Foucault with theologians in 1980. Cf. Bernauer, 'The prisons of man: an introduction to Foucault's negative theology', *International Philosophical Quarterly*, vol. 27, no. 4, issue 108, 1987, pp. 356–80, and Bernauer, *Force of Flight*.

[13] Bernauer, *Force of Flight*, pp. 158ff.

Bernauer's book-length study, regarded by David Macey as one of the best intro-ductions,[14] offers an excellent reading of Foucault by examining the nature of his 'thought', and in consequence appreciates both the style and process of Foucault's thinking. The central aspect of this thought, according to Bernauer, 'is precisely this dynamic movement of relentless questioning that refuses to remain with one specific area of study and draw out fully the implications of a particular investigation'.[15] Foucault is seen as formulating a series of experiments to escape the contemporary prisons of thought. Bernauer traces this intellectual journey through the 'extra-ordinary experience that we call thinking'.[16] He is shown to struggle with the Kantian limits, to build an anti-humanist stance against psychology and phenomenology, to enter a 'cathartic' exercise in The Order of Things, to play 'dissonant' sounds in his archae-ological method, to demonstrate 'dissident' thinking in his political tasks and finally to discover the ecstasy of relinquishment in an ethical space of intellectual freedom.[17]

It is within the area of ethical thinking – which Bernauer regarded later with Mahon as a politics of self – that Bernauer found substantial theological significance, regarding Foucault's thinking as 'ecstatic' and referring to it as 'a worldly mysticism'.[18] These phrases could be powerful metaphors indicating a position outside the dominant lines of thinking, but they also contain presuppositions about the nature of mysticism; for as Grace Jantzen and Richard King have argued, mysticism is not separate from the politics of gender (Jantzen) and colonial power (King).[19] Bernauer's suggestion is not, as he points out, 'an arbitrary imposition', but arises from a series of enigmatic references to negative theology by Foucault himself.[20] Although negative theology does not necessarily equate with 'mysticism' Bernauer opened up a series of oblique references in Foucault's texts in order to ascertain the theological relevance of negative theology in relation to Foucault's work. Foucault first made references to negative theology in his 1966 piece on Blanchot and later returned to this theme in his lecture at the Collège de France on 30 January 1980.[21] Foucault had also made the suggestion that his thought was a negative theology in a private meeting with Bernauer on 12 March 1980. At this meeting he supported the suggestion that his work could be compared to negative theology, but as applied to the human sciences not the divine sciences.[22] Foucault was therefore drawing a parallel between his own negations in The Archaeology of Knowledge in relation to the human sciences and the theological tradition of

---

[14] Private discussion. Cf. D. Macey, The Lives of Michel Foucault, Hutchinson, London, 1993, pp. xxi; 133; 481 (American edition: Vintage, New York, 1995).

[15] Bernauer, Force of Flight, p. 6.

[16] Bernauer, Force of Flight, p. 24.

[17] Bernauer, Force of Flight, p. 175ff.

[18] Bernauer, Force of Flight, p. 178. Cf. Bernauer and Mahon, 'The ethics of Michel Foucault' in Foucault: The Cambridge Companion, ed. G. Gutting, Cambridge University Press, Cambridge, 1994, pp. 141–58.

[19] Jantzen, Power, Gender and Christian Mysticism, pp. 4–25 and R. King, Orientalism and Religion: Post-colonial Theory, India and the 'Mystic East', Routledge, London, 1999.

[20] Bernauer, Force of Flight, p. 178.

[21] Foucault, 'Maurice Blanchot: the thought from the outside'; private meeting with James Bernauer, who was present at the 30 January lecture at the Collège de France.

[22] Bernauer–Foucault meeting 12 March 1980. I am extremely grateful to James Bernauer for this material and for his generous support during my research work. Bernauer, Force of Flight, p. 178.

Pseudo-Dionysius. It is however important to emphasise that Foucault is at this point comparing styles of thought rather than aligning his work with theology.[23]

The theological parallel however enabled Bernauer creatively to explore Foucault's work as a 'negative theology' based on Foucault's 'negative anthropology', to link the negation of 'man' to the theological negations of God. Bernauer develops Foucault's work by inextricably linking theology with anthropology similarly to the way Foucault links the death of man to the death of God. Recalling his meeting with Foucault, Bernauer writes: 'Foucault's negative theology is a critique not of the conceptualisation employed for God but of that modern figure of finite man whose identity was put forward as capturing the essence of human being.'[24]

Bernauer argues that Foucault's work is more adequately understood as a 'negative theology' than a 'negative anthropology' because 'its flight from man is an escape from yet another conceptualisation of the Absolute'.[25] Bernauer attempts to isolate one particular theological dimension of Foucault's anti-humanism, but does not enter into the specific theological content of Foucault's views or critically examine the nature of his wider theological and religious ideas. What Bernauer offers is a theological vignette to stimulate further analysis, a fragment from Foucault's religious discourse. His aim is therefore to highlight the 'relevance' of Foucault's work for religion, to provide possibilities of theological dialogue, and, principally, to 'invite interest' from the theological tradition.[26] Bernauer's work assumes an historical significance both in his personal engagement with Foucault and in setting the intellectual agenda for theology, but the task remains to be completed. This volume of texts is itself an attempt to extend Bernauer's invitation for a theological dialogue with Foucault and open up a new territory of religious thinking.

In my own work I am seeking to take seriously the religious fragments of Foucault's work in order to rescue his silenced discussion of Christianity brought about by his death. Foucault left behind sufficient fragments in his lectures and interviews for us to see the outer contours of his final unpublished work. There are also sufficient reflections in his earlier work to thread together a fascinating tapestry of Foucault's own religious questions – both in formal writings, lectures, interviews and in more casual interactions. I have written about these ideas in greater depth elsewhere, but this volume seeks to bring together the most important of Foucault's extraneous writings on religion and culture.[27] Before I outline the texts in detail I want, as a way of introduction, to examine some of the central issues which have arisen in Foucault studies since his death in 1984. First, I want to examine briefly the question of the gendered nature of Foucault's work. I want to explore how Foucault scholarship can responsibly engage with Foucault's work on religion in the light of

[23] Foucault does not regard his own work as supporting a link with negative theology in any literal sense. He was not making theological statements, but rather noting structural parallels. For a wider discussion of my opposition to those who wish to link Foucault to negative theology see J. R. Carrette, *Foucault and Religion*, Routledge, London and New York, 2000.

[24] Bernauer, *Force of Flight*, p. 178. Cf. Bernauer, 'The prisons of man', pp. 375ff.

[25] Bernauer, *Force of Flight*, p. 178.

[26] Bernauer, 'The prisons of man', pp. 366–7.

[27] See J. R. Carrette, 'Male theology in the bedroom: Foucault, de Sade and the body', *John Rylands Bulletin*, vol. 8, no. 3, autumn 1998, pp. 215–33, and Carrette, *Foucault and Religion*.

feminist thinking. I then want to examine in greater detail the issue of religion in the biographies of Foucault – particularly the controversial work by James Miller – in order to explore how Foucault's work on religion has been presented and in some cases positively distorted. I hope that by clearing the ground to think more critically about Foucault's work on religion a new appreciation of Foucault's work can be developed – and perhaps one day his unpublished work may see the light – not in contravention of Foucault's will but as a confirmation of what he had already delivered in lectures and published in articles.

Foucault, religion and the question of gender

The Christian pastoral prescribed as a fundamental duty the task of passing everything having to do with sex through the endless mill of speech. (Foucault, *History of Sexuality Volume One: An Introduction*, p. 21)

Foucault's later work on religious ideas, and some of his earlier studies, are to a large extent shaped by his examination of the 'emergence' of sexuality inside the Christian technology of the self. In his later work Foucault highlights the influence of Christianity in the construction of the Western sexual subject, and in his earlier work we find the links between the sexual body and religious thought; for example, Foucault's archival research on madness reveals the historical misogyny of religious thinking, and his work on Bataille and Klossowski bring together sexuality and theology. However, the absence of any gender critical perspective in these writings on religion and sexuality has not surprisingly been the focus of much feminist analysis, and it raises the question of how to read Foucault's work on religion in a gendered context. How are the ideas which Foucault formulates on religion inscribed with a gendered perspective? How far has Foucault been complicitous with the religious institutions which have silenced and abused women and distorted men? How do we read Foucault's texts on religion with an awareness of the politics of gender?

The relationship between feminist writers and Foucault over the last twenty years has rightly been one of 'continual contestation', to quote Sawicki.[28] The initial relationship, which has been characterised variously as a kind of 'flirting' (Morris 1979), 'loving' (Fraser 1989), 'dancing' (McNeil 1993) and 'friendship' (Diamond and Quinby 1988), soon became focused in the realisation that there was an awkward alliance with a 'malestream theorist' (Hekman 1996).[29] What remained, according to

[28] J. Sawicki, 'Feminism and the power of Foucauldian discourse' in *After Foucault: Humanistic Knowledge, Postmodern Challenges*, ed. J. Arac, Rutgers University Press, New Brunswick, New Jersey, 1991, p. 176.

[29] M. Morris [1979], 'The pirate's fiancée: feminists and philosophers, or maybe tonight it'll happen' in *Feminism and Foucault: Reflections on Resistance*, Northeastern University Press, Boston, 1988, p. 26; N. Fraser, *Unruly Practices: Power, Discourse and Gender in Contemporary Social Theory*, Polity Press, Cambridge, 1989, p. 65; M. McNeil, 'Dancing with Foucault: feminism and power-knowledge' in *Up Against Foucault: Explorations of Some Tensions between Foucault and Feminism*, Routledge, London, 1993, p. 147; I. Diamond and L. Quinby, ed., 'Introduction' in *Feminism and Foucault: Reflections on Resistance*, Northeastern University Press, Boston, 1988, p. ix; and S. Hekman, ed., *Feminist Interpretations of Michel Foucault*, Pennsylvania State University Press, Philadelphia, Pennsylvania, 1997, p. 1.

Lois McNay, in the feminist dialogue with post-structuralist writers such as Foucault, was a 'stimulating crossover'.[30] Foucault offered a critical framework for social and political analysis but was seen at times to destabilise the force of emancipatory politics by questioning the power of agency in the idea of docile bodies and ignoring women in his analysis of the historical conditions of knowledge. Foucault was also seen to be guilty of employing male normative models of the body and sexuality and holding an analysis of violence which did not take adequate account of the specific violence against women in rape.[31]

However, in an attempt to appreciate the diversity of positions in Foucault's work, Lois McNay highlighted the value of Foucault's late work on the aesthetics of the self as a critique of his earlier excesses. McNay renewed the possibility of a fundamental affirmation of the self and autonomy in the feminist dialogue with Foucault – she believed that Foucault's work allowed for a critical struggle to overcome the oppressive which in turn allowed for a positive affirmation of what one may become.[32] There is however some dispute in feminist circles as to whether Foucault's late work is so distinct form his earlier ideas. Amy Richlin's critical essay on Foucault's *History of Sexuality* has powerfully asserted the unacceptability of the 'erasure of the female' from studies in late antiquity.[33] Richlin is sharply critical of McNay and other feminist philosophers who are prepared to accept so easily Foucault's (misogynist) reading of late antiquity.[34] These tensions are in part about the different political priorities and disciplinary value of Foucault to feminist philosophers and feminist historians. Foucault is tactically useful to philosophers to undermine the dominant patriarchal structures of much Anglo-American analytical thinking by historicising knowledge, something (on the whole) less urgent for historians – different disciplinary knowledges have different political strategies. In the continuing dialogue what does become clear is that however much Foucault has helped feminist thinking in the late twentieth century he remains caught in an androcentric paradigm.[35] The resolution of this dilemma will always plague feminist appropriations of Foucault.

Following the work of Amy Richlin and others we cannot walk away from the fact that Foucault's *History of Sexuality* (and his other works) are principally focused on male paradigms. Foucault's limited representation of women in his *History of Sexuality* is simply an injustice to the literature of ancient Greece or Rome. 'Ancient women', as Richlin states, 'did write'.[36] What are we to make of the absent voices in the history of madness, medicine, the prison and the history of sexuality? Do we to simply 'move

[30] L. McNay, *Foucault and Feminism*, Northeastern University Press, Boston, 1992, p. 195.

[31] See McNay, *Foucault and Feminism*, pp. 33; 45–6.

[32] McNay, *Foucault and Feminism*, pp. 197–8; McNay, *Foucault: A Critical Introduction*, Polity Press, Cambridge, 1994, p. 145.

[33] See M. Lloyd, 'A feminist mapping of Foucauldian politics' in *Feminist Interpretations of Michel Foucault*, ed. S. Hekman, Pennsylvania State University Press, Philadelphia, Pennsylvania, 1996, pp. 251–3; Richlin, 'Foucault's *History of Sexuality*: a useful theory for women?' in *Rethinking Sexuality: Foucault and Classical Antiquity*, ed. D. H. Larmour, P. A. Miller and C. Platter, Princeton University Press, Princeton, New Jersey, 1998, p. 142.

[34] Richlin, 'Foucault's *History of Sexuality*', pp. 166–7.

[35] Hekman, *Feminist Interpretations*, p. 1.

[36] Richlin, 'Foucault's *History of Sexuality*', p. 153.

on', as Richlin suggests, or is there a political value in looking at Foucault's texts from a new gender-awareness which can strategically acknowledge the omissions and rescue the value of his work? If Foucault's writings carry the injustice of gender-blind analysis, if the construction of otherness, sexuality and ethical subjects exclude women, and if Foucault has uncritically read the ancient texts, what are we to make of Foucault's work? What is the value of Foucault's project and why has his work so powerfully attracted so much attention? Why should we be bothered to struggle with the texts? The feminist responses, as we have seen, have been varied, and in approaching Foucault's work on religion we need constantly to bear in mind the problems and values of Foucault's work.

There are, as pro-Foucault feminist writers have argued in relation to his wider critical projects, numerous reasons for wrestling with Foucault's work on religion. First, Foucault's work provides a critical apparatus in which to challenge the epistemo-logical assumptions of religious and theological thinking. He provides us with new ways to reconceptualise and 'think differently' about religion. Foucault's work is a critical project which strategically breaks open the hegemonic structures which have ordered Western religious thinking and subjectivity. He provides ways to allow 'difference' and the 'Other' a voice. While he oppressively omits to explore the position of women his methodological stance creates the conceptual space to critique Foucault's own exclusions. What Foucault offers is a project of political disruption, not an anarchic chaos, but a 'problematisation' of the practices of normalisation and control.

It is true that my attitude isn't a result of the form of critique that claims to be a methodical examination in order to reject all possible solutions except for the valid one. It is more on the order of "problemization" – which is to say, the development of a domain of acts, practices, and thoughts that seem to me to pose problems for politics.[37]

Foucault's writings on religion offer a series of critical interventions that question the conditions of religious knowledge. He questions the alliance of medicine and church, disruptively locates (male) sexuality at the site of the death of God, examines the politics of mystery in literature, he reveals the power of religious revolts, uncovers the disciplinary regimes of religious institutions and exposes technological practices which shape the Western ethical subject and give birth to the emergence of (male) sexuality. The texts in this volume give clear witness to the range and depth of Foucault's 'problematisation' of religion.

It is however precisely the radical displacement of religious knowledge that so powerfully brings to light the omission of gender in such critical enquiry. For all the tactical and strategic disruption of religion, Foucault fails to acknowledge the gendered nature of the religious practices. Foucault's work in consequence requires a dialogue with feminist theologians and feminist historians who struggle to overcome the oppression of patriarchy. The voices of feminist theologians and historians of religion

---

[37] Foucault [1984], 'Polemics, politics, and problemizations' in *The Foucault Reader*, ed. Paul Rabinow, Penguin, London and New York, 1991, p. 384. On the idea of 'problematisation' see also Foucault, *The Use of Pleasure*, Penguin, London, 1992, pp. 10–13 (American edition: Pantheon, New York, 1985) and Foucault [1983], 'Problematics' in *Foucault Live: Collected Interviews, 1961–1984*, 2nd edition, ed. S. Lotringer, Semiotext(e), New York, 1996, pp. 416–22.

writing at the same time as Foucault in the 1960s, 1970s and early 1980s need to be brought into dialogue with Foucault's texts. Foucault's world needs to be opened up to the critique developed by Mary Daly, Rosemary Radford Ruether, Elizabeth Fiorenza, Carol Christ, Judith Plaskow, Naomi Goldenberg and Luce Irigaray, to name only a few of the leading names within feminist theology at the time.[38] To rescue Foucault's texts on religion without engaging with these thinkers is to have missed a revolution in religious and theological thinking – the difficult (and humbling) task for us all is to join the fragments of differing revolutions in order to fight against all forces of oppression.

Foucault's texts are 'without women' but they are also, as Richlin notes, 'without Jews … without Africans … without children, babies, poor people, slaves'.[39] Foucault scholarship needs to register the lacunae in Foucault's reading of religious history, it needs to register that the death of God is often the death of a masculine divinity, that the explorations of Islam and Buddhism are not informed by the discourse of Orientalism and postcolonial theory, it needs to register all the selective readings and omissions, but there needs also to be a recognition of what Foucault's work does offer, there needs to be acknowledgement of how effective Foucault's work has been in drawing out the regimes of power and political constructions of knowledge.

Devoney Looser's incisive bibliographical essay on feminist theory and Foucault shows precisely why feminist thinkers continue to struggle with Foucault's texts.[40] Foucault may be problematic for feminists but his ideas have also been instrumental in transforming the discussion of gender, bodies, sexuality, power and the politics of knowledge. In approaching Foucault's writings on religion it is therefore necessary to find ways of reading Foucault that are open to his theoretical insights while holding a critical awareness of the gender bias. The feminist appraisal of Foucault is similar in this sense to the feminist appraisal of Christianity and religion: there can be either a rejection, a selective or critical acceptance or a critical adaptation. What we need to learn, as Earl Jackson in his writings on queer theory makes clear, is 'how to read and write from responsibly identified positions'.[41] We need in effect to find ethically responsible ways of reading and writing that take account of the multivalent forces which shape our world.

[38] See for example M. Daly, *Beyond God the Father*, Beacon Press, Boston, 1973; R. R. Ruether, *Sexism and God-talk*, SCM Press, London, 1983; E. S. Fiorenza, *In Memory of Her: A Feminist Theological Reconstruction of Christian Origins*, SCM Press, London, 1983; C. P. Christ and J. Plaskow, ed., *Womanspirit Rising: A Feminist Reader in Religion*, Harper and Row, New York, 1979; N. Goldenberg, *Changing of the Gods: Feminism and the End of Traditional Religion*, Beacon Press, Boston, 1979; L. Irigaray [1984], 'Divine women' in *Sexes and Genealogies*, Columbia University Press, New York, 1993. For an overview of feminist thinking and religion see A. Loades, 'Feminist theology' in *The Modern Theologians*, 2nd edition, ed. D. F. Ford, Blackwell, Cambridge, 1997, pp. 575–84, and U. King, ed., *Religion and Gender*, Blackwell, Cambridge, 1995.

[39] Richlin, 'Foucault's History of Sexuality', p. 139.

[40] D. Looser, 'Feminist theory and Foucault: a bibliographic essay', *Style*, vol. 26, no. 4, winter 1992, pp. 593–603. Looser's essay is a useful discussion of literature up to 1992. Since then a number of important texts and collections have been published. Hekman, *Feminist Interpretations*, is a more up-to-date reflection on the range of positions in the 'continual contestation' between feminist theory and Foucault.

[41] E. Jackson, *Strategies of Deviance: Studies in Gay Male Representation*, Indiana University Press, Bloomington and Indianapolis, 1995, p. 267. I am grateful to David Halperin for introducing me to this work.

It is in the work of queer theory (theory which, as David Halperin notes, benefits not only lesbians and gay men but anyone challenging heteronormative powers) that Foucault's work has found one of its most positive receptions. As David Halperin makes clear in his reading of *The History of Sexuality*:

Foucault's project has a special importance, resonance, and urgency for lesbians and gay men, who for too long have been the objects rather than the subjects of expert discourses of sexuality – who have been the objects, in particular, of murderously pathologizing, criminalizing, and moralizing discourses, one of whose comparatively minor effects has been to deauthorize our subjective experiences and to delegitimate our claims to be able to speak knowledgeably about our own lives.[42]

Halperin's valuable recognition of the importance of Foucault for gay and lesbian studies enables us to see how Foucault's work has provided 'effective histories' through which to question and challenge the dominant ideologies within Western society. Foucault's work has so easily been criticised from the perspective of the archive that it should now be apparent that Foucault is not an 'historian' in any traditional sense but someone using historical material to illuminate 'specific' struggles. Cousins and Haussins made this point early on in Foucault scholarship. They saw Foucault's works as more like 'case studies' than historical records, and to confuse the genres is to misunderstand Foucault.[43] The case study selectively uses material to make a therapeutic, or in Foucault's case, a 'political' statement. The value of Foucault's work is in what it changes rather than in what it creates. Foucault's writings on religion and theology should be seen in terms of this interventionist and strategic engagement.

One of the problems in reading Foucault, as Gayatri Spivak points out, is that because of 'discipleship' Foucault is being read as a 'universal' rather than as a 'specific' intellectual.[44] Foucault is not providing a complete systematic analysis of religion or any other cultural phenomena. His work rather raises problems and questions.

The role of the intellectual is not to tell others what they have to do. By what right would he do so? ... The work of an intellectual is not to shape others' political will; it is, through the analysis that he carries out in his field, to question over and over again what is postulated as self-evident, to disturb people's mental habits, the way they do and think things, to dissipate what is familiar and accepted, to reexamine rules and institutions and on the basis of this re-problematization (in which he carries out his specific task as an intellectual) to participate in the formation of a political will (in which he has his role as citizen to play).[45]

---

[42] D. Halperin, 'Historicizing the subject of desire: sexual preferences and erotic identities in the Pseudo-Lucianic *Erôtes*' in *Foucault and the Writing of History*, ed. J. Goldstein, Blackwell, Cambridge, 1994, p. 23.

[43] M. Cousins and A. Hussain, *Michel Foucault*, Macmillan, London, 1984, p. 3.

[44] G. C. Spivak, *The Post-colonial Critic: Interviews, Strategies, Dialogues*, Routledge, London, 1988, p. 4. For Foucault's discussion of the 'universal' and 'specific' intellectual see Foucault [1976], 'Truth and power' in *Power/Knowledge: Selected Interviews and Other Writings 1972–1977*, ed. Colin Gordon, Harvester Wheatsheaf, London, 1980, pp. 126–31 (American edition: Pantheon, New York, 1980).

[45] Foucault [1984], 'The concern for truth' in *Politics, Philosophy, Culture: Interview and Other Writings 1977–1984*, ed. L. D. Kritzman, Routledge, London and New York, 1988, p. 265.

The rejection of the 'old prophetic function' of the intellectual and Foucault's own acknowledgement of the historical context and location of discursive practices makes Foucault's work more amenable than most androcentric writers to feminist analysis. There is a certain paucity and openness in Foucault's strategic operations that enables his work to avoid the constraints of dogmatic assertion. As well as recognising the value of such a position it is important to acknowledge the parameters and limitations of this living process of Foucault's texts. It is necessary to appreciate what feminist standpoint theory identifies as the 'material circumstances' of Foucault's writing. While feminist standpoint theory shares Foucault's appreciation of the 'contingent, partial and historically situated character' of knowledge it significantly extends the rational framework to include the sex/gender dimension.[46] Reading Foucault from this position of feminist standpoint theory reinforces the 'specificity' of Foucault's project. It allows us to read Foucault's work on religion from the position of a white male writing from within the corridors of the French academic elite, but it also enables us to see that Foucault's sexual orientation meant that he was not always (contrary to Nancy Hartsock's belief) 'with power', meaning that he did not always understand the world from 'the perspective of the ruling group'.[47]

The attempt to locate Foucault's work in the personal/political circumstances of his writing and take it outside of the 'universal' assumptions offers new ways of reading Foucault's work on religion. I have attempted elsewhere to read Foucault's avant-garde religious themes of sexuality and the death of God as related to specific issues of male sexuality.[48] Jerrold Seigel in an intriguing article has attempted to identify a 'hidden level of homosexual reference in many of Foucault's writings' and following this line of thought Mark Vernon seeks to open a series of questions from within Foucault's work for the emerging dialogue between queer theory and religion.[49] Foucault's interest in the construction of the Other, of Same and Difference, his fascination with the nature of silence and his critique of the subject can all be read through his gay identity. Indeed Earl Jackson sees a direct link between the critique of the subject and the gay identity: 'In this light, it seems neither accidental nor incidental that two very influential post-structuralist essays of the 1970's, "What Is an Author?" and "The Death of the Author", were written by gay men, Michel Foucault and Roland Barthes, respectively.'[50]

---

[46] N. Hartsock, 'The feminist standpoint: developing the ground for a specifically feminist historical materialism' in *Discovering Reality*, ed. S. Harding and M. B. Hintikka, Reidel, Dordrecht, 1983, pp. 283ff., and N. Hartsock, 'Foucault on power: a theory for women?' in *Feminism/Postmodernism*, ed. L. G. Nicholson, Routledge, London, 1990, p. 158; Fraser and Nicholson, 'Social criticism without philosophy: an encounter between feminism and postmodernism' in *Feminism/Postmodernism*, p. 26.

[47] Hartsock, 'Foucault on power', p. 167. Many feminist writers have failed to appreciate the politics of sexual orientation.

[48] See Carrette, 'Male theology in the bedroom'.

[49] J. Seigel, 'Avoiding the subject: A Foucaultian itinerary', *Journal of the History of Ideas*, vol. 51, part 2, 1990, pp. 273–99; M. Vernon, 'Following Foucault: the strategies of sexuality and the struggle to be different', *Theology and Sexuality*, no. 5, September 1996, pp. 76–96. See Mark Vernon's postscript in this volume.

[50] Jackson, *Strategies of Deviance*, p. 35.

I have already noted how David Halperin sees Foucault's work as central to the articulation of gay and lesbian sexuality, and his *Saint Foucault* stands as a passionate demonstration of how Foucault's work offers new possibilities for queer identity.[51] These attempts to locate Foucault in the context of 'specific' struggles of his life are one response to the feminist challenge to Foucault. These readings however should not be seen as an excuse or as ways to ignore the tensions in Foucault's work but as part of those 'responsibly identified positions' of reading.

The feminist critique of Foucault extends and enriches Foucault's critical approach to religion and sexuality. It both contributes to and broadens the critical framework. As Foucault stated in 1977:

> I dream of the intellectual who destroys evidence and generalities, the one who, in the inertias and constraints of the present time, locates and marks the weak points, the openings, the lines of force, who is incessantly on the move, doesn't know exactly where he is heading nor what he will think tomorrow for he is too attentive to the present; who, whenever he moves, contributes to posing the question of knowing whether the revolution is worth the trouble, and what kind (I mean, what revolution and what trouble), it being understood that the question can be answered only by those who are willing to risk their lives to bring it about.[52]

If Foucault's project was about questioning and unsettling the intellectual certainties, the 'continual contestation' between Foucault and feminism must be part of the very 'Foucauldian' project of questioning and unsettling Foucault's work on religion.

Mystical illusions? Foucault, religion and biography

To be sure, bringing the words mystical, eroticism and atheism together attracts attention. (M. Blanchot, *The Infinite Conversation* [1969] 1993, p. 202)

The examination of Foucault's work on religion has been limited. There have, as I indicated earlier, been a number of studies which have briefly examined specific theological and religious issues in relation to Foucault's work but they have failed to appreciate the full scope of Foucault's writings on religious and theological themes.[53] James Bernauer's initial invitation for theological engagement is still very much open and awaits some critical and creative dialogue. In the absence of any detailed assessment of Foucault's work on religion we have to rely on the partial and even distorted pictures of Foucault's religious engagement interlaced in the wider examinations of Foucault's life and work. In order to unravel the complexity of Foucault's religious thinking and to show how it has at times been misappropriated I

---

[51] D. Halperin, *Saint Foucault: Towards a Gay Hagiography*, Oxford University Press, Oxford, 1995.

[52] Foucault [1977], 'Power and sex' in *Politics, Philosophy, Culture: Interview and Other Writings*, ed. L. D. Krizman, Routledge, London, 1988, p. 124.

[53] See, for example, A. MacIntyre, *Three Rival Versions of Moral Enquiry*, Duckworth, London, 1990; J. Milbank, *Theology and Social Theory: Beyond Secular Reason*, Blackwell, Oxford, 1990, pp. 278ff; C. Davies, *Religion and the Making of Society: Essays in Social Theology*, Cambridge, Cambridge University Press, 1994. See also note 10 above.

want to examine the present biographical accounts[54] of Foucault's life in terms of their representation of Foucault's work on religion, focusing in particular on James Miller's 'narrative account'. This is particularly important given the way these studies have transformed Foucauldian scholarship in their examination of Foucault's wider intellectual and political context. The richness of these biographical studies has been highlighted by Kate Soper in her review of the literature and they provide useful registers for considering not only the significance of Foucault's work on religion but the ways this has at times been seriously misunderstood.[55]

All of Foucault's biographers, to a greater or lesser extent, pick up the religious strands of Foucault's life and work, but with considerably different emphasis, style and orientation, creating a fragmented and varied picture of Foucault's religious concerns. The varied assessment of Foucault's writings on religious themes ranges from minor allusions in the first biography by Didier Eribon to what I shall show to be wild exaggerations and misrepresentation in the most controversial account by James Miller.[56] However the signposts of Foucault's interest in religion are documented more efficiently in David Macey's work. He refrains from marginalisation and excessive commentary by plotting the main features of Foucault's intellectual interest in theological and religious themes. The clear demarcation of religious themes in Macey confirms in this respect David Halperin's own assessment of the work as providing one of the best biographical studies: 'Macey's book can reasonably claim to be the single best source to date of complete and accurate information about Foucault's life.'[57] One of the particular strengths of David Macey's biography is the way it captures the political life of France and in consequence monitors the peripheral influence of the Catholic church in such affairs. The Catholic inheritance of many significant French intellectuals, including Foucault, is succinctly noted and the political and intellectual force of the church highlighted.[58] These social influences are not mere cosmetics, they reflect the importance of the church in France's social history and the influences which mark Foucault's historical documentation of psychiatry, medicine and the prison.[59]

---

[54] D. Eribon, *Michel Foucault*, Faber & Faber, London, 1992 (American edition: Harvard University Press, Cambridge, Massachusetts, 1991); Macey, *The Lives of Michel Foucault*; and J. Miller, *The Passion of Michel Foucault*, Harper Collins, London, 1993.

[55] K. Soper, 'Ruling passion strong in death', *Radical Philosophy* 66, spring 1994, pp. 44–6.

[56] Eribon takes note of the Catholic context of Foucault's upbringing and notes in the general outline of his work a number of references to religious ideas. See Eribon, *Michel Foucault*, pp. 5; 7; 9; 11; 33; 35; 75; 78; 157; 217; 221; 254; 271; 273; 277; 285-91; 309–13; 317–24. I will discuss J. Miller, *The Passions of Michel Foucault*, in greater detail in this chapter.

[57] Halperin, *Saint Foucault*, p. 140.

[58] Macey, *The Lives of Michel Foucault*, pp. 24; 27; 64; 147; 192.

[59] All of Foucault's archaeological and genealogical studies identify aspects of church history in shaping contemporary thought and practice. See for example, Foucault [1961], *Madness and Civilization: A History of Insanity in the Age of Reason*, Routledge, London, 1991, pp. 241ff. (American edition: Pantheon, New York, 1965); and Foucault [1975], *Discipline and Punish: The Birth of the Prison*, Penguin, London, 1991, p. 212 (American edition: Pantheon, New York, 1977). As Foucault stated in 1970: 'Religious discourse, juridical and therapeutic as well as, in some ways, political discourse are all barely dissociable from the functioning of a ritual that determines the individual properties and agreed roles of the speakers.' Foucault [1970], 'The discourse of language' in *The Archaeology of Knowledge*, Pantheon, New York, 1972, p. 225 (also Harper Colophon, New York, 1976; British edition: Routledge, London, 1989).

Macey's biography signposts the major religious contours of Foucault's work, from his work on religious experience in French literature in 1958, through his engagement with the literary avant-garde and the death of God, his interest in Islamic spirituality in Iran and Japanese Zen, and the final studies of religion and sexuality; a catalogue of engagements which remain unexamined in any detail.[60] Macey also uncovers the intriguing taped discussions Foucault had with the hitch-hiker Thierry Voeltzel in 1975. Although the printed version of these discussions, *Vingt ans et après*, is only a selection of transcripts, they do provide a rare glimpse into Foucault's attitudes to religion. (See 'On religion' in this volume.) The comments are brief and of little weight against his actual writings, but we learn about his fascination with religious ritual; an interest which in 1978 made him miss an interview in order to watch the installation of John Paul II on television.[61]

Macey's work also provides illuminating asides to wider religious issues by documenting intriguing episodes such as Maurice Clavel's reaction to Foucault's *The Order of Things*. Clavel, novelist, critic and teacher, who according to Macey had 'recently discovered a headily mystical Catholicism', had found in Foucault's work a confirmation of his faith. This is certainly surprising given that, as Macey also indicates, Foucault was an acknowledged atheist.[62] Clavel's remarks however arose from a similar basis to those which fascinated Bernauer, the intrinsic relationship between God and 'man' in Foucault's work. Clavel was able to lecture on Foucault 'before the altar' because 'the man whose death was proclaimed in *Les mots et les choses* was "man without God"'.[63] This episode may be dismissed as a misconceived religious reading of Foucault by Clavel but what it does reveal is the significance of the theological material inside Foucault's texts. Foucault may have been an atheist but his interests led him to spend the final years of his life in the Bibliothèque du Saulchoir, a Dominican library, where his archive was preserved until 1997. Macey's work, without attempting any secondary analysis of the material, is thus able to demarcate the boundaries of Foucault's religious question by providing glimpses of a wider French Catholic interface to Foucault's life and work – the space for a theological examination is left open.

Where Macey and Eribon, as Halperin has noted, stop short of overt interpretative strategy, Miller's account reorganises and distorts the religious features.[64] While such an amplification may be beneficial in highlighting the importance of the religious content of Foucault's work, its failure lies in a lack of critical theological insight which can correctly position Foucault's work. The fundamental problem in Miller's reading of the religious content of Foucault's work, and also inadvertently of Bataille's work, is the way he retains the 'traditional attitudes' and religious perspectives which both suspend.[65]

---

[60] Macey, *The Lives of Michel Foucault*, pp. 80; 90; 99; 120; 138ff.; 256ff.; 416; 465.

[61] Macey, *The Lives of Michel Foucault*, pp. 372-3. Cf. pp. xxi–xxii; 399; 406; 408; James Bernauer private interview, October 1995.

[62] Macey, *The Lives of Michel Foucault*, pp. 192; 415.

[63] Macey, *The Lives of Michel Foucault*, p. 192.

[64] Halperin, *Saint Foucault*, p. 162, cf. pp. 142–3; 159.

[65] The idea that there is a problem of 'traditional attitudes' in reading Bataille is taken from M.-C. Lala, 'The conversions of writing in George Bataille' in *On Bataille:Yale French Studies*, no. 78, ed. A. Stoekl, Yale, University Press, New Haven, 1990, p. 237.

Miller fails to appreciate the critical understanding of religious ideas employed by Foucault and instead builds a confusion of ideas in a fascination with the conjunction of mysticism, eroticism and atheism.[66] This distortion of religious ideas is part of a wider problem with Miller's 'narrative account' exposed by David Halperin.

Halperin's critique of Miller's work reveals the complications within the biographical accounts of Foucault in terms of his gay identity and the politics of homosexuality.[67] The force of Halperin's critique is directed to Miller's study in particular because of the way it misrepresents aspects of Foucault's life. Miller, he argues, assumes a 'privileged access to the "truth" of Foucault's psychopathology', selectively drawing out fragments of text, fabricating and interpolating passages and, finally, developing distorted interpretations about his life in terms of a preoccupation with death and sado-masochism.[68] The entire structure of Miller's biographical account is seen to operate on a 'normalising judgment' about Foucault's 'psychosexual being'.[69] Halperin's criticism is severe and brings into focus, from the position of gay politics, the way Foucault's life is 'reconstituted' according to a particular (straight) 'narrative'.[70]

Halperin condenses his severely critical argument into a short incisive paper with a few striking examples. He is interested in the broader significance of Miller's biographical portrayal only in so far as it supports his central concerns about the 'politics of writing a gay life'.[71] However, the stylisation of Foucault in Miller's work, to which Halperin is so opposed, unwittingly rests on a particular religious distortion of Foucault. Miller not only 'normalises' Foucault's psychosexual being, but builds into this portrayal a powerful religious iconography. The gay life is projected through a particular mystification of death, excess and the limit. Religious authority, in this sense, not only controls through its prohibition of gay sexuality but also enforces control by allowing certain experiences to exist as marginal. Mysticism has historically given voice to marginalised groups, such as women, who were denied access to the wider corridors of church power.[72] Miller's demarcation of Foucault's gay experience as existing within a mystical framework is not, as it may appear, an affirmation, but a controlled mapping within a particular religious ideology.

Miller reads Foucault's religious ideas according to a popular 'normalisation' (a social construction which restricts, controls and limits practice and identity) of 'mystical experience' which in turn supports a sexual 'normalisation'. Although Halperin's use of the title Saint Foucault was an 'ironic appropriation' of his critics, the use of religious iconography is particularly significant given the sub-text of Miller's

[66] M. Blanchot [1969], The Infinite Conversation, University of Minnesota, Minneapolis, 1993, p. 202.
[67] Halperin, Saint Foucault, pp. 126–85. Halperin's critique was originally published in Salmagundi, 1993, pp. 63-93.
[68] Halperin, Saint Foucault, pp. 164–5; 167.
[69] Halperin, Saint Foucault, p. 145.
[70] Halperin, Saint Foucault, p. 164.
[71] Halperin, Saint Foucault, p. 137.
[72] See Jantzen, Power, Gender and Christian Mysticism.

work – it sets up a tension between saint and mystic.[73] The idea of a 'hagiography' was also introduced into the debate by Alasdair MacIntyre, who saw Miller's own work as a 'secular hagiography'.[74] This demonstrates how religious ideas carry a weight and veracity in creating certain frameworks of value in the reading of Foucault's work. By providing access to Foucault's writings on religious themes it is possible to provide a critical context for such interpretations.

In order to understand the religious nature of Foucault's work it is important to isolate and define the iconography which surrounds and informs the reading of his texts. It is necessary to separate the distorted images and 'mysticalisation' of Foucault from his actual texts and comments on religion. There is a multi-layered reading and reorganisation of religious ideas which demands careful scrutiny. The first task therefore is to extinguish the mystical iconography which clouds the religious understanding of Foucault's work, a popularisation which revolves around the avant-garde and is turned back on Foucault. In this respect I want to examine Miller's misrepresentation of Foucault in order to clear the ground for a more comprehensive consideration of Foucault's religious question, which will indirectly support Halperin's own critique of Miller's portrayal of the gay life. I will spend some time examining Miller's work, because it provides such a striking concoction of religious ideas which both confuses and obscures the nature of Foucault's own writings on religion. Miller's work forms a negative from which to draw out the central theoretical issues underpinning Foucault's work on religion.

MILLER'S RELIGIOUS ICONOGRAPHY

In the postscript to his 'narrative account' of Foucault's life, Miller acknowledges his fascination with the style of Foucault's writing and a certain 'aura' in the works. Commenting on his reading of Foucault's texts, Miller states: 'Much of Foucault's prose now seemed to me suffused with a strange kind of aura, both morbid and vaguely mystical.'[75] And, lecturing at Tokyo University in 1991 on the theme of his biography, he stated: 'Besides being a master of a certain type of positive historiographic inquiry, he was, I believe, a kind of mystic – philosophically; sexually; politically.'[76] Miller defends his work by stating how he attempts to 'evoke the color and mood of Foucault's imaginative universe'.[77] He admits to using 'interpretative techniques' but the strands of imaginative interplay are never clearly articulated and oscillate around the text without any rigorous substantiation. There is some doubt in Miller's mind as to whether he 'was reading something into him [Foucault]', but

[73] David Halperin, private discussion. 'Saint Foucault' was originally given as the title of David Halperin's review of Didier Eribon's biography in the Lesbian and Gay Studies Newsletter, vol. 19, no. 2, July 1992, pp. 32–5; reprinted from Bryn Mawr Classical Review, vol. 3, no. 2, 1992, pp. 104–9. The title 'Saint Foucault' also appeared in G. G. Harpham, The Ascetic Imperative in Culture and Criticism, Chicago University Press, Chicago, 1987, pp. 220–35; 292–5. I am grateful to David Halperin for this brief genealogy of the term.

[74] A. MacIntyre, 'Miller's Foucault, Foucault's Foucault', Salmagundi, no. 97, winter 1993, p. 60.

[75] Miller, The Passions of Michel Foucault, p. 376.

[76] J. Miller, 'Foucault's politics in biographical perspective', Salmagundi, no. 97, winter 1993, p. 42.

[77] J. Miller, 'Policing discourse: a response to David Halperin', Salmagundi, no. 97, winter 1993, p. 97.

'seduced by his literary style' Miller becomes immersed into a particular dimension of the work connected with death and cruelty.[78] Miller in this process indexed a whole series of 'recurrent images and motifs' in, he admits, his 'own crude way'.[79] In his postscript there is a clear admission of a presentation of Foucault based on a magnification of certain images. We discover at the end of the work how Miller had intuitively taken the notion of the 'vaguely mystical' and slowly built a whole religious iconography into the life and work of Foucault. Every tangential link with the idea of the 'mystical' is exploited, such as rewriting Foucault's reporting of the Iranian Revolution as reflecting 'his essentially mystical vision of politics as a "limit-experience"' and merging the discussion of Christian self-sacrifice with the mystical erotics of Bataille.[80]

There is a whole series of ideas built into Miller's text which support and reinforce this mystical iconography. We find alongside the central ideas of the Nietzschean quest and the 'limit-experience', religious and occult terminology such as 'hermetic', 'esoteric', 'visionary', 'erotic ecstasy', 'ascetic' and even 'gnomic'; terms which would more freely be associated with Crowley, Gurdjieff and Jung than with Foucault.[81] These ideas are not just passing metaphors, rather key imaginative reconstructions of Foucault's life and work in terms of a misreading and distorted emphasis of Foucault's religious texts and secondary influences.

Many assertions about the religious nature of Foucault are prefixed with the phrase 'a kind of'; Foucault is 'a kind of spiritual medium' and 'a kind of visionary', but most of Miller's iconography has no such weak escape clause.[82] Miller reads the texts of Foucault that examine religion and the religious influences of the avant-garde as confirming a notion of the 'mystical' – but no detailed qualification is provided and Miller shows no sign of reading the texts of Christian 'mysticism' or any other 'mystical' tradition.[83] The seeds of distortion are sown and obscure religious ideas are planted in a landscape of sensation and effect; no doubt Foucault would again, to use his own dismissal of identity, be over there laughing.[84]

In order to focus the many disparate strands of Miller's mystical reading of Foucault I want to organise my discussion around four interrelated areas: mysticism

[78] Miller, *The Passions of Michel Foucault*, pp. 376–7.

[79] Miller, *The Passions of Michel Foucault*, p. 376.

[80] Miller, *The Passions of Michel Foucault*, pp. 314; 324. With reference to 'mystical experience' and Iran see Miller, *The Passions of Michel Foucault*, pp. 306–7; 460 n.92; cf. Jambet [1989], 'The constitution of the subject and spiritual practice'.

[81] There are a whole range of references to this terminology and I list the principal examples: Miller, *The Passions of Michel Foucault*: 'hermetic' pp. 7; 33; 124; 281; 294; 319; 335; 'esoteric' pp. 7; 88; 321; 'visionary' p. 8, cf. pp. 339 n.59; 445 n.122; 'erotic/ecstasy' pp. 72; 87–8; 154–5; 313; 319; 324; 'divine agony' p. 87; 'ascetic' pp. 334; 342; 344; 'gnomic' pp. 5; 318; 332; and, 'mystical' pp. 30; 88–9; 154; 279; 306–7; 314; 376.

[82] Miller, *The Passions of Michel Foucault*, pp. 8; 118; 155; 162.

[83] As will already be apparent, the terms 'mysticism' and 'mystical' have a complex genealogy. See Jantzen, *Power, Gender and Christian Mysticism*, and King, *Orientalism and Religion*, for a more detailed discussion of these terms. When I refer to these terms in relation to Miller I have in mind the modern stereotypical construction of intense psychological experiences, developed in the work of William James, which is distinct from, although related to, the varied use of the term in Christian history. See G. Jantzen, 'Mysticism and experience', *Religious Studies*, vol. 25, 1989, pp. 295–315.

[84] Foucault [1969], *The Archaeology of Knowledge*, Routledge, London, 1991, p. 17.

and the 'limit-experience'; sado-masochism and religious suffering; transgression and transcendence; Gnosticism and the occult. These four areas constitute the central theoretical operations underpinning Miller's work which is developed from a mixture of theological naivety, popular misconception and a misreading of Foucault's engagement with the religious themes of the avant-garde. It is through the writings of the avant-garde that Miller supported and enhanced the mystical reading, referring specifically to de Sade, Artaud, Bataille, Blanchot, Beckett and Char (Miller, chapters 3–4). These writings are then written across a description of sado-masochism, confirming the precarious way religious themes are imported from the avant-garde without any critical appreciation of theology or Foucault's own work (Miller, chapters 8–10).

MYSTICISM AND THE 'LIMIT-EXPERIENCE'

The mystical reading of Foucault's life and work is built from an understanding of the notion of 'limit-experience', which in turn is grafted on to a spurious reading of mysticism. The idea of 'limit-experience' is in fact the central linchpin of Miller's entire narrative work, forming the basis of reading Foucault and his life.

Foucault's lifelong preoccupation with 'experience' and its limits thus represents more than a dramatic and sometimes disturbing aspect of one philosopher's quest for truth: it also suggests a new way of looking at his major texts and assessing their significance; and of reexamining how a profound modern skeptic, avowedly 'beyond good and evil', handled the vocation of philosophy, the making of political commitments, and the shaping of a public 'self'.[85]

Miller develops the significance of the idea of 'limit-experience' from three sources: the foreword to the original 1961 edition of Histoire de la folie; the 1978 interview with the Italian journalist Duccio Trombadori; and a private meeting with Foucault's partner Daniel Defert in 1990.[86] These fragmentary pieces are taken alongside the Nietzschean quest to formulate a 're-creation' of Foucault's inner 'daimon'.[87] This is an interesting imaginative exercise and one which has certainly captured a level of public interest and popular appeal.[88] But whether it captures Foucault's inner drive or whether it has any textual justification is another matter entirely. The desire to find a single motivating source of any great life is tempting; but, as many commentators have shown, such attempts at coherence in a thinker like Foucault contradict his entire enterprise.[89] To subsume Foucault's lifelong attempt to understand and articulate his gay sexuality under the idea of 'limit-experience' is itself a reductive exercise which attempts to imprison a multifariously embodied living into a narrow conceptual

---

[85] Miller, The Passions of Michel Foucault, p. 32.

[86] Miller, The Passions of Michel Foucault, pp. 29–31; 380; 398–9 n.49, 52, 58.

[87] Miller, The Passions of Michel Foucault, p. 70.

[88] Miller's work became the subject of a British television programme, and even though this programme began by mentioning the 'three' published biographies it discussed only Miller's work. David Macey had been interviewed at length for the programme but no mention or footage of this appeared. The importance of Didier Eribon's ground-breaking study was also never fully acknowleged. This is a clear demonstration of media sensation preceding academic validity and indicates the problems and dangers of Miller's popular sensationalisation of Foucault's sexuality. See 'The Late Show', BBC television, 1993.

[89] Halperin, Saint Foucault, pp. 127ff.

framework. Would Miller have done the same with the sexuality of a straight man? The inner motivations of Foucault's work will always lie in the realms of speculation and are certainly not reducible to a singular factor. These issues extend far beyond the domains of this enquiry; the more immediate concern here is how the idea of the 'limit-experience' forms the central basis for Miller's reading of Foucault's religious texts and how it is linked to the idea of mysticism.

Miller very quickly links the idea of 'limit-experience' with mysticism in the description of 'aspects of human existence that seemed to defy rational under-standing' in Foucault's *Madness and Civilization*. The 'tormented vision of Goya', the 'cruel erotic fantasies of Sade' and the 'insane glossolalia of Artaud' are linked, not by Foucault but by Miller, to 'a mystical kind of experience'.[90] This association and preoccupation occurs throughout Miller's work and examples abound through the text. The idea of the 'limit-experience' becomes the nucleus around which to develop a series of ideas from the mysterious to the mystical, and the esoteric to the ecstatic, each a way of positioning and understanding Foucault's concerns about death, sexuality and the desire to think differently.

In the light of such incongruous associations with Foucault we may legitimately ask: how and why has this process of 'mysticalization' been devised in Miller's work? The answer to this resides in a confused reading of Foucault's religious texts, particularly in those essays from the 1960s. One of the strengths of Miller's work was to highlight the influences of the surrealist and avant-garde writers on Foucault and it is this emphasis which at times simultaneously distorts. In the writings of the avant-garde there were a number of religious and theological concerns used to disrupt the dominant rational order and re-create a sense of the 'sacred'. During what is known as his 'literary period', Foucault engaged with a number of these works, picking up a series of religious ideas. (See for example 'Preface to transgression' in this volume.) As I have stated elsewhere, Foucault created a fascinating theological sub-text through the encounter with the avant-garde, but this entry into the theological realm is very specific and there is no substantial textual evidence to support the view that Foucault regarded his work in any way as 'mystical'.[91] There are, as Bernauer noted, a number of isolated comments on 'negative theology' but these were very specific and can in no way justify interpreting his entire works and experiences in a mystical framework. The key to Miller's mysticalisation of Foucault is a misreading of the 'limit-experience' and, as I will demonstrate, a hidden Jamesian notion of mysticism which operates behind Miller's text.

The idea of 'limit-experience' in Foucault's work is derived from the avant-garde writer Georges Bataille, who wrote a powerful essay on the experience of the 'impossible' and the 'unknown' which he entitled *Inner Experience*.[92] The nature of Bataille's text is deliberately obfuscating and it weaves together a number of experiences which it simultaneously suspends, such as laughter, ecstasy, poetry and eroticism, in order to reach a realm of 'unknowing', a place which shatters the

---

[90] Miller, *The Passions of Michel Foucault*, p. 30.

[91] Carrette, 'Male theology in the bedroom'.

[92] G. Bataille [1954], *Inner Experience*, SUNY, New York, 1988, pp. 3; 12–13; 39; 137.

'known'. Bataille with great intensity and struggle attempts to create an indefinable space utilising the familiar 'known' in order to postulate an 'unknown', to reach what is uncontainable. It seeks through 'torment' and 'anguish' to break the boundaries of 'ordinary' knowing in order to reach a space of 'non-knowledge', an 'inaccessible unknown'.[93] 'I wanted experience to lead where it would, not to lead it to some end point given in advance. And I say at once that it leads to no harbour (but to a place of bewilderment, of nonsense).'[94]

Bataille makes the point in his study that what he designates as 'inner experience', the elusive point of the impossible and non-knowledge, is understood by what 'one usually calls "mystical experience": the states of ecstasy, of rapture, at least of meditated emotion'.[95] The 'mystical' certainly informs Bataille's study and he refers to such paradigm 'mystics' as Eckhart, St John of the Cross and St Ignatius, but to presume that Bataille's idea of 'inner experience' is referring to a history of Christian mysticism (whichever way this may be defined) or a stereotypical mystical experience is to misunderstand the complexity of Bataille's work.[96]

Bataille explicitly uses a mystical frame of reference in order to suspend it; it is a useful arena of experience to point towards his idea of 'inner experience'. He borrows the ideas of mysticism in order to grasp an 'experience laid bare, free of ties, even of origin'.[97] In fact he does not like the word mysticism because, as he rightly assumes, it is difficult to use without 'inviting confusion'.[98] Bataille entertains but specifically rejects experiences like mysticism because they are formed by predetermined religious and theological ideas.[99]

There is a specific rejection of the theological in Bataille, his work Inner Experience forming part of his three-volume 'La somme athéologique'.[100] Christian mystical experience for Bataille is formed and constructed in relation to known objects and beliefs, it holds theological presuppositions and can be seen as a 'fiction' and 'art'.[101] There is a distinct process of valuing certain experiences which have theological validity and then discarding them as inadequate. 'God', according to Bataille, 'differs from the unknown'.[102] In this sense Bataille regards his work, alongside that of Blanchot, as offering a 'new theology' of the 'unknown'.[103] This rejection of Christian mysticism

[93] Bataille, Inner Experience, p. 179.
[94] Bataille, Inner Experience, p. 3.
[95] Bataille, Inner Experience, p. 3.
[96] Bataille, Inner Experience, pp. 4; 12; 47; 119. I am here making a distinction between a broad collection of thinkers in the Christian tradition located under the term 'mystical' and the modern psychological reconstruction of this tradition in the work of William James.
[97] Bataille, Inner Experience, p. 3.
[98] Bataille, Inner Experience, p. 174.
[99] Bataille, Inner Experience, p. 175. As Bataille states: 'A "mystic" sees what he wants – this depends on powers which are relative. And in the same way, he discovers – what he knew. No doubt there are wills, beliefs which are unequally favourable, but as such [man?] experience introduces nothing which has not at first been a part of one's understanding – if not the contestation of understanding as the origin of beliefs.'
[100] Bataille's 'La somme athéologique' consisted of On Nietzsche [1945], Paragon House, New York, 1992; Inner Experience [1954], SUNY, New York, 1988; and Guilty [1961], Lapis Press, California, 1988.
[101] Bataille, Inner Experience, pp. 4-5; 73
[102] Bataille, Inner Experience, p. 5.
[103] Bataille, Inner Experience, p. 102; Cf. M. Blanchot [1950], Thomas the Obscure (New Version), Davis Lewis, New York, 1973; and N. Greene, 'Thomas, come back', Novel, vol. 8, no. 2, winter 1975, pp. 175–7.

by Bataille is clearly supported by Richardson in his discussion of Bataille's work:

> While Bataille's experience is entirely framed by Western concepts and he does retain some of the terminology of Christian mysticism, nevertheless there can be no doubt that the experience he conveys has nothing to do with union with a transcendent God ... As such it certainly goes beyond anything that is proper to Western mysticism.[104]

Bataille's complex exploration at the 'limits' of thought and experience brushes up against a series of ideas in recent scholarship on mysticism initiated by Katz, who examines whether it is possible to have 'raw experience' unmediated by culture and tradition.[105] Katz and others have tried to ascertain whether mystical experience exists outside the historical and social traditions of a particular religion in a similar way that Bataille is trying to point to an 'inner experience' outside the categories of mysticism. Foucault's own work on the social construction of experience would not support any idea of 'raw experience', but the desire to push the boundaries of social identity and reshape the self is very much in support of Bataille's project. Bataille's struggle is to break the confines of thinking and 'experience' the 'ungraspable', the 'extreme limit of the possible'.[106] Bataille is wrestling with the tortuous limits and suffering found in human life and the desire to extend beyond it. The central notion behind this work for Foucault, in his own essay on Bataille, is 'contestation', a concept Bataille takes over from Blanchot.[107] As Bataille explains: 'inner experience is linked to the necessity, for the mind, of putting everything into question – without any conceivable respite or rest.'[108] The idea of limit and transgression has currency for Foucault in terms of his anti-humanist stance and the attempt to suspend the categories of Enlightenment thought. It was Bataille, along with Blanchot and Klossowski, who enabled Foucault to break with the traditional philosophy of the subject.[109] Foucault carries forward the force of 'contestation' in his own questioning of the idea of 'man' and the 'subject', but this does not lead to a state of mystical rapture, which would be to fall back into the traditional categories of theological authority, and, as occurs in Miller's work, psychological individualism.

Foucault's post-structuralist spirit utilises the 'contestation' of Bataille and Blanchot to push the boundaries of thought. Such thinkers support Foucault's radical vision and it is not surprising that every reference to the concept of 'limit-experience' in his 1978 interview with Trombadori is couched in terms of the reorganisation of

---

[104] M. Richardson, *Georges Bataille*, Routledge, London, 1994, p. 113. cf. pp. 112–16. Richardson points out that to see Bataille's thinking as 'mystical' is 'misconceived'. See M. Richardson, 'Introduction' in *The Absence of Myth: Writings on Surrealism by George Bataille*, ed. M. Richardson, Verso, London, 1994, pp. 18; 20f. Cf. G. Bataille, *Visions of Excess: Selected Writings 1927–1939*, Minneapolis, University of Minneapolis, 1985, p. 236 and N. Calas (1945), 'Acephalic mysticism' in *Transfigurations: Art Critical Essays in the Modern Period*, UMI Research Press, Ann Arbor, 1985.

[105] See S. T. Katz, ed., *Mysticism and Philosophical Analysis*, Sheldon, London, 1978.

[106] Bataille, *Inner Experience*, p. 37.

[107] Foucault [1963], 'A preface to transgression' in this volume, p. 61 n. 13. Cf. Foucault [1966], 'Maurice Blanchot: the thought from the outside', p. 22.

[108] Bataille, *Inner Experience*, p. 175. Cf. Blanchot, *The Infinite Conversation*, p. 202ff.

[109] Foucault [1978], *Remarks on Marx*, Semiotext(e), New York, 1991, pp. 31; 40–1; 46; 48; 52; 56–8; 68–9; 70–1. Cf. Foucault [1980], 'About the beginning of the hermeneutics of the self' in this volume, p. 160.

knowledge and the deconstruction of the subject; ideas which specifically offered Foucault a way out of the traditional philosophy of the subject. As Foucault makes clear:

And then in Bataille, the theme of the 'limit-experience' in which the subject reaches decomposition, leaves itself, at the limits of its own impossibility. All that had an essential value for me. It was the way out, the chance to free myself from certain traditional philosophical binds.[110]

The notion of 'limit-experience', irrespective of its place and meaning in Bataille, inspired the wider operation of 'de-subjectifying' Western thought. It was an attempt to step outside the experience of the 'subject', to write, to articulate and to think without the 'subject'.[111] Madness, death, sexuality and crime were all examined in terms of breaking the 'limits' of preconceived rationality and subjective orientation, and not as an inner mystical event.[112] At no point does Foucault make a direct association of the 'limit-experience' with mysticism, which remains a strategy of Bataille's argument. To read Bataille's mystical analogies back into Foucault's life and work, as Miller does, is to distort the evidence.

Miller's work on the 'limit-experience' misreads both Bataille and Foucault by translating the term into a contemporary psychological event, which as Grace Jantzen's study on mystical experience reveals is developed from a Jamesian interpretation of mysticism.[113] Jantzen exposes the way modern interpretations of mysticism are seen as 'subjective psychological states or feelings of the individual', a position she sees as emerging from an over-reliance in contemporary thought on William James's definition of mysticism in *The Varieties of Religious Experience*.

William James, according to Jantzen, built his idea of mysticism from the Romantic tradition of Schelling and Schleiermacher, emphasising the qualities of intense ineffable experience.[114] This position was in turn a response to Kant's critical philosophy which prevented any rational understanding of God. While aware of a broad range of mystical experiences James was, as Jantzen indicates, 'drawn to these fringes of experience' in order to 'circumvent Kantian strictures on the experience of the supernatural'.[115] In his turn Miller falls into this reading of the mystical in his own focus on the 'limit-experiences' and in the process presents a confused understanding of Foucault. What is perhaps more intriguing is that Miller's reliance on a post-Kantian mysticism is circumvented by Foucault in his own essay on Bataille.

Foucault recognises that the idea of the 'limit' comes from Kant's reflections on metaphysical discourse, but he also acknowledges that such an opening was simultaneously closed when Kant 'relegated all critical investigations to an anthropological

[110] Foucault, *Remarks on Marx*, p. 48.

[111] Foucault, 'A preface to transgression', pp. 65–6.

[112] Foucault, *Remarks on Marx*, pp. 99–100.

[113] See Jantzen, 'Mysticism and experience'.

[114] Jantzen, 'Mysticism and experience', pp. 298–9; cf. Jantzen, *Power, Gender and Christian Mysticism*, pp. 278ff.

[115] Jantzen, 'Mysticism and experience', p. 302; cf. I. Kant [1793], *Religion within the Limits of Reason Alone*, Harper Torchbooks, New York, 1960 and W. James [1901–2], *The Varieties of Religious Experience*, Collins, Glasgow, 1960.

question'.[116] Foucault relies on Nietzsche, and those post-Nietzschean thinkers like Bataille, to break the anthropological subject. There is a tension in Miller – noted in passing by Alasdair MacIntyre in his own critique – between Nietzsche's project and the 'cult of extreme experiences with its roots in nineteenth century romanticism'.[117] Miller misunderstands Foucault and mysticism by his failure to see beyond a post-Kantian anthropology.

Miller not only misreads Bataille's understanding of the 'inner experience' and Foucault's understanding of Bataille but he also injects a Romantic notion of mysticism developed by James to support his narrative. It would even be possible to say that Miller's underlying 'passion' is to read (perhaps unconsciously) Foucault and his life through the intellectual climate of The Varieties of Religious Experience, through the 'extreme experiences' which for Miller are psychological and religious.[118] Such confusions in reading the works of Foucault as mystical demand greater scrutiny of his religious texts and expose the need to understand the religious nature of French avant-garde writing.

Miller's work has obviously dominated a lot of current interest in Foucault. However, the value of Miller's work is not in presenting an accurate understanding of Foucault, but in allowing greater exposure to some intriguing details of Foucault's work. (Miller's research if not accurate is prolific.) Miller in effect sets the 'mystical' cat among the 'religious' pigeons. It is up to those who follow to reorganise Foucault against the backdrop of Miller's fanciful narrative. This narrative has twisted the writings of avant-garde writers, such as Bataille, to substantiate a preconceived idea about Foucault's work. In order to extinguish the religious distortions in Miller's work I want to follow three less dominant, but none the less significant, strands of Miller's 'mysticalization', the first two of which are linked directly to the idea of 'limit-experience'.

SADO-MASOCHISM AND RELIGIOUS SUFFERING

In his critique of Miller's work Halperin warns the reader to 'check Miller's quotations of Foucault against their original contexts', a procedure particularly necessary in the light of the 'extraordinary critical acrobatics' and the 'frenetic orgy of citations'.[119] This becomes most acute in relation to Miller's account of sado-masochism (S/M) and the way he links this to mystical and ecstatic experience. The pleasure from

---

[116] Foucault, 'A preface to transgression', p. 63.

[117] A. MacIntyre, 'Miller's Foucault, Foucault's Foucault', p. 56.

[118] I am not suggesting that Miller is developing his idea of mysticism directly from William James. He provides no genealogy for his use of the term. It would be more reasonable to assume that Miller's stereotypical notion of the mystical is derived from the popular culture of the 1960s that operated on, absorbed and developed notions of mysticism reconstructed through a psychological discourse, which goes back to William James. See, for example, the popular literature, influencing and arising from the 1960s, such as A. Huxley [1954; 1956], The Doors of Perception; Heaven and Hell, Granada, London, 1977 and A. Maslow [1964], Religions, Values and Peak-experiences, Penguin, New York, 1970.

[119] Halperin, Saint Foucault, pp. 172; 167; 181. Miller in response to Halperin's critique acknowledged the importance of his footnotes to allow readers to make their own judgement. While Miller's footnotes and sources are substantial, the utilisation of the material, as Halperin has clearly identified, is spurious. Miller, 'Policing discourse', pp. 94–9.

physical pain in martyrdom or religious suffering and S/M opens a vast area of study, and, while it is not in question that at some level they may constitute a parallel event and hold a common denominator in the suffering body, there are huge epistemological quandaries in understanding the so-called 'limit-experience' of S/M as religious. What is erotic is not necessarily religious and vice versa, and whereas it may be just a question of definitions, the context and belief behind a particular infliction of pain on the body is surely crucially important.[120]

Miller continually amalgamates themes in Foucault's writing with religious ideas of self-sacrifice and martyrdom; for example, he takes Foucault's desire to obliterate identity, the 'shattering of the philosophical subject', the death of the author and Foucault's interest in St Anthony in order to position the experience of S/M within a mystical framework.[121] Miller fails to appreciate the different order of these experiences and face the central fact that activities in S/M are not acts of missionary zeal, a desire to die for Christ, or attempts to find union with God in any specific theological sense. There are also huge social and political differences in the conception of suffering in the Californian bathhouses and that of religious martyrs of the Middle Ages, and to suggest that Foucault understood his own experience theologically is seriously to misread his work on religion. The question remains as to how Miller formulates such a misconstrued argument.

Once again the central confusion arises from Miller's misreading of Foucault through Bataille, this time principally through his later study, *Eroticism*. In this work Bataille makes a clear link between erotic experiences and mysticism. They hold a 'structural' similarity in the sense of creating a feeling of continuity in a state of discontinuity.[122] Foucault is fully aware of this discussion and confirms the link between Christian mysticism and spirituality to sexuality.[123] The link between Christian experience and sexuality forms a central part of Foucault's engagement with religion, and his *History of Sexuality* is underpinned by such a discussion of Christian history. (See Part 3 in this volume.) The fact that Foucault develops a fascinating study

---

[120] See E. Scarry, *The Body in Pain: The Making and Unmaking of the World*, Oxford University Press, New York, 1985. There is an interesting anomaly related to this mixture of discourses when we consider the original location of the Foucault archive in the Dominican library, the Bibliothèque du Saulchoir. St Dominic, in his identification with Christ, idealised, with so many of his time, the state of martyrdom and suffering. He wrote with passion: 'Do not offer me a swift death, I beg you, but rather tear off my limbs one by one – I should wish to be no more than a limbless trunk, eyes torn out, rolling in my own blood that I might conquer a more beautiful crown of martyrdom' (from Jourain de Saxe (1891), *Opera*, Fribourg, p. 549, quoted in Zoé Oldenbourg, *Le Bûcher de Montségur*, Gallimard, Paris, 1959, p. 97). These words of St Dominic parallel the opening passages of Foucault's *Discipline and Punish*, and form an intriguing connections with S/M, but the epistemology and hermeneutics of suffering in each case operates at an entirely different level. Dominic's experiences in the thirteenth century is set around the politics of the Inquisition and a religious understanding of dying for Christ; this is not the same as the politics of punishment in the eighteenth century or the erotics of twentieth-century gay bathhouses. The simple linking by Miller of these events gives no consideration to their social location and is cause for much distortion. Similarly, although Miller correctly notes Foucault's interest in St Anthony and the images of suffering, there is no evidence to suggest that Foucault equates this with S/M. See Miller, *The Passions of Michel Foucault*, pp. 341–4. (I am grateful to Richard Townsend for providing the example of St Dominic.)

[121] Miller, *The Passions of Michel Foucault*, pp. 30; 324; 342–4.

[122] G. Bataille [1957], *Eroticism*, Marion Boyars, London, 1987, p. 15.

[123] Foucault, 'Preface to transgression', p. 57.

of religious ideas and sexuality is not under question; what is questioned is the view that Foucault saw modern sexuality as being linked to the idea of mysticism.

The crucial fact is that Foucault makes a distinction between the shaping of sexuality in Christian history and modern sexuality. Modern sexuality from Sade to Freud has not according to Foucault 'found the language of it logic or of its natural process', it exists in an 'empty zone', at the site of a 'dead God'.[124] Modern sexuality is a post-theological position, it inherits Christian models of the flesh but is not Christian or mystical. These are fundamental ideas in Foucault's religious sub-text and they offer little support to a view of contemporary sado-masochistic experience as constituting a mystical or religious event. It is important to remember that Foucault makes a clear division between the Christian heritage of sexuality and the modern sexual condition, sufficient evidence to show it is unlikely that Foucault would have seen his own experience of S/M as specifically Christian, let alone Christian mystical.

In his own discussion of S/M in 1984 Foucault saw S/M as the 'eroticization of power', it held 'new possibilities of pleasure'. There was no hint of any Christian or mystical experience in Foucault's words. More importantly, Foucault recognised S/M as the '"use" of a strategic relationship' not before sex (as in heterosexual relationships) but 'inside sex'. Foucault even points out in passing that while the institution of courtly love in the Middle Ages held a strategic relationship (to God) it remained outside the sexual act. Although Foucault does not mention religious suffering in his discussion of S/M it can, according to his own analysis, be seen as a 'strategic relationship' to God and oneself which may create pleasure but which does not necessarily operate within sex.[125] The S/M relationship exists inside a hermeneutics of sexual pleasure rather than a theology of suffering.

It soon becomes clear that Miller's argument links erotic and sexually ecstatic events to the notion of 'limit-experience' as a way of justifying the mystical dimension, which as we have seen holds no textual support.[126] Foucault's texts are reconstituted by Miller in terms of Bataille's account of mystical experience and eroticism and show no appreciation of the shifts in direction and changes of emphasis that take place in Foucault's own reflections. Miller uses the enigmatic nature of Foucault's writing to insert his own reconstructions, by placing Bataille's account of mystical rapture and erotic behaviour alongside 'typically oblique' passages from Foucault; Miller thus creates a false religious atmosphere out of Foucault's own understanding of S/M.[127] Foucault may have taken his experience in California as 'limit-experiences' as Daniel Defert suggested to Miller, but, as I have shown, Foucault did not take such 'limit-experiences' as 'mystical'. The continual compounding of misinformation builds huge fantasies; fantasies Halperin believes to be Miller's own.[128]

[124] Foucault, 'Preface to transgression', p. 57.

[125] Foucault [1982], 'Michel Foucault: an interview: sex, power and the politics of identity', *The Advocate*, no. 400, 7 August 1984, pp. 27–30. Cf. Foucault [1982], 'The social triumph of the sexual will', *Christopher Street*, no. 64, May 1982, pp. 36–41.

[126] Miller, *The Passion of Michel Foucault*, pp. 87–8; 154–5; 278–9.

[127] Miller, *The Passion of Michel Foucault*, pp. 88–9. Cf. Halperin, *Saint Foucault*, p. 168.

[128] Halperin, *Saint Foucault*, p. 181.

The mysticalisation of Foucault and the erotic is given extra weight by Miller when he uses the key passage on 'negative theology' from Foucault's essay on Blanchot to magnify his narrative. Foucault's essay on Blanchot examines the idea of 'the thought from the outside', and Foucault suggests this type of thinking may be linked to the mystical writings of Pseudo-Dionysius.[129] This 1966 allusion has been completely misunderstood by Miller. What Miller fails to realise is that Foucault, like Bataille before, suspends the mystical idea as soon as it is introduced. Foucault and Bataille are attempting to demarcate a new space in literature with inadequate old language. Miller provides no context for Foucault's remarks and introduces 'a kind of mystical thinking' into the modern period inaugurated by Sade. Foucault holds no such position and only indicates how Sade 'gives voice to the nakedness of desire as the lawless law of the world'; no 'kind of mystical thinking' is implied.[130]

Miller's technique is to extrapolate any possible fragments from Foucault's work, or from influential writers related to Foucault, to support a process of mysticalisation. This can be seen in the way Miller interjects Deleuze's idea of 'perverse mysticism' into his Sadeian recreation of S/M, a passage which Halperin believes shows no real understanding of the practices of gay bathhouses.[131] Miller also shows no real appreciation of Deleuze's idea of 'perverse mysticism', which exists in a very specific discussion of the historical influences on the writings of Leopold von Sacher-Masoch, the writer from whom Krafft-Ebing invented the pathology of 'masochism'. Deleuze believes Masoch to have been 'treated unjustly' because his work was neglected while his name 'passed into current usage'.[132] Miller commits a similar injustice to both Masoch and Foucault, neglecting Foucault's writing for the popular fascination with gurus, icons and erotics.

TRANSGRESSION AND TRANSCENDENCE

In the process of Miller's iconography there is a significant interplay and slippage between the ideas of transformation, transgression and transcendence which supports his distortion of Foucault. The religious cosmology is stimulated by interweaving these terms and performing some intricate (possibly unconscious) linguistic juggling in order to allow sufficient ambiguity to create a religious space in Foucault's writing, a strategy reinforced by fusing 'transcendence' with the 'limit-experience'.

Miller accurately registers Foucault's interest in personal transformation, a theme which emerges in the 1978 Trombadori interview, a text crucial to Miller's narrative.[133] Foucault continually tried to hide his private self and attempted to escape classification; he wanted to step outside of the normalising categories of the 'subject'. This desire to 'shatter the philosophical subject' and write from the place of the death of the author does provide a framework for considering Foucault's attempt to make 'transform-ations' both intellectual and personal. Klossowski, according to Macey, saw Foucault's

[129] Foucault, 'Maurice Blanchot', p. 16.
[130] Foucault, 'Maurice Blanchot', p. 17.
[131] Miller, The Passion of Michel Foucault, pp. 279–80; Halperin, Saint Foucault, pp. 181–2.
[132] G. Deleuze [1967], Masochism, Zone Books, New York, 1991, p. 13.
[133] Foucault, Remarks on Marx, p. 37; Miller, The Passion of Michel Foucault, p. 32.

goal, with Deleuze, as 'the liquidation of the principle of identity'.[134] The confusion arises when Miller links this to a religious transcendence, as opposed to a self-transcendence, in his concept of the 'limit-experience'.[135]

The complication in Miller's work occurs when he introduces Heidegger's idea of '"transcends" pure and simple' and aligns it with Foucault's idea of 'transgression'.[136] This marriage of ideas escalates rapidly when sado-masochism is seen to 'illuminate the enigma of transcendence' and when 'the object of transgression' is viewed as being able to 'tap the untamed energy of transcendence'.[137] A very simplistic metaphysical structure is being developed here by Miller and it shows no respect for the infinite complexities in this terminology. The cacophony is increased when Miller advances a strange litany of figures in his 'transcendent' musical; Kant's 'freedom' and Nietzsche's 'will to power' join with Heidegger to mark out the space of trans-cendence.[138] The noise is unbearable and the reader is left deafened in any attempt to ascertain the meaning, especially when these ideas are all linked to 'a mysterious (and perhaps divine) spark within'.[139]

It would seem that Miller's narrative forms an unintended intellectual mockery of Foucault and Western philosophy, but, inaccurate as it is, it does allow us to draw attention to a central problem in understanding the idea of 'transcendence' in Foucault and its relationship to 'transgression'.[140] This is brought further into focus when Miller in two footnotes explains that he translates the French word franchissement in Foucault's 1983 essay on Kant's 'What is Enlightenment?' as 'transcendence', rather than following Catherine Porter's translation in The Foucault Reader of 'transgression'.[141] Miller justifies his decision to alter the translation on the grounds that after criticising Bataille in his 1976 History of Sexuality: An Introduction he stopped using the French word 'transgression'. Miller may be correct to question the use of the word 'transgression', despite the fact that it remains faithful to the spirit of Foucault's work, but Miller's use of the word 'transcendence' is equally problematic.

The introduction of the word 'transcendence' into an essay offering alternative methods to Kant's 'transcendental' opens up the danger, as we have already seen in Miller's symphony, of confusing 'transcendental' (a Kantian mode of argumentation) with 'transcendence' (primarily a religious notion).[142] The situation is complicated by a certain amount of slippage between these terms in Foucault as well, but what is clear is that through the historical processes Foucault challenged both the 'transcend-

---

[134] Macey, The Lives of Michel Foucault, p. xv.

[135] Miller, The Passion of Michel Foucault, pp. 13ff.

[136] Miller, The Passion of Michel Foucault, pp. 46; 88; 143.

[137] Miller, The Passion of Michel Foucault, pp. 88; 143.

[138] Miller, The Passion of Michel Foucault, p. 305; cf. pp. 105; 116.

[139] Miller, The Passion of Michel Foucault, p. 348.

[140] See Carrette and King's discussion of 'transcendence' in J. Carrette and R. King, 'Giving "birth" to theory: critical perspectives on religion and the body', Scottish Journal of Religious Studies, Special Edition, 'Beginning with birth', vol. 19, no. 1, spring 1998, pp. 123–43.

[141] Miller, The Passion of Michel Foucault, pp. 445 n.124; 456 n.45. Cf. Foucault (1983), 'What is Enlightenment?' in The Foucault Reader, ed. Paul Rabinow, Penguin, London and New York, 1991, p. 45.

[142] Foucault, 'What is Enlightenment?', p. 46; Miller, The Passion of Michel Foucault, p. 88; Foucault, 'A preface to transgression', p. 62.

ental' and the idea of 'transcendence'. While the confusion may be apparent, his challenge to these ways of thinking is not, as Foucault defending his archaeological method in 1969 states: 'But because it seemed to me that, for the moment, the essential task was to free the history of thought from its subjection to transcendence.' And later in the same paragraph: 'My aim was to cleanse it [history] of all transcendental narcissism.'[143] In order to avoid these complications the translation of franchissement should perhaps have retained the more literal sense of a 'crossing over', specifically as Foucault could have used the words 'transgression' or 'transcendence' (the same in French and English) if he had wanted to be precise. I do not wish to place too much emphasis on this particular text and its translation, but it serves to demonstrate how easily the slippage in terminology can occur, particularly in the light of Miller's religious iconography.

Foucault's thinking on the 'transcendent' exists in a complex trajectory of philosophical thought arising from Kojève's lecture on Hegel and Nietzschean avant-garde thought. Miller's work only demonstrates the misleading results of an uncritical use of this term, hovering between a general idea of 'self-transcendence/transformation' and a more theological notion, which he then interchanges with 'transgression'. The discussion of these problems is made more complex by a Gnostic reading of Klossowski, yet another idea Miller imports into Foucault.

GNOSTICISM AND THE OCCULT

The linking of Foucault's thought with the occult and Gnosticism is perhaps one of the most intriguing and fascinating strands of Miller's narrative, the meaning of which is often concealed in footnotes and brief allusions. As is the case with other areas of Miller's work, he is correct to identify Gnostic influences in the work of the avant-garde and surrealism, but totally inaccurate in assuming that this is carried forward in any significant way in Foucault's own understanding.

The principle force behind Miller's narrative was to see Foucault as engaging in a 'hermetic quest' according to Nietzsche's 'gnomic injunction "to become what one is"'.[144] The hermetic mystery seems to be supported by Miller's response to Foucault's style, which can be seen from the way he links a 'hermetic impulse' to his discussion of Roussel and perceives a 'hermetic abstractness' in his earlier works such as The Order of Things.[145] The use of the word 'hermetic' may have been a useful metaphor to describe the deliberately oblique styles and poetical ellipses Foucault inherited from avant-garde discourse, but when Miller also refers to the 'occult' in regard to Foucault's work, such descriptions take on an entirely different meaning and begin to form part of the sophisticated tapestry of Miller's underlying mysticalisation of Foucault.

The hermetic quest forms part of a seemingly innocent smattering of terms from 'occult' literature, including 'esoteric', 'visionary' and 'ascetic'.[146] The misuse of these

---

[143] Foucault, The Archaeology of Knowledge, p. 203; cf. Foucault [1972], 'An historian of culture' in Foucault Live: Collected Interviews, 1961–1984, 2nd edition, ed. S. Lotringer, Semiotext(e), New York, 1996, p. 99.

[144] Miller, The Passion of Michel Foucault, pp. 5; 319.

[145] Miller, The Passion of Michel Foucault, pp. 33; 124; cf. pp. 281; 294; 335; 348.

[146] Miller, The Passion of Michel Foucault, pp. 7; 8; 88; 321; 342; 344. cf. pp. 399 n.59; 445 n.122.

terms to create an occult visionary out of Foucault is exposed when Miller makes a few passing remarks to the 'occult', a word, it should be added, which is left precariously to drift in the text without definition or any substantiation. Miller sees the end of Foucault's *History of Sexuality Volume One*, presumably the essay entitled 'Right of death and power over life', as holding 'occult possibilities' in the sense of the erotic pleasure of death and violence, a view he associates with Foucault's own S/M practice.[147] There is no evidence to suggest that Foucault viewed his S/M practices in 'occult' terms and we can conclude only that this forms part of the wider wave of distortion operating throughout Miller's fantasy. Miller seems to use the word 'occult' merely to signify an assumed erotic pleasure of sacrifice and shows no appreciation of the very diverse historical and social practices which have been labelled as 'occult'; it forms a kind of literary strategy to cause sensation. This is precisely the force behind Halperin's critique of Miller: gay sexual practices are sensationalised and wrapped in an elaborate and esoteric language so as to divorce them from the more immediate pleasures of gay men erotically losing control. Miller's (straight) narrative is able to contain Foucault's sexuality in terms which have no, or at least very little, relationship to Foucault's own work.

Foucault did write about the themes of witchcraft, the devil and Gnosticism in the early 1960s, but specifically in terms of the history of madness and the work of Pierre Klossowski.[148] The essay on Klossowski directly discusses aspects of Gnosticism, a theme which sits alongside that of the occult and forms according to Miller 'an unspoken subtext' to his interpretation of 'Foucault's peculiar brand of "asceticism"'.[149] Miller argues, in a fascinating footnote, that Foucault has a 'subterranean link, via his affinities with Klossowski, to a Manichean Gnosticism'.[150] And, commenting on Foucault's discussion of St Anthony in a similar context, Miller writes:

As should be clear by now, I take 'all' of Foucault's work to be an effort to issue a license for exploring this 'daimonic' possibility – and also as a vehicle for expressing, 'fictively', his own Nietzschean understanding of this harrowing vision of a gnosis beyond good and evil, glimpsed at the limits of experience.[151]

The final strand of Miller's mysticalisation of Foucault is completed with the alignment of Foucault with Gnosticism.

The Gnostic nature of Foucault's work is never really developed fully by Miller and largely remains, as he stated, his own 'unspoken subtext'. The 'unspoken subtext' in Miller's work appears to be focused on an interpretation of Foucault's 1980 Howison lectures concerned with Christian self-sacrifice, coupled with some residue of Foucault's 1963 essay on Klossowski. As Miller flamboyantly writes: 'Testing the soul like a moneychanger tested gold in a fire, the Christian ascetic struggled with a diabolical double, conjuring up this demonic other in order to defeat and drive out,

---

[147] Miller, *The Passion of Michel Foucault*, pp. 279; 348. Cf. p. 304.

[148] Foucault [1962/8], 'Religious deviations and medical knowledge', and Foucault [1964], 'The prose of Actaeon', both in this volume.

[149] Miller, *The Passion of Michel Foucault*, p. 445 n.129.

[150] Miller, *The Passion of Michel Foucault*.

[151] Miller, *The Passion of Michel Foucault*, pp. 458–9 n.73.

through a kind of spiritual combat, this despicable self.'[152] The Gnostic language is Miller's devised by joining Foucault's description of the Christian (not Foucault's) hermeneutics of the self and the idea of the 'double' in Foucault's description of Klossowski's writing where the Same and the Other, God and the Devil, are joined together.[153] However, Foucault's interest in Klossowski's language (see 'The prose of Actaeon' in this volume) is in framing a thought 'outside dialectics', where everything is 'simulacrum', a mirror of itself.[154] Klossowski offers Foucault a way out of theological dialectics in the attempt to 'sidestep all the Alexandrianism of our culture', which reads the simulacra as signs. The 'time of theologians' is one which divides and immerses itself in the 'ambiguous play of signs', as Foucault states:

Catholics scrutinise signs, Calvinists have no trust at all in them, because they only believe in the election of souls. But what if we were neither signs nor souls, but merely the same as ourselves (neither visible sons of our works, nor predestined), and thereby torn apart in the discrete distance of the simulacrum?[155]

According to Foucault we would be richer if we abandoned the divisions of Christian theology. This is not Gnostic theology but a commentary on the value of Klossowski's work in the contemporary literature of France.[156] Foucault may see Klossowski as bringing Christianity under the spell of the Demon, but in the space of the simulacrum Foucault sees the disappearance of theology. Foucault is at this point developing a critique of theology and not, as Miller suggests, developing a Gnostic discourse.

Miller's work demonstrates how he is unable to separate Foucault from the avant-garde writers before him, confusing the works of Bataille and Klossowski with those of Foucault. Many post-structuralist writers, as Goodall has demonstrated in relation to Artaud, focus selectively on issues from the avant-garde and surrealism to serve their own anti-humanist venture. Gnosticism was well suited to undermine Western humanism and provided a rich language to undermine the securities of knowledge: it was as Goodall suggests an 'older and absolute assault' to stand with Nietzsche's own philosophical critique.[157] Miller therefore falls into a double trap in appropriating Gnostic ideas, confusing both Gnosticism and Foucault's use of Klossowski's Gnostic works. The distinction between Klossowski's thinking and Foucault's is given even greater support when we consider how Foucault's political interests took him away from Klossowski's literary influences, a fact made clear by David Macey, who interviewed Klossowski for his own biographical study of Foucault. Commenting on the relationship between Foucault and Klossowski, Macey writes: 'There were, on the other hand, limits to their common interests and Klossowski never really succeeded in interesting Foucault in the gnostics who mean so much to him.'[158]

[152] Miller, *The Passion of Michel Foucault*, p. 323
[153] Foucault, 'The prose of Actaeon', pp. 75–6.
[154] Foucault, 'The prose of Actaeon', p. 77.
[155] Foucault, 'The prose of Actaeon', p. 81.
[156] Foucault 'The prose of Actaeon', p. 84.
[157] J. Goodall, *Artaud and the Gnostic Drama*, Clarendon Press, Oxford, 1994, pp. 217–20.
[158] Macey, *The Lives of Michel Foucault*, p. 157.

The Gnostic fantasy provides yet further evidence to show how Miller's religious iconography stands as a testimony to misreading Foucault through writers like Bataille and Klossowski. There are many religious fragments and deposits from the avant-garde literature in Foucault's work but none which suggests Foucault is either a mystic or a Gnostic.

Foucault's writing is not, as Miller suggests, 'weird', it makes sense in certain philosophical and literary traditions of French culture, his 'cryptic utterances' are not those of a mystical guru, and he is not captured in such media epithets as 'postmodern sphinx' or 'metaphysical Eraserhead', he is a thinker, to note Bernauer, struggling to escape certain 'prisons' of Western thought and to understand his own sexuality.[159] Miller's work can only be seen, at best, as an unfortunate misreading of the source material, and, at worst, as an outrageous distortion of the gay life and Foucault's engagement with religious ideas.

Miller has left a confused series of religious images floating in Foucault scholarship which need to be critically evaluated. Foucault's work on religious and theological themes needs in this respect to be re-examined with some urgency. There are many religious strands operating in Foucault's work, and more importantly in the writers who influenced his work, that remain unexplored and confused. The texts in this volume provide a new opportunity to explore Foucault's work on religion in order to create a better understanding of Foucault and open again Bernauer's invitation for religious and theological engagement.

Foucault on religion and culture: the texts

I believe that somebody who writes has not got the right to demand to be understood as he had wished to be when he was writing; that is to say from the moment when he writes he is no longer the owner of what he says, except in a legal sense. (Foucault, 'Michel Foucault and Zen', 1978)

Foucault's work on religion is not a systematic treatment of the subject but a series of somewhat fragmented interventions and tactical manoeuvres. They are attempts to 'problematise' religion in terms of either discursive history, literature, governmentality, sexuality, power or an ethics of the self. Religion for Foucault was always part of a set of force relations and discursive practices which order human life. Foucault's work thus presents a reading of religion outside theological traditions and belief – a reading that does not position religion in some separate realm but inside a political struggle of knowledge-power. In this way Foucault provides a radical framework to question the politics of all religious and theological thinking. He brings religion back into history and back into the immanent struggle of identity and subjectivity.

This volume of texts does not seek to present the religious tropes of Foucault's main work (interesting and significant as they are) but to bring together some previously untranslated texts from *Dits et écrits* and other pieces outside his main work which are either largely inaccessible or thematically important for his work on

[159] Miller, *The Passion of Michel Foucault*, p. 320; Bernauer, *Force of Flight*, pp. 1 ff.

religion. As Arnold Davidson has noted: 'With the publication of Michel Foucault's *Dits et écrits* in 1994, we are in a new position to begin to assess the significance of his work.'[160] The Foucault that has been constructed and made into an academic icon in the secondary literature needs to questioned and broadened in the context of his wider work found in *Dits et écrits*, the Collège de France lectures and other archival material. We need to understand the complexity of Foucault's texts and take them out of the simplistic epithets which attempt to package his key ideas neatly.[161] One aspect in appreciating the wider scope of Foucault's work is to rescue the important religious dimensions of his writings. Such an archival process reveals the complexity of a life and a work inescapably reduced in the boundaries of its presentation.

In each of the texts in this volume Foucault opens religion to scrutiny and suspicion according to the concerns that dominate his work at the time. Religion in this sense is always a subsidiary category, a cultural deposit influencing and informing his wider historical and philosophical interests. Religion is a part, a central part, of the cultural conditions of knowledge. In this sense it is very difficult to separate religion and culture; they are interconnected parts of each other. This argument has been developed by Richard King, who has adopted a broadly Foucauldian methodology in developing the idea of 'a mutual imbrication of religion, culture and power'. King argues that the category of religion has been subject to a series of contestations and was isolated from the cultural dynamic, and perceived as an autonomous realm, only after the Enlightenment.[162] Foucault's work directly questions the separation between religion and culture by including it within his 'analysis of the cultural facts' and later collapsing the division between religion and politics in an ethics of the self.[163] Foucault's work can therefore be seen to move within a discursive space of 'religion and culture' – where one mutually informs the other. As Foucault's work demonstrates, a culture cannot understand itself without first understanding its implicit connection and development within the constructs of religious belief and practice. Contemporary culture is born out of religious traditions and the conditions of our knowledge are therefore embedded in religious discourse. The so-called secular space is itself a hybrid of past religious traditions, and in order to understand contemporary culture Foucault recognised (and was fascinated by) the religious influences upon thought and practice.

[160] A. I. Davidson, 'Structures and strategies of discourse: remarks towards a history of Foucault's philosophy of language' in *Foucault and His Interlocutors*, ed. A. I. Davidson, University of Chicago Press, Chicago, 1997, p. 1.

[161] Take for example Foucault's work on the body. Most commentators examine Foucault's work on the body from 1975 onwards, viewing the body as a passive object, but there is a more complex trajectory behind Foucault's thinking. In Foucault's 1954 introductory essay on Ludwig Binswanger's 'Dream and existence' there are fragments of an imagining body, in 1963 we find an active Sadean body and in 1966 Foucault recognises the 'ambiguous space' of the body. See Foucault [1954], 'Dream, imagination and existence' in *Dream and Existence: Michel Foucault and Ludwig Binswanger*, ed. K. Hoeller, Humanities Press, Atlantic Highlands, New Jersey, 1993; Foucault [1963], 'A preface to transgression' in this volume, and Foucault [1966], *The Order of Things*, Routledge, London, 1989, p. 314 (American edition: Pantheon, New York, 1970).

[162] King, *Orientalism and Religion: Post-colonial Theory, India and the 'Mystic East'*, Routledge, London, 1999. See chapter 2, 'Disciplining religion', and chapter 9, 'Beyond Orientalism?'

[163] See Foucault [1967], 'Who are you, Professor Foucault?', p. 91 in this volume, and Part 3, pp. 153–97.

The texts in this volume are divided for convenience into three parts. Part 1 deals with Foucault's work on religion in the study of madness and in his literary avant-garde work in the 1960s; Part 2 brings together a number of disparate religious themes from the 1970s, including the emergence of Foucault's concern with Christianity and pastoral power; and Part 3 groups together texts from the early 1980s when Foucault extended his work on early Christian history – originally started in the late 1970s. The final part constitutes work for Foucault's unpublished final volume of the *History of Sexuality*. It marks out the hidden contours of Foucault's work on Christianity. By bringing Foucault's late work on Christianity alongside earlier texts and extracts I am seeking to open up the trajectory of Foucault's religious thought – to provide an account of Foucault on religion and culture. Together these texts provide a unique chronicle of one of the most influential twentieth-century thinkers encountering religion and theology. Finally, these texts attempt to rescue Foucault's unpublished work on religion and open a dialogue terminated by his death.

PART 1: MADNESS, RELIGION AND THE AVANT-GARDE

Following the publication of *Histoire de la folie* in 1961 Foucault was very much in demand to speak. In May 1962 he took part in the Royaumont conference on 'Heresy and society in pre-industrial Europe', contributing a paper on 'Religious deviations and medical knowledge'. This paper continued themes from Foucault's earlier study of madness but instead of focusing on the earlier question of 'silence' and 'unreason' he explored the 'system of the transgressive'. The paper examines the interrelationship between the religious deviation of the demonic and the medicalisation of this parareligious experience. This medicalisation did not replace the supernatural with the pathological but rather established the relationship between the excluded and the included in fantasy. 'Paradoxically doctors of the sixteenth century freed up from the demonic only those things which were inanimate, they placed the demonic in the immediate environs of the soul, at the surface of the body.' There was in effect an alliance or 'annexation' between medicine and religious cosmology. The idea of an 'annexation' was introduced into Foucault's revision of *Maladie mentale et personalité* in 1962, reflecting the nature of his research at this time.[164] The church and medical institutions formed a 'network ' or 'apparatus' to control and exclude. These early lines of thought are important in the way they reveal the oppressive mechanisms of Christianity. Foucault's later work can be seen to examine in greater detail these embryonic ideas of religious exclusion in the religious concept of the demonic in his technology of the self. The notion of the Devil is also significant in so far that it depicts the Other of religious discourse. In Foucault's later essay on the Devil/Other in the work of Klossowski these ideas assume greater significance. Foucault's essay on the demonic and madness can be seen therefore as part of his wider concerns with the marginalised and prohibited which dominates so much of his work, not least in relation to religion.

[164] Foucault [1962], *Mental Illness and Psychology*, University of California Press, Berkeley, 1987, p. 65 (also Harper & Row, New York, 1976).

While writers like Midelfort, Sedgwick and Porter have questioned the historical evidence behind Foucault's history of madness, its revisionist approach has none the less been very influential in questioning the progressive models of history.[165] 'Religious deviations and medical knowledge' supplements Foucault's early work on the history of madness by drawing out Foucault's understanding of the history of madness as intrinsically carrying forward religious ideas. It serves to support Foucault's view that the 'complex problem of possession does not belong directly to the history of madness, but to the history of religious ideas'.[166] The religious dynamics of madness in European history form a central, and as yet unexplored, part of Foucault's work. From the 'foolishness' of the Cross to religion as a 'safeguard' of reason in the asylum, there is an important recognition by Foucault of the centrality of Christian imagery to the history of madness. In both *Mental Illness and Psychology* and *Madness and Civilization* Foucault noted how the church and medical establishment interwove complex webs of order around the voice of 'unreason'. The particular focus on religion takes its force not merely from the fact that religious ideas inform Western knowledge but from the way Foucault's history unearths the power of images which shape and order 'madness'. Foucault is interested in the imagination that informs the understanding of madness.

Foucault's work on madness is concerned with 'iconographic powers' in the shaping of madness. It is concerned with an 'imaginary landscape' and the 'reactivation of images'.[167] This particular focus accounts for the many literary allusions in *Madness and Civilization* but it also indicates why Foucault is so concerned with religious ideas. Foucault's work on madness is in fact a twofold imaginative study. He reclaims images of madness from the archive and then inserts his own powerful images into a new history. Foucault realises that it is the imagination which constructs madness.

'Religious deviations and medical knowledge' continues the examination of the religious 'image' by considering how the sixteenth-century writers understood the nature of Satanic possession and the body. Foucault is attempting to show how the imagination is rooted in the physical body through a fusion of religious and medical practices. 'Development of medical knowledge in the sixteenth century is not linked to the replacing of the supernatural by the pathological, but to the appearance of transgressive powers of the body and of the imagination.'

The importance of the imagination, the body and madness is often lost in the examination of Foucault's study of madness, but it relates to the continuing influence

---

[165] H. C. E. Midelfort, 'Madness and civilization in early modern Europe: a reappraisal of Michel Foucault' in *After the Reformation: Essays in Honor of J. H. Hexter*, ed. Barabara C. Malament, Manchester University Press, Manchester, 1988, pp. 247–65; P. Sedgwick, *PsychoPolitics*, Pluto Press, London, 1982, pp. 125–48; R. Porter, *Mind-Forg'd Manacles*, Penguin, London, 1987, pp. 5–9. Cf. W. F. Bynum, R. Porter and M. Shepherd, 'Introduction' in *The Anatomy of Madness: Essays in the History of Psychiatry*, Tavistock, London, 1985, vol. 1, 'People and ideas', p. 7.

[166] Foucault, *Mental Illness and Psychology*, p. 64.

[167] Foucault [1961], *Madness and Civilization*, pp. 72; 205–6; 211.

of themes in Foucault's early work on Binswanger. In the foreword to Binswanger's *Dream and Existence* Foucault briefly discusses Spinoza's reflections on the prophetic dream where two sorts of imagining are examined; the imaginings dependent on the body, as in delirium, and the embodied imagination which is a specific form of knowledge.[168] According to Foucault, Spinoza's *Tractatus theologico-politicus* operates on these two levels. The prophetic imagination is tied to the body (the affliction of Jeremiah and the anger of Elias) but also holds a meaning, 'the link of imagination to truth' (the language of God). In 'Religious deviations and medical knowledge' Foucault draws out a similar dynamic in the sixteenth century. Spirit (the demonic) and the body are joined in the imagination which allows for an interweaving of religious and medical terminology. Foucault's argument is that the processes of exclusion and inclusion operate in the sixteenth century across religious and medical languages through the dynamic of imagination and the body. As Foucault concludes: 'I believe finally ... that there is a unity of madness with a certain number of phenomena of religious territoriality and that it would be useful to carry out structural study of the whole, a synchronous study, because the system is quite obviously different in each period.'

Foucault's work on the 'transgressive' in religion and madness is also informed by the work of Bataille. It was Bataille who also led Foucault to consider a series of religious questions in relation to sexuality. In a series of pieces for such journals as *Critique* and *Tel Quel*, and in his 1966 work *The Order of Things*, Foucault unfolded a complex series of theological issues around the work of Bataille, Blanchot and Klossowski. This work reveals a significant religious sub-text exploring such issues as eroticism and the death of God. In his 1963 essay 'A preface to transgression' for *Critique* Foucault entertained a number of post-Nietzschean religious themes in Bataille's work. This essay is important because it shows how Foucault adapts and extends Bataille's religious work. Foucault is not simply adopting Bataille's position, as James Miller suggests, but rather interlacing the themes of language, sexuality and the death of God in a new construction of religious discourse. This religious discourse develops Bataille by locating his work in the context of anti-humanist philosophy and contemporary theories of language. As Foucault declares: 'Perhaps the importance of sexuality in our culture, the fact that since Sade it has persistently been linked to the most profound decisions of our language, derives from nothing else than this correspondence which connects it to the death of God.'

The trope of the 'death of God' is a major part of Foucault's engagement with Nietzsche and the avant-garde in the 1960s. Foucault's reading of Nietzsche's death of God is coupled with the death of man and forms the basis for Foucault's own death of God theology in *The Order of Things*. In order to elucidate this key notion I have included a very short interview ('Philosophy and the death of God') which provides an important clarification of how Foucault understands the idea of the death of God. It shows how he distinguishes Nietzsche's use of the term from other philosophers. The text forms an important 'footnote' supplement to Foucault's use of Nietzsche and

[168] Foucault [1954], 'Dream, imagination and existence', p. 45.

Foucault's reworking of Bataille through language and the death of God.[169] What we discover is that death of God leaves an empty space: it has not been filled – the theological space remains open.

Foucault's reflections on avant-garde theological ideas offer new ways of developing an embodied theology from the empty space. With the death of God, the body and sexuality assume a greater importance in the finitude of existence. Elsewhere I have argued that this embodied theology lacks any gender specificity and needs to be critically explored as reflecting a series of masculine models of spirituality which emerge out of French avant-garde religious thinking.[170] From an early stage we see how Foucault's work interweaves religion, the body and sexuality but surprisingly this is often neglected in the literature on religion and body theory.[171] What is also not sufficiently appreciated is how the emergence of such glorious ideas as 'body theology,' 'polymorphously perverse theology' and 'indecent theology' were already theoretically mapped out by the avant-garde and surrealist writers that Foucault examined.[172]

The avant-garde religious themes are continued in other essays from Foucault's 'literary period'. In his opening comments to a major conference on the novel in 1963 ('The debate on the novel'), organised by the Tel Quel group, Foucault explored the relationship between the literature of the 'new novel' and surrealism. In this discussion Foucault made a significant allusion to 'spiritual experiences'.

I am struck by the fact that, in Sollers's reading yesterday and in the novels of his that I've read, reference is constantly made to a certain number of experiences – experiences, if you like, that I will call, in quotation marks, 'spiritual experiences' (although 'spiritual' is not quite the right word) – such as dreams, madness, folly, repetition, doubling [le double], the disruption of time, return [le retour], etc. These experiences form a constellation that is doubtless quite coherent. I was also struck by the fact that this constellation was already mapped out in surrealism.

This passage was picked up by James Bernauer in one of the first attempts to explore Foucault's religious writings and opens a huge debate about how Foucault understood the 'spiritual'.[173] Foucault returns to the idea of the spiritual through out his writings, particularly from the late 1970s, with the idea of a 'political spiritualité' and the idea of

---

[169] As Foucault in The Order of Things points out: 'God is perhaps not so much a region beyond knowledge as something prior to the sentences we speak; and if Western man is inseparable from him, it is not because of some invincible propensity to go beyond the frontiers of experience, but because his language ceaselessly foments him in the shadows of his laws: "I fear indeed that we shall never rid ourselves of God, since we still believe in grammar" [Nietzsche].' Foucault [1966], The Order of Things, p. 298. Cf. F. Nietzsche [1889], Twilight of the Idols/The Anti-Christ, Penguin, London, 1968, p. 38; and N. Schiffers, 'Analysing Nietzsche's "God is Dead"' in Nietzsche and Christianity, ed. C. Geffré and J.-P. Jossua, T. and T. Clark, Edinburgh, 1981. See my own discussion of Foucault's use of the death of God in J. Carrette, 'Male theology in the bedroom'.

[170] See Carrette, 'Male theology in the bedroom' and J. R. Carrette, Foucault and Religion.

[171] For an overview of some of the literature on religion and the body see J. Carrette and R. King, 'Giving "birth" to theory'.

[172] See, for example, J. Nelson, Body Theology, W/JKP, Louisville, Kentucky, 1992; H. Eilberg-Schwartz, God's Phallus, Beacon, Boston, 1994, p. 242; M. Althaus-Reid, 'Sexual strategies in practical theology: indecent theology and the plotting of desire with some degree of success', Theology and Sexuality, no. 7, 1997, pp. 45–52; and, J. Carrette, Foucault and Religion.

[173] See Carrette, Foucault and Religion.

spirituality as a 'mode of being' inside a technology of the self.[174] I have included the extract from 'Débat sur le roman', and other short sections from Foucault's early work, to show the evolution of Foucault's religious thinking inside his wider concerns. This movement in and out of the sphere of religious discourse serves to illustrate the centrality of religion to the cultural conditions of knowledge and throws light on Foucault's later work.

In Foucault's 1964 essay on Klossowski, 'The prose of Actaeon', the literary exploration of religious themes continued. As with Foucault's essay on Bataille, there is always a great danger of confusing Foucault's work with the avant-garde writers he entertained. While Foucault entertains many religious concepts from avant-garde writers he does not necessarily adopt their position. This is particularly true in the case of Foucault's essay on Klossowski. Klossowski incorporated many Gnostic themes into his writing but Foucault, as I have indicated earlier, was never fully convinced by these ideas.[175] Foucault's discussion of Klossowski's work is however important in so far as it demonstrates his challenge to the binary oppositions between spirit and matter. This is a central theme developed in many earlier surrealist writers and Foucault supports these ideas from his own anti-humanist position.

Concluding the section on Foucault's avant-garde work on religious ideas is an interview from September 1967, 'Who are you, Professor Foucault?' This interview provides a broad overview of Foucault's work up to 1967 and shows the nature of Foucault's philosophical critique. It confirms the importance of Nietzsche, Blanchot and Bataille to Foucault's (religious) thinking and also indicates the importance of Georges Dumézil and Claude Lévi-Strauss. It is through Dumézil (specialist in Indo-European religions and mythologies) and Lévi-Strauss (anthropologist of religion) that we see the tentative emergence of a 'functionalist' view of religion.[176] Foucault sees religion, alongside ideologies, philosophies and systems of metaphysics, as part of the mechanism for controlling the function of human life. These ideas would later develop into Foucault's conceptualisation of religion as a political power and a 'technology of self'. It shows how Foucault is interested not so much in religious beliefs as in the practice or function of religion.[177]

[174] Foucault [1978], 'Questions of method' in The Foucault Effect: Studies in Governmentality, ed. G. Burchell, C. Gordon and P. Miller, Harvester Wheatsheaf, Hemel Hempstead, 1991, p. 82; [1984], 'The ethic of care for the self as a practice of freedom' (Interview) in The Final Foucault, ed. J. Bernauer and D. Rasmussen, MIT Press, Cambridge, Massachusetts, 1991, p. 14.

[175] Macey, The Lives of Michel Foucault, pp. 154–7.

[176] Throughout his work Foucault acknowledged a great debt to the historian of religion Georges Dumézil. See, for example, Foucault's inaugural lecture at the Collège de France, where Foucault stated: 'I believe I owe much to Monsieur Dumézil, for it was he who encouraged me to work at an age when I still thought writing a pleasure. But I owe a lot, too, to his work … It is he who taught me to analyse the internal economy of discourse quite differently from the traditional methods of exegesis or those of linguistic formalism. It is he who taught me to refer the system of functional correlations from one discourse to another by means of comparison. It was he, again, who taught me to describe the transformations of a discourse, and its relations to the institution' (Foucault, 'The discourse of language' in The Archaeology of Knowledge, Pantheon Books, New York, 1972 [appendix] p. 235). For a discussion of the influence of Dumézil on Foucault see: Macey, The Lives of Michel Foucault, pp. 77–8, and n. 20. pp. 492–3; Eribon, Michel Foucault, pp. 75–6; Miller, The Passion of Michel Foucault, pp. 135–6.

[177] This approach to religion was developed by Bryan Turner in his 'materialist theory of religion'. See B. Turner, Religion and Social Theory, p. 13.

PART 2: RELIGION, POLITICS AND THE EAST

Part 2 attempts to show the diversity of Foucault's religious interests in the late 1970s. It brings together a series of interventions, from casual interviews discussing religious rituals to formal lectures on the history of pastoral power. It is during this period that we see not only Foucault's interest in the East but the development of Foucault's view of religion as a political force. It was also during the 1970s that Foucault began to work on Christian confession for his 1976 *The History of Sexuality Volume One: An Introduction*; and in consequence firmly established the influence of Christianity in the emergence of discourses of sexuality in the West. Following this work Foucault, around 1977,[178] started to read the work of the father of Christian monasticism, John Cassian, and thus began the long and awkward journey through the literature of late antiquity. Foucault's *History of Sexuality* from this point on was to face continual reorganisation and postponement as Foucault discovered problems with his original project. This meant that the work on Christianity would be delayed and, as it turned out, remain unpublished. We will explore the shape of the unpublished volume in Part 3, but in the 1970s Foucault would firmly ground religion in the political realm.

One of the most intriguing set of comments Foucault made about religion occurred in a series of taped interviews with Thierry Voeltzel, 'a young hitch-hiker picked up by Foucault in 1975'.[179] The document was originally brought to light by Claude Mauriac and published as *Vingt ans et après* (*Twenty Years and After*). It was brought to the notice of the English-speaking world through the biographical work of Didier Eribon and David Macey in the early 1990s. It reveals Foucault in a more relaxed mood talking about a whole range of issues. A small section of these interviews, 'On religion', contained some revealing comments by Foucault's about the church and religious rituals. Although this interview cannot be held in the same light as his other work, it does throw a wider perspective on Foucault's interest in religion. It reveals the fascination, intrigue and passion Foucault held for religion and his understanding of religion as a political force. Some may regard the dialogue with Thierry Voeltzel as insignificant but it provides an insight into Foucault's personal interest in religion, an aspect picked up by many who knew Foucault personally.[180] No doubt this interest was in part motivated by Foucault's French Catholic background.

In 1978 Foucault made a second trip to Japan, the first trip having taken place in 1970.[181] During the visit Foucault had a busy schedule and gave a series of lectures and interviews. His visits to Japan had opened up his interest in Zen Buddhism, and in an interview with a Zen Buddhist priest Foucault briefly explored the relationship between Eastern and Western religious thinking. The interview, 'Michel Foucault and Zen: a stay in a Zen temple', also reflects upon a variety of issues such as meditation,

---

[178] Tape C16 'Discussion with philosophers, 23 October 1980, Berkeley, California' in the Foucault Archive, Paris.

[179] Macey, *The Lives of Michel Foucault*, p. xxi.

[180] I have been pleased to discover in talking to those who knew Foucault in the USA that they remember his real fascination with religion, and the Voeltzel piece perhaps captures this personal interest.

[181] For an account of Foucault's visit to Japan see Macey, *The Lives of Michel Foucault*, pp. 399–401 and Eribon, *Michel Foucault*, p. 310.

mysticism and Marxism. Although Foucault's understanding of Zen is simplistic and the concept of 'mysticism' has since been deconstructed with Foucault's own methodology, the interview is important in so far as it shows the scope of Foucault's interest in Eastern religious thinking.

It is possible to identify a small strand of comparative philosophical work on the boundaries of Foucault's writings but it always remains marginal and open to Orientalist critique. We find, for example, the famous passage from the Chinese encyclopaedia at the beginning of *The Order of Things*, regarded by Larson as 'poetic projection', and the contrast between 'ars erotica' of Eastern traditions and the Western 'scientia sexualis'. There are also brief comparisons between Greek, Christian and Chinese constructions of the desiring subject.[182] Uta Liebmann Schaub has gone as far to argue that there is an Oriental sub-text in Foucault's work and that a correspondence can be established between Foucault's early writing and Oriental concepts, such as those found in the Mahayana Buddhist tradition of Nāgārjuna.[183] Foucault's early work on language and the avant-garde does offer striking parallels with non-dualist philosophical ideas, and perhaps minor strands of Eastern thinking do emerge but we need to be critical of the Orientalist assumption behind such tropes and ask whose interests are served through such comparative engagement.[184] This of course is not to diminish Foucault's peripheral interest in Eastern traditions and from the interview at the Zen temple we have a sense of how seriously he takes religious ideas and his respect for cultures of 'silence'. As Foucault reflected in 1982, no doubt to some extent recalling his experiences in Japan:

Silence may be a much more interesting way of having a relationship with people … I think silence is one of those things that has unfortunately been dropped from our culture. We don't have a culture of silence; we don't have a culture of suicide either. The Japanese do, I think. Young Romans or young Greeks were taught to keep silent in very different ways according to the people with whom they were interacting. Silence was then a specific form of experiencing a relationship with others. This is something that I believe is really worthwhile cultivating. I'm in favour of developing silence as a cultural ethos.[185]

One of the many lectures given during Foucault's 1978 visit to Japan was delivered at the University of Tokyo. This paper, 'Sexuality and power', is important in so far as it brings together themes from Foucault's 1976 *History of Sexuality* and new ideas from his 1977–8 Collège de France lectures on 'Security, territory, and population'. In these lectures Foucault began to explore the theme of 'governmentality', examining the 'procedures and means employed to ensure, in a given society, the "government of

---

[182] G. J. Larson, 'Introduction: the "age-old distinction between the same and the other" in *Interpreting Across Boundaries: New Essays In Comparative Philosophy*, ed. G. J. Larson and E. Deutsch, Motilal Banarsidass, Delhi, 1988, p. 4; Foucault [1966], *The Order of Things*, p. xv; Foucault [1976], *The History of Sexuality Volume One: An Introduction*, p. 59; Foucault [1983], 'On the genealogy of ethics', p. 359; 'Discussion with Michel Foucault', April 1983, manuscript D250 (12), Foucault Archive, Paris.

[183] U. L. Schaub, 'Foucault's Oriental subtext', *PMLA*, vol. 104, 1989, pp. 306–16.

[184] For a more detailed discussion of Nāgārjuna (second century CE) in his context and the Orientalist problematic, see R. King, *Indian Philosophy: An Introduction*, Edinburgh University Press, Edinburgh, 1999. I am grateful to Richard King for his reflections on Nāgārjuna and comparative philosophy.

[185] Foucault, 'The minimalist self', interview in June 1982, in *Politics, Philosophy, Culture*, p. 4; for a discussion of Foucault and silence see Carrette, *Foucault and Religion*.

men".[186] This analysis of government included an exploration of pastoral power in Hebrew and Christian society. Pastoral power, as Foucault indicated in his Collège de France course outline, is a

power that individualizes by granting, through an essential paradox, as much value to a single one sheep as to the entire flock. It is this type of power that was introduced into the West by Christianity and took an institutional form in the ecclesiastical pastorate: the government of souls was constituted in the Christian Church as a central, knowledge-based activity indispensable for the salvation of each and everyone.[187]

This interest in the pedagogical and spiritual dimension of government was to open Foucault's study of Christianity. It extended the work on confession and psychoanalysis into a wider technology of self.

The 1978 Tokyo lecture reflects the beginnings of Foucault's analysis of the Christian 'hermeneutics of the self'. It firstly restates the dynamic of confession and then secondly draws out the structures of pastoral power through the dynamics of obedience and salvation. Foucault's overriding concern in this work is the relationship of the subject to truth – the way Christianity produces a certain 'truth' of the individual. 'Truth, the production of interior truth, the production of subjective truth, is a fundamental element in the practice of the pastor.' These ideas would be developed in greater detail in the 1980s and lead to the paradox of the Christian care of the self in 'renunciation'.[188] It is striking to see how many of the late themes of Foucault's work were present in 1978. In the Tokyo lecture we already see Foucault arguing that Christianity is introducing 'new techniques' for sexuality rather than 'new moral ideas'. This argument would form the underlying force of the second and third volumes of his *History of Sexuality* and indicates how Foucault shaped the study of the Graeco-Roman world around his earlier understanding of Christianity.

The theme of pastoral power returned to prominence just over a year later when Foucault delivered the Tanner Lectures on Human Values at Stanford University in October 1979. In this lecture, originally titled 'Omnes et Singulatim: towards a criticism of political reason' (in this volume 'Pastoral power and political reason'), Foucault brings together his themes of the government of individuals and the government of the state. He attempts to outline the origin of pastoral power and its alignment with the secular political rationality of the state. Foucault's overall aim is to demonstrate the 'development of power techniques oriented towards individuals' – the way the state orders the truth of subjects. According to Foucault the state is the centralised power and pastorship is the 'individualising power'. These techniques of power are joined together in a secular form in the problem of the welfare state. Many of these issues directly reflect the concerns in Foucault's lectures at the Collège de France on issues of 'biopolitics', by which he meant 'the endeavour, begun in the

---

[186] Foucault, 'Security, territory, and population' in *Ethics, Subjectivity and Truth: The Essential Works of Foucault*, ed. Paul Rabinow, New Press, New York, 1997, p. 67.

[187] Foucault, 'Security, territory, and population', p. 68.

[188] See Foucault, 'About the beginnings of the hermeneutics of the self' in this volume, and Foucault [1984], 'The ethic of care for the self as a practice of freedom', pp. 5–9. Cf. Foucault [1982], 'Technologies of the self' in *Technologies of the Self*, pp. 16–49.

eighteenth century, to rationalize the problems presented to governmental practice by the phenomena characteristic of a group of living human beings constituted as a population.'[189] It is through this work that Foucault is able to break down the separation between the individual and the political. The individual is always for Foucault inescapably caught within the wider political technologies of control.

Political rationality has grown and imposed itself all through the history of Western societies. It first took its stand on the idea of pastoral power, then on that of reason of state. Its inevitable effects are both individualisation and totalisation.

In the Tanner Lectures we see Foucault's growing interest in ancient Christian literature, with reference to Chrysostom, Cyprian, Ambrose, Jerome and Cassian, and his recognition of the importance of self-examination and the guidance of conscience for Christian living. This material would eventually form the basis of his 1980 lecture series at the Collège de France and bring Christianity to the centre of Foucault's work. (See 'On the government of the living' in this volume). The religious practices of Christianity, and the insights from the Graeco-Roman world, had introduced a complex structuring of the self.

We can say that Christian pastorship has introduced a game that neither the Greeks nor the Hebrews imagined. A strange game whose elements are life, death, truth, obedience, individuals, self-identity; a game which seems to have nothing to do with the game of the city surviving through the sacrifice of the citizens.

It is through the creative deployment of the concept of 'governmentality' as the 'techniques and procedures for directing human behaviour' that Foucault is able to bring the state and individual together inside the idea of pastoral power.[190] There is a fusing of the political and the individual which leads in turn to a collapsing of the boundaries between politics, religion and the ethics of self. For Foucault it is the interlocking of the government of self and the government of state that forms the basis of a 'political spirituality'. As Foucault wrote in 1978:

How can one analyze the connection between ways of distinguishing true and false and ways of governing oneself and others? The search for a new foundation for each of these practices, in itself and relative to the other, the will to discover a different way of governing oneself through a different way of dividing up true and false – this is what I would call 'political *spiritualité*'.[191]

Religion for Foucault is always part of a political technology governing the self.

The location of religion inside the political arena took on a new dimension when Foucault became interested in the Iranian Revolution in 1978/9 and carried out a series of journalistic 'reportages' for the Italian newspaper *Corriere della Sera*.[192] Foucault's interest in Iran is important to the development of Foucault's views on religion in so far that Foucault sees religious inspiration as bringing about political change. The Iranian Revolution in 1978 fascinated Foucault precisely because of its religious basis. In a 1979 interview Foucault suggested that religion for the Iranian people 'was like

---

[189] Foucault, *The Essential Foucault*, p. 73.
[190] Foucault [1980], 'On the government of living', see pp. 154–7 in this volume.
[191] Foucault [1978], 'Questions of method', p. 82.
[192] See Stauth, 'Revolution in spiritless times', and Macey, *The Lives of Michel Foucault*, pp. 406–11.

the promise and guarantee of finding something that would radically change their subjectivity'.[193] Here again we see the interlocking of the political ideology of the state with the construction of the religious subject.

Although many commentators now feel that Foucault misjudged the Iranian question in his journalist 'reportages', the issues of a 'political spirituality' relate to important aspects of Foucault's interest in governmentality and his wider attempt to understand the politics of religion.[194] In 1979, after receiving criticism for his report-ing of the Iranian Revolution, Foucault wrote an article for Le Monde reflecting on the situation. In this article ('Is it useless to revolt?') Foucault examined the religious motivation behind the Iranian Revolution. The article shows clearly the dilemma Foucault faced between an intellectual interest in 'live revolts' and the political consequences. The paper however does provide a valuable insight into how Foucault sought to extend his ideas of a 'political spirituality' into a non-Christian context. The negative responses to his reports of the Iranian Revolution may have disillusioned Foucault in his attempt to understand state politics and religion, but his examination of a 'political spirituality' was to continue in his examination of early Christian literature and the ethics of the self – the final and unfinished project.

PART 3: CHRISTIANITY, SEXUALITY AND THE SELF: FRAGMENTS OF AN UNPUBLISHED VOLUME
In a discussion with Paul Rabinow and Hubert Dreyfus in 1983 Foucault explained he had written a book on the early Christian experience of the flesh, sex and desire.[195] Foucault explained how the work examined the new techniques of the self introduced by Christianity, a featured already indicated in the Tokyo lecture of 1978. At this point Foucault seemed to think 'the Christian book', as he came to call it, would appear after L'usage des plaisirs (The Use of Pleasure) but Foucault would juggle the material around again to allow for another volume, Le souci de soi (The Care of the Self).[196] The Christian book had from the beginning of the project on sexuality been the intended second volume.[197] In 1977, a year after the publication of the first introductory text, Foucault was grappling with Tertullian and the church in late antiquity in preparation for such a volume: 'We have had sexuality since the eighteenth century, and sex since the nineteenth. What we had before that was no doubt the flesh. The basic originator of it all was Tertullian.'[198] Foucault actually finished a version of the work on Christianity, presumably in the late 1970s. The work however faced a number of unforeseen

[193] Foucault, 'Iran: the spirit of a world without spirit' in Politics, Philosophy, Culture, Routledge, London and New York, 1988, p. 218.

[194] See Foucault [1978], 'Governmentality', pp. 87–104.

[195] Foucault, 'Discussion with Michel Foucault: 19 April 1983', Mss. D250(5)* and Tape C27*, Foucault Archive, Paris.

[196] Foucault [1983], 'On the genealogy of ethics: an overview of work in progress' in The Foucault Reader, ed Paul Rabinow, Penguin, London and New York, 1991, p. 358; Foucault [1984], The Use of Pleasure: The History of Sexuality Volume Two; Foucault [1984], The Care of the Self: The History of Sexuality Volume Three, Penguin, London, 1990 (American edition: Pantheon, New York, 1986).

[197] The back cover of the first volume of the History of Sexuality in 1976 had indicated that a second volume entitled La chair et le corps (Flesh and Body) would appear but owing to the problems outlined below it was postponed, reshaped and retitled. See Eribon, Michel Foucault, pp. 273–4.

[198] Foucault [1977], 'The confession of the flesh' (a discussion) in Power/Knowledge, p. 211.

43

problems and multiple reworkings. Foucault recognised that his introductory 'clichés' about the Graeco-Roman world, the first forty pages in his planned second volume on Christianity, contained many errors and needed to be substantially corrected.[199] He realised he could not write about the Christian tradition until he had explored its antecedents.

I wondered what the technology of the self before Christianity was, or where the Christian technology of the self came from, and what kind of sexual ethics was characteristic of ancient culture. And then I was obliged after I finished *Les Aveux de la chair*, the book about Christianity, to reexamine what I said in the introduction to *L'Usage des plaisirs* about the supposed pagan ethics, because what I has said about pagan ethics were only clichés borrowed from secondary texts.[200]

The change of order in Foucault's *History of Sexuality* was coupled with new developments in Foucault's thinking about 'governmentality' and 'techniques of the self'. The material on Christianity was thus reconfigured in terms of a genealogy of ethics – an ethics conceived as *rapport à soi* (the relationship to oneself).

In the Christian book – I mean the book about Christianity! – I try to show that [Greek] ethics has changed. Because the telos has changed: the telos is immortality, purity, and so on. The asceticism has changed, because now self-examination takes the form of self-deciphering. The *mode d'assujettissement* [mode of subjection] is now divine law. And I think that even the ethical substance has changed, because it is not *aphrodisia*, but desire, concupiscence, flesh, and so on.[201]

The ethical themes in Graeco-Roman and Christian ethics were the same but the techniques of the self were substantially different. Foucault in effect identified a different ethical 'formula' in Christianity which placed the emphasis on the control of desire.[202] *Les aveux de la chair* (*Confessions of the Flesh*) was thus rewritten and transformed in the mind of Foucault – in lectures, interviews and articles – but it did not appear in final print.

Part 3 in this volume is an attempt to bring together some of the fragments behind Foucault's final volume. It does not represent every lecture and article which would have shaped the contours of Foucault volume but brings together a selection of the central documents, including a course outline, lecture transcripts and a published extract. These pieces, with the material from the 1970s, undoubtedly constitute research work for *Les aveux de la chair*. There are other fragments from interviews and lectures in the early 1980s which further supplement these central texts but on the whole the other pieces only replicate or elaborate material contained in this selection.[203]

According to the final advertising statement for the *History of Sexuality*, written by Foucault and distributed in June 1984, *Les aveux de la chair* would 'treat the experience of the flesh in the early centuries of Christianity and the role played by hermeneutics and the purifying process of deciphering desire'.[204] Each of the pieces included in this

---

[199] See Foucault, 'Discussion with Michel Foucault: 19 April 1983', Mss. D250(5)*, Tape C27*, Foucault Archive, Paris.

[200] Foucault, 'On the genealogy of ethics', pp. 341–2.

[201] Foucault, 'On the genealogy of ethics', p. 358.

[202] Foucault, 'On the genealogy of ethics', p. 359.

[203] See, for example, Foucault, 'Technologies of the self'; Foucault, 'The ethic of care for the self as a practice of freedom', pp. 1–20.

[204] Quoted in Eribon, *Michel Foucault*, pp. 320–1.

selection covers material under this brief remit. The outline of the book undoubtedly covers work on John Cassian and monasticism, some work on Augustine,[205] and undoubtedly sections on the Christian hermeneutics of the self – themes captured in the material for this volume. Until the final editing and shape of *Les aveux de la chair* is made known through publication we will have to rely on the fragments that remain.

The first 'fragment' of documentation reflecting Foucault's rethinking of *Les aveux de la chair* is the course summary of 1980, 'On the government of the living'. This summary, as with the other course outlines, stands as a crucial benchmark in the evolution of Foucault's work. It firmly locates the broad parameters of Foucault's work on Christian history in terms of the government of self, the examination of conscience, confession and monastic practice. It shows the continuing importance of John Cassian to Foucault's thinking and also indicates how Foucault has extended his original work on Christian confession. These excursions into Christian themes were enhanced by Foucault's move to the Bibliothèque du Saulchoir, a Dominican library in the southeast of Paris, which contained a valuable collection of works on Christianity in late antiquity.

In 1980 Foucault also gave a series of lectures in the United States on themes of early Christian history and sexuality. The next two 'fragments' are taken from this series of lectures. The first of the two texts is the transcript of the lectures given at Dartmouth College, New Hampshire, which incorporates slight changes from the Howison Lectures given earlier at Berkeley. 'About the beginning of the hermeneutics of the self' consists of two lectures, one on Greek philosophy and the other, following similar issues on the genealogy of the modern subject, on Christian confession. These lectures reveal how Foucault had formulated in his late work a new framework around the technology of self in both Greek and Christian history. The lecture on Christianity explored the work of Tertullian, John Chrysostom and John Cassian in terms of confession and self-examination. In his examination of these thinkers Foucault uncovered the techniques through which the Christian self was constructed. As Foucault stated:

In the Christian technologies of the self, the problem is to discover what is hidden inside the self; the self is like a text or like a book that we have to decipher, and not something which has to be constructed by the superposition, the superimposition, of the will and the truth.

These lectures link very strongly with Foucault's 1982 lectures at the University of Vermont on *The Technologies of Self*. They show clearly the structure of thinking behind the final volume of Foucault's *History of Sexuality* as located in techniques of the self and ethics.

The second American lecture in this section is the 1980 James Lecture, entitled 'Sexuality and solitude', given at the Institute for Humanities in New York. This lecture starts in a similar fashion to the other 1980 American lectures but notably focuses

[205] Foucault not only makes reference to Augustine in the James Lecture, included in this collection, but he also responds to questions on Augustine in his discussion with philosophers at Berkeley in 1980. See Foucault, 'Discussion with philosophers: 23rd October 1980', Tape C16*, Foucault Archive. It is reasonable to assume that sections on Augustine are included in the unpublished volume. Cf. Foucault, 'On the genealogy of ethics', p. 347.

45

more on St Augustine. In this lecture Foucault compares a text by the pagan philosopher Artemidorus on dream interpretation with the fourteenth book of St Augustine's *City of God*. The comparison enables Foucault to demonstrate how Christianity established a 'new type of relationship' between sex and subjectivity. Foucault establishes that Augustine's sexual ethic is concerned with male sexuality and the issue of the internal control of the libido. As Foucault states:

The question is not, as it was in Artemidorus, the problem of penetration: it is the problem of erection. As a result, it is not the problem of a relationship to other people, but the problem of the relationship of oneself to oneself, or, more precisely, the relationship between one's will and involuntary assertions.

The techniques of self-examination in Christianity were the main focus of Foucault's study of Christianity and are shown clearly in Foucault's essay on the monastic writer John Cassian. In his 1982 essay 'The battle for chastity', an extract from the unpublished fourth volume, Foucault shows the extent of self-analysis in the Christian monastic tradition. In Cassian's work there is 'a whole technique for analysing and diagnosing thought, its origins, its qualities, its dangers, its potential for temptation and all the dark forces that lurk behind the mask it may assume'. In his focus on Cassian, Foucault showed the detailed techniques for rooting out desire and the procedures for renouncing the self. It was with this ultimate tension and paradox of Christianity – a self opposed to God's will and a self found in the renunciation of self – that Foucault brought his *History of Sexuality* to a conclusion. Perhaps Foucault's *History of Sexuality* had been a long struggle to overcome the oppression of Christianity and its denial of the body, desire and the flesh. As Foucault concluded his Dartmouth lectures:

Maybe our problem is now to discover that the self is nothing else than the historical correlation of the technology built in our history. Maybe the problem is to change those technologies. And in this case, one of the main political problems would be nowadays, in the strict sense of the word, the politics of ourselves.

In Didier Eribon's biography of Foucault we learn from an interview with Pierre Nora that Foucault had expressed the wish for 'no "posthumous publications"'.[206] This did not affect Foucault's Collège de France lectures, which were apparently 'open to discussion' and which started to appear in publication in 1997.[207] However, the final volume of his *History of Sexuality* which required only minor 'editorial tidying up' and was possibly one or two months away from completion, could not be published. It was in effect locked, at the point of Foucault's death, in the debates about Foucault's intended wishes. It remains a mystery to Foucault scholarship, a mystery similar to the final enigmatic work of Roussel, *How I Wrote Certain Books*, a work simultaneously revealing and concealing.[208] *Les aveux de la chair* holds a similar key to Roussel's enigma.

---

[206] Eribon, *Michel Foucault*, p. 323.

[207] *'Il faut défendre la société': Cours au Collège de France, 1976*, Hautes Études, Gallimard/Seuil, Paris, 1997. The Collège de France lectures are due to appear in English translation.

[208] See Foucault [1963], *Death and the Labyrinth: The World of Raymond Roussel*, Athlone, London, 1987 (American edition: Doubleday, New York, 1986).

It is the pivotal work of the *History of Sexuality* and, according to Pierre Nora, 'the part most important to Foucault'.[209] Yet for all its near-completion and the fact that many close to the Foucault archive have seen it, *Les aveux de la chair* remains unpublished. What makes this even more surprising is the fact that parts of the work already exist in the pieces which Foucault had agreed to publish before his death. Foucault's death denied him and those he left behind the completed work – the fragments however remain.

[209] See Eribon, *Michel Foucault*, p. 324.

PART I

Madness, religion and the avant-garde

CHAPTER ONE

Religious deviations and medical knowledge (1962)

Originally delivered at the Royaumont conference on 'Heresy and society in pre-industrial Europe' in May 1962.[1] The paper was first published as 'Les deviations religieuses et le savoir médical' in the conference proceedings: Jacques Le Goff, ed., *Hérésies et sociétés dans l'Europe pré-industrielle 11–18 siècles*, Mouton, Paris, 1968, pp. 19–29. It was subsequently published in *Dits et écrits*, vol. I, Gallimard, Paris, 1994, pp. 624–35.

Translation by Richard Townsend

There is certainly, in any culture, a coherent series of gestures of separation; among these, prohibition of incest, the marking out of madness and perhaps certain religious exclusions are only particular cases. The function of these gestures is, in the strict sense of the term, ambiguous: just when they mark the limit, they open out a space whose transgression is always possible. This space thus measured and open has its own configuration and its laws: it forms for each period what we might call the 'system of the transgressive'. It is right to say that it coincides neither with the illegal or the criminal, nor with the revolutionary, nor with the monstrous or the abnormal, nor with the addition of all these deviant forms; but each of these terms marks it out, at least indirectly, and sometimes allows it to be revealed in part. It is the space which, for all these terms taken as a coherent whole, is the condition of possibility and historical appearance.

The modern consciousness tends to order, as distinct from the normal and the pathological, the ability to mark out the irregular, the deviant, the unreasonable, the illicit and also the criminal. To all which consciousness finds foreign it gives the status of exclusion, when it is necessary to judge, and inclusion, when it is a question of explaining. The ensemble of fundamental dichotomies which, in our culture, lays out on both sides of the limit the conforming and the deviant, finds here a justification and gives the appearance of having a sound basis. Such marvels should not create an

---

[1] [The original text reads like a transcript and contains a number of technical difficulties when presented as a written document.]

illusion: they were set up at a recent date; the very possibility of tracing a line between the normal and the pathological was not formulated much earlier than this, since we must acknowledge that this possibility was something entirely new in the texts of Bichat at the turn of the eighteenth and nineteenth centuries. Strange as that may seem, the Western world knew, and had known for thousands of years, a form of medicine which rested upon an understanding of illness whose fundamental categories were not organised in terms of the normal and the pathological.

The debate that took place between the medical consciousness and certain forms of religious deviation, at the turn of the sixteenth century, may serve as an example. We will limit ourselves here to the belief in a changing of the physical powers of man due to the effect of a demonic intervention.

Let us first note that between partisans and adversaries of this multiplication [of religious deviation], what is at issue is not really punishment. The often cited indulgence[2] of Molitor and Wier is relative and very much partial. Molitor acquitted the witches of any real action, but only to condemn them more surely to the death sentence, 'because by their apostasy and their corruption these women have completely denied God and given themselves up to the devil' (*Des sorciéres et devineresses*, 1489, p. 81).[3] Doubtless, Wier was indignant that the judge did not show enough trust in the anger of God and that 'for a storm which has fallen on young corn [...] he had arrested a few mad and simple minded women', but he condemns with even more rigour the magicians who made pacts with the Devil 'in all awareness, free will and knowledge' (*Des illusions et impostures des diables*, 1579, pp. 164, 362).[4] As to Erastus, who held 'that witches were absolutely unable to perform the marvels that were commonly believed of them', he asks for the death penalty against them: 'I believe that I have shown sufficiently that witches should be punished, not so much for the things that they do or that they wish to do; but for their apostasy and their revolt against obedience to God. Similarly for their alliance contracted with the Devil' (*Dialogues touchant le pouvoir des sorcières*, 1579).[5]

This problem of indulgence is secondary. The essential point is that neither Molitor, at the end of the fifteenth century, nor Weir or Erastus, in the sixteenth century, dismisses the demonic. The debate with Sprenger, Scribonius or Bodin does not contest either the existence of the demon or his presence amongst men; rather it ponders upon the ways in which he shows himself and the manner in which his action is transmitted and hidden by appearances. This is not a conflict between nature and the supernatural but rather a difficult debate on the type of truth of the illusion. Here are a few points of reference:

---

[2] [The remission of sins.]

[3] U. Molitor, *De laniis et phitoniciis mulieribus tractatus*, C. de Zyrickzee, Cologne, 1489 (*Des sorcières et des devineresses*, trans. E. Nourry, Bibliothèque magique des XVe and XVIe siècles, Paris, vol. 1, 1926, p. 81).

[4] J. Wier, *De praestigiis daemonum et incantationibus ac veneficiis*, J. Oporinum, Basel, 1564 (*Cinq livres de l'imposture et tromperie des diables, des enchantements et sorcelleries*, trans. J. Grévin, 2nd edition, J. Du Puys, Paris, 1579, book III, chap. XVI).

[5] T. L. Erastus, *Deux dialogues touchant le pouvoir des sorcières et la punition qu'elles méritent*, Frankfurt, 1579. Re-edited in J. Wier, *Histoires, disputes et discours des illusions et impostures des diables, des magiciens infâmes, sorcières et empoisonneurs*, ed. D. Bourneville, Bibliothèque diabolique, Paris, 1885, first dialogue, p. 426.

First, Satan, an evil angel, but above all an angel, remained spirit even when he acquired a body. It is with spirits that he can communicate most easily; for these are free, whereas things of the earth submit to the laws which God prescribed for them. If then Satan acts upon bodies this can only be with God's special permission and a sort of miracle. If he acts upon souls, it is following this general permission which God gave him after the Fall; it is the universal consequence of sin. It was in this way that Erastus defined the possibilities of the action of the Devil: he has little power over things and bodies, less even than man to whom God confided the care of the world; but a great influence over spirits that he wishes to trick and seduce, and which are now the very domain of his ill doings, unless God, by special grace, consents to distancing him from hearts and minds.

Second, among those hearts and minds, Satan will choose by preference and ease the most fragile, those in whom will and piety are the weakest. *Women* first of all: 'The Devil, sharp, crafty and sly enemy, invades easily the feminine sex, which is inconstant by its make up; the fickle faith, mischievous, impatient, melancholic because it does not have command of its affections, and principally those old, simple minded and stupid women of wavering spirit' (Wier p. 300).[6] *Melancholics* also, who 'are saddened by little loss or other things, as said Chrysostom in these words: "All those whose the Devil tricks he tricks by irritation and sadness"' (p. 298).[7] Finally, the *mad*: 'And just as by humours and vapours the use of reason is interested in drunkards and fanatics, so also the Devil who is a spirit can easily and through God's permission move them, adapt them to his illusions and corrupt reason' (p. 313).[8] Thus, the Devil, without overturning any of this natural order, over which he has so little power, knows how to take advantage of the weaknesses and the failings this order may provoke in souls, in order to take them over. He has passed from an order of the world to which he is subject to the disorders of the soul which in turn he subjects. Sprenger's *Malleus Maleficarum* (*The Hammer of Witches*) said as much when it explained that the demon took advantage of the fact that 'the brain is the most humid of all the parts of the body' and of the influence of the 'moon, which [itself has power to] incite humours' (p. 40).[9]

Third, the demon – power disarmed against nature but all-powerful against souls – will act above all by trickery: nothing will be changed in the order of external things; but all will be overturned in their appearance, in the images which are transmitted to the soul. Because man has power, as Sprenger explained, to recover by his own will the images of things which no longer exist, the demon, even more so, holds a similar power: is it not he who when man's will is asleep commands dreams? (p. 50).[10] The demon is the master of dreams, the great tricking power; and, as he does not have the

[6] Wier, *Cinq livres*, book III, chap. VII, p. 300.

[7] Wier, *Cinq livres*, book III, chap. V, p. 298.

[8] Wier, *Cinq livres*, book III, chap. XIII, p. 313.

[9] H. K. Institoris and J. Sprenger, *Malleus maleficarum*, Jean Prüss, Strasbourg, 1486. *Malleus maleficarum*, trans. Rev. Montague Summers, The Hogarth Press, London, 1969, p. 40 (*Le marteau des sorcières*, trans. A. Danet, Plon, coll. 'Civilisations et mentalités', Paris, 1973, question V, p. 194). [The quotation is taken from the English translation which is slightly different from Foucault's rendition of the French translation.]

[10] Institoris and Sprenger, *Le marteau des sorcières*, question III, p. 165.

power to suspend the laws of nature, he only gives to men, by dreams and images, the full certainty that he holds this power: 'It is false that witches run thousands of leagues in the silence of the night to reach the sabbath;[11] they are the toy of dreams or some powerful illusion ... that the devil has imprinted in their brain' (Molitor).[12] Demonic action will not take place in the world itself but between the world and man, all along the surface which is that of the 'phantasy' and senses, there where nature is transformed into image. It is precisely this operation which he overturns, in no way changing the truth of nature, but clouding all appearances:

He knows ... how to show diverse figures, artificially shape useless idols, cloud vision, dazzle the eyes, put forward the false for true, and by a singular dexterity stop us from noticing his deceptions; hiding the things that are true, in order that they should not appear to be foregrounding things which are not true, and yet making them appear ... He is accustomed also to spoiling the phantasy of men by the mockery of many phantoms, troubling those who keep watch at night, astonishing by dreams those who sleep, making stray from the straight road those who travel, and to laughing at those who fail and others also! scaring them, confusing them and mixing up many things by the inexplicable labyrinths of opinion (Wier, pp. 55–6)[13]

Fourth, the intervention of the Devil then is clearly localised. This does not reduce at all its complexity nor its marvellous power, because it can be only in a whole system of complicity and correspondences. Of all the faculties of the soul, the imagination is the most material, or rather, it is in the imagination that the transition from body to soul and from soul to body is effected. And if it's no doubt true that, under the impetus of a whole religious evolution, the thinkers of the sixteenth century increasingly spiritualised the power of the Devil, they only gave him more complete powers over the body's interior machinery. All that is at the limits of the soul, just this side of the image, of fantasy and of dream, that is to say the senses, nerves, humours, become by association the privileged domain of the Devil: 'This evil spirit is more use to moving the humours [of the body], to trouble the source of the nerves which is the brain' (Wier, p. 58).[14] Satan knows how to mobilise all the solids of the body: when he shakes the nerves next to the brain, he needs at the same time to excite the organs of the senses, so that the fantasy can be taken for reality itself and that the body can be taken in by this great trickery, which makes the Devil appear to the enfeebled spirit of witches. But this mechanism, in itself complicated, is still not sufficient. That which the witch sees, others must see in their turn. In the mind of spectators the same fantasies must be born. And so the demonic operation, which spreads out from the imagination to the nerves and from there to the organs of the senses, extends itself, gains the body of others, their senses, their brain and their imagination, forming a dense vegetation which, excluding the outside world, is none the less real. (It is by this collection of co-ordinated artifices that 'the evil spirit knows how to bring out, craftily from the body of one possessed and into the sight of all', hair entangled, sand,

---

[11] [The references to the sabbath in this text refer to the 'witches sabbath' – a gathering of demons, witches and sorcerers presided over by the Devil.]

[12] Molitor, De laniis, p. 80.

[13] Wier, De praestigiis daemonum, book I, chap. XII.

[14] Wier, De praestigiis daemonum, book I, chap. XII, p. 58.

nails of iron, bones, waste, 'which he does after having dazzled our vision'.)[15]

Fifth, this power, limited to the space of the imagination, finds itself by that very fact redoubled in depth. It can in this way trick not only victims or accomplices, but those very individuals whose piety should be most resistant to temptations: those who hound out sorcerers because they have really been to the sabbath, or because they have turned themselves into wolves; but this is only trickery, and, therefore, the Devil tricks both the feeble spirits and the believers whose solid faith cannot be circumvented directly. Believing in the reality of all these physical powers is also a way of submitting to Satan: those who affirm in order to condemn, the real transport to the sabbath, are 'the principal slaves of their master Belzabuth who glorifies himself for having been well served, above all under the mantle of the Church' (Wier, pp. 255–6).[16] But, conversely, to deny the physical modifications because the operations which make them up are imaginary is to be in turn victim of the marvels of Satan: in only addressing oneself to already agitated imaginations and proceeding through fantasies and dreams, Satan knew well that we would fear him less and we would finish by no longer believing in his power; thus, disarmed, one becomes its victim, the peak of the illusion being to believe that his physical powers are only an illusion. According to Scribonus, it is the case with Wier himself, when he

proclaims that witches imagine only that they have committed crimes where in reality they have done nothing ... I speak frankly with Bodin: I believe that Wier who defended in all circumstances the witches and poisoners is himself a witch and a mixer of poisons. Ah, if only a man like him had never been born or at least had never written a single word! Whereas he and his books offer to people so many opportunities for sin and to sink into the kingdom of Satan.[17]

In any case, this empire triumphs and we do not come out of the realm of the demonic; we confirm its existence if we harry it in order to condemn it; we bring him succour if we deny his physical powers. Satan is always there precisely at the point from which we have just chased him; the place which he leaves empty is still the mark of his victory.

In this order of physical powers, which is henceforth only a universe of fantasies, Satan has become he who is perpetually absent. But it is in this very absence that his presence becomes assured and is shown; the less he can be assigned in his transcendental presence to a particular place in the world and in nature, the more his operations become universal, the more they gain in invisible subtlety, slipping into all truth and each appearance. A sort of 'ontological' argument is established: a discourse which does not go in a straight line from idea to existence, but from image (fantasy present to the dazzled mind) right up to the absence (because it only consists of a fantasy), then to he who has dug out or excavated the void, and is the solid figure of his own absence. When we take the image of Satan not for Satan but for an illusion, then Satan shows by this abusive lack of belief that he does exist; and when we take

---

[15] Wier, *De praestigiis daemonum*, book I, chap. XII, p. 57.

[16] Wier, *De praestigiis daemonum*, book II, chap. XVII, p. 255.

[17] W. A. Scribonius, *De sagarum natura et potestate. Contra joannen Ewichium*, Pauli Egenolphi, Frankfurt, 1588. *Liber primus: De sagis*, pp. 97–8.

the image of Satan not for an illusion, but for Satan, then Satan shows by this belief that, once again, he exists.

The demonic has not been dismissed; quite the opposite, it is brought closer, and infinitely so: embedded in the joining of spirit and body where the imagination is born. Paradoxically doctors of the sixteenth century freed up from the demonic only those things which were inanimate; they place the demonic in the immediate environs of the soul, at the contact surface of the body. Wier, as with Molitor and Erastus, neither more nor less than their adversaries, by assigning physical powers to the imagination, rooted the demonic in the body. Much later, this did indeed allow a naturalistic reduction of the demonic, but it by no means determined that reduction in an absolute sense in the sixteenth century, a period where the imaginary is not non-existent, and where the body is not nature.

Third consequence: when located at this point, the demonic commands all access to truth; its power is identified with the very possibility of error; it covers in any case the same surface, and it is there that it takes on its own dimensions. We are subject to the Devil only to the extent that we can be subject to error. But when we escape error we are still not escaping Satan because although we have uncovered and denounced this fantasy, we do not know at all if we are triumphing over Satan by revealing the derisory truth of the error he imposed, or if we are still mystified by he who wants to have us believe that he is not a fantasy. At the centre of the physical powers that are being challenged, there is an experience of the demonic, it is the great uncertainty of experience and truth, of being and non-being, and what Wier, with his contemporaries, named as the 'dazzling' of the spirit.

We can therefore say that there was a 'medicalisation' of this parareligious experience. But this medicalisation:

- has no reducing value, because it is an *a fortiori* and an inevitable demonstration of its existence;
- does not have the sense of a naturalistic explanation, because it is a rather complex operational analysis of demonic intervention;
- does not refer us to psychology, because it is to do with bodily supports of the 'fantasy';
- does not fix the innocent limits of the pathological, since what we are dealing with is the fact that fault and error belong to one another in a confused but essential way.

The development of medical knowledge in the sixteenth century is not linked to the replacing of the supernatural by the pathological, but to the appearance of transgressive powers of the body and of the imagination. Doctors such as Molitor or Wier were not able to naturalise the demonic under the form of illness; they turned the Devil into the subtle doctor able to bend the body to its trickery and impose upon it the false image of its powers. We were to have the proof of this in the seventeenth century, when, through internment, we were to subject visionaries, fanatics, the mad and all those who imagine and are mistaken to the same type of exclusion.

In the entire course of the development of which we have just marked out a few stages, the terms of the dichotomy have not changed: the same elements are accepted and the same refused (movement in space, birth of monsters, operations at a distance, discovery of objects in the body). What has been changed is the relationship between the excluded and the included, between the recognised and the rejected: this relationship is now established on the level of the possibilities of the deviation of the body, or rather in the margins of the game which surround the exercise of the soul and the body. The *real* place of transgression has become the fantasy and all forms of the unreal. The body with its madnesses marks at this time, and for a long time afterwards (our own period is a witness to this), the point at which transgression exploded.

[This paper was followed by a series of brief responses from conference delegates and a final short comment by Foucault confirming a unity between madness and aspects of a 'religious territoriality'. Foucault concluded by recognising the need for more research on the distinctive features of this relationship in each historical period.]

CHAPTER TWO

A preface to transgression (1963)

First published in *Critique*, no. 195–6, *Hommage à Georges Bataille*, August–September, 1963, pp. 751–70. It was subsequently reprinted in *Dits et écrits*, vol. I, Gallimard, Paris, 1994, pp. 233–50. This translation was originally published in *Language, Counter-Memory, Practice*, ed. Donald F. Bouchard, Cornell University Press, Ithaca, New York, 1977, pp. 29–52.

Translated by Donald F. Bouchard and Sherry Simon

We like to believe that sexuality has regained, in contemporary experience, its full truth as a process of nature, a truth which has long been lingering in the shadows and hiding under various disguises – until now, that is, when our positive awareness allows us to decipher it so that it may at last emerge in the clear light of language. Yet, never did sexuality enjoy a more immediately natural understanding and never did it know a greater 'felicity of expression' than in the Christian world of fallen bodies and of sin. The proof is its whole tradition of mysticism and spirituality which was incapable of dividing the continuous forms of desire, of rapture, of penetration, of ecstasy, of that outpouring which leaves us spent: all of these experiences seemed to lead, without interruption or limit, right to the heart of a divine love of which they were both the outpouring and the source returning upon itself.[1] What characterises modern sexuality from Sade to Freud is not its having found the language of its logic or of its natural process, but rather, through the violence done by such languages, its having been 'denatured' – cast into an empty zone where it achieves whatever meagre form is bestowed upon it by the establishment of its limits. Sexuality points to nothing beyond itself, no prolongation, except in a frenzy which disrupts it.[2] We have not in the least liberated sexuality, though we have, to be exact, carried it to its limits: the limit of consciousness, because it ultimately dictates the only possible reading of our unconscious; the limit of the law, since it seems the sole substance of universal taboos; the limit of language, since it traces that line of foam showing just how far speech may advance upon the sands of silence. Thus, it is not through sexuality that

[1] [For Bataille's analysis of Christian mysticism, see *Eroticism*, trans. Mary Dalwood, John Calder, London, 1962, pp. 117–28, 221–64.]

[2] [See below in this essay, p. 70, for a discussion of the non-representational nature of the language of sexuality.]

we communicate with the orderly and pleasingly profane world of animals; rather, sexuality is a fissure[3] – not one which surrounds us as the basis of our isolation or individuality, but one which marks the limit within us and designates us as a limit.

Perhaps we could say that it has become the only division possible in a world now emptied of objects, beings and spaces to desecrate. Not that it proffers any new content for our age-old acts; rather, it permits a profanation without object, a profanation that is empty and turned inward upon itself and whose instruments are brought to bear on nothing but each other. Profanation in a world which no longer recognises any positive meaning in the sacred – is this not more or less what we may call transgression? In that zone which our culture affords for our gestures and speech, transgression prescribes not only the sole manner of discovering the sacred in its unmediated substance, but also a way of recomposing its empty form, its absence, through which it becomes all the more scintillating. A rigorous language, as it arises from sexuality, will not reveal the secret of man's natural being, nor will it express the serenity of anthropological truths, but rather, it will say that he exists without God; the speech given to sexuality is contemporaneous, both in time and in structure, with that through which we announced to ourselves that God is dead. From the moment that Sade delivered its first words and marked out, in a single discourse, the boundaries of what suddenly became its kingdom, the language of sexuality has lifted us into the night where God is absent, and where all of our actions are addressed to this absence in a profanation which at once identifies it, dissipates it exhausts itself in it, and restores it to the empty purity of its transgression.[4]

There indeed exists a modern form of sexuality: it is that which offers itself in the superficial discourse of a solid and natural animality, while obscurely addressing itself to Absence, to this high region where Bataille placed, in a night not soon to be ended, the characters of *Eponine*:

In this strained stillness, through the haze of my intoxication, I seemed to sense that the wind was dying down; a long silence flowed from the immensity of the sky. The priest knelt down softly. He began to sing in a despondent key, slowly as if at someone's death: *Miserere mei Deus, secundum misericordiam magnam tuam.* The way he moaned this sensuous melody was highly suspicious. He was strangely confessing his anguish before the delights of the flesh. A priest should conquer us by his denials but his efforts to humble himself only made him stand out more insistently; the loveliness of his chant, set against the silent sky, enveloped him in a solitude of morose pleasures My reverie was shattered by a felicitous acclamation, an infinite acclamation already on the edge of oblivion. Seeing the priest as she emerged from the dream which still visibly dazed her senses, Eponine began to laugh and with such intensity that she was completely shaken; she turned her body and, leaning against the railing, trembled like a child. She was laughing with her head in her hands and the priest, barely stifling a clucking noise, raised his head, his arms uplifted, only to see a naked behind: the wind had lifted her coat and, made defenceless by the laughter, she had been unable to close it.[5]

---

[3] [See Foucault, *The Order of Things*, Pantheon Books, New York, 1970, p. 314.]
[4] [See Nietzsche, *The Gay Science*, 108, Vintage Books, New York, 1974, p. 167.]
[5] [Bataille, *Oeuvres complètes*, Gallimard, Paris, 1973, vol. III, pp. 263–4.]

Perhaps the importance of sexuality in our culture, the fact that since Sade it has persistently been linked to the most profound decisions of our language, derives from nothing else than this correspondence which connects it to the death of God. Not that this death should be understood as the end of his historical reign or as the finally delivered judgement of his non-existence, but as the now constant space of our experience. By denying us the limit of the Limitless, the death of God leads to an experience in which nothing may again announce the exteriority of being, and consequently to an experience which is *interior* and *sovereign*. But such an experience, for which the death of God is an explosive reality, discloses as its own secret and clarification, its intrinsic finitude, the limitless reign of the Limit, and the emptiness of those excesses in which it spends itself and where it is found wanting. In this sense, the inner experience is throughout an experience of the *impossible* (the impossible being both that which we experience and that which constitutes the experience). The death of God is not merely an 'event' that gave shape to contemporary experience as we now know it: it continues tracing indefinitely its great skeletal outline.

Bataille was perfectly conscious of the possibilities of thought that could be released by this death, and of the impossibilities in which it entangled thought. What, indeed, is the meaning of the death of God, if not a strange solidarity between the stunning realisation of his non-existence and the act that kills him? But what does it mean to kill God if he does not exist, to kill God *who has never existed*? Perhaps it means to kill God both because he does not exist and to guarantee he will not exist – certainly a cause for laughter: to kill God to liberate life from this existence that limits it, but also to bring it back to those limits that are annulled by this limitless existence – as a sacrifice; to kill God to return him to this nothingness he is and to manifest his existence at the centre of a light that blazes like a presence – for the ecstasy; to kill God in order to lose language in a deafening night and because this wound must make him bleed until there springs forth 'an immense alleluia lost in the interminable silence'[6] – and this is communication. The death of God does not restore us to a limited and positivistic world, but to a world exposed by the experience of its limits, made and unmade by that excess which transgresses it.

Undoubtedly it is excess that discovers that sexuality and the death of God are bound to the same experience; or that again shows us, as if in 'the most incongruous book of all', that 'God is a whore'.[7] And from this perspective the thought that relates to God and the thought that relates to sexuality are linked in a common form, since Sade to be sure, but never in our day with as much insistence and difficulty as in Bataille. And if it were necessary to give, in opposition to sexuality, a precise definition of eroticism, it would have to be the following: an experience of sexuality which links, for its own ends, an overcoming of limits to the death of God. 'Eroticism can say what mysticism never could (its strength failed when it tried): God is nothing if not the surpassing of God in every sense of vulgar being, in that of horror or impurity; and ultimately in the sense of nothing.'[8]

---

[6] [*Eroticism*, p. 271.]

[7] [*Eroticism*, p. 269; and on excess, pp. 168–73.]

[8] [*Eroticism*, p. 269.]

Thus, at the root of sexuality, of the movement that nothing can ever limit (because it is, from its birth and in its totality, constantly involved with the limit), and at the root of this discourse on God which Western culture has maintained for so long – without any sense of the impropriety of 'thoughtlessly adding to language a word which surpasses all words'[9] or any clear sense that it places us at the limits of all possible languages – a singular experience is shaped: that of transgression. Perhaps one day it will seem as decisive for our culture, as much a part of its soil, as the experience of contradiction was at an earlier time for dialectical thought. But in spite of so many scattered signs, the language in which transgression will find its space and the illumination of its being lies almost entirely in the future.

It is surely possible, however, to find in Bataille its calcinated roots, its promising ashes.

Transgression is an action which involves the limit, that narrow zone of a line where it displays the flash of its passage, but perhaps also its entire trajectory, even its origin; it is likely that transgression has its entire space in the line it crosses. The play of limits and transgression seems to be regulated by a simple obstinacy: transgression incessantly crosses and recrosses a line which closes up behind it in a wave of extremely short duration, and thus it is made to return once more right to the horizon of the uncrossable. But this relationship is considerably more complex: these elements are situated in an uncertain context, in certainties which are immediately upset so that thought is ineffectual as soon as it attempts to seize them.

The limit and transgression depend on each other for whatever density of being they possess: a limit could not exist if it were absolutely uncrossable and, reciprocally, transgression would be pointless if it merely crossed a limit composed of illusions and shadows. But can the limit have a life of its own outside of the act that gloriously passes through it and negates it? What becomes of it after this act and what might it have been before? For its part, does transgression not exhaust its nature when it crosses the limit, knowing no other life beyond this point in time? And this point, this curious intersection of beings that have no other life beyond this moment where they totally exchange their beings, is it not also everything which overflows from it on all sides? It serves as a glorification of the nature it excludes: the limit opens violently onto the limitless, finds itself suddenly carried away by the content it had rejected and fulfilled by this alien plenitude which invades it to the core of its being. Transgression carries the limit right to the limit of its being; transgression forces the limit to face the fact of its imminent disappearance, to find itself in what it excludes (perhaps, to be more exact, to recognise itself for the first time), to experience its positive truth in its downward fall?[10] And yet, towards what is transgression unleashed in its movement of pure violence, if not that which imprisons it, towards the limit and those elements it contains? What bears the brunt of its aggression and to what void does it owe the

[9] [Eroticism, p. 269.]

[10] [This can serve as a description of Foucault's technique in Madness and Civilization and also as the basis, in The Order of Things, of his statement that 'modern thought is advancing towards that region where man's Other must become the same as himself' (p. 328).]

unrestrained fullness of its being, if not that which it crosses in its violent act and which, as its destiny, it crosses out in the line it effaces?

Transgression, then, is not related to the limit as black to white, the prohibited to the lawful, the outside to the inside, or as the open area of a building to its enclosed spaces. Rather, their relationship takes the form of a spiral which no simple infraction can exhaust. Perhaps it is like a flash of lightning in the night which, from the beginning of time, gives a dense and black intensity to the night it denies, which lights up the night from the inside, from top to bottom, and yet owes to the dark the stark clarity of its manifestation, its harrowing and poised singularity; the flash loses itself in this space it marks with its sovereignty and becomes silent now that it has given a name to obscurity.

Since this existence is both so pure and so complicated, it must be detached from its questionable association to ethics if we want to understand it and to begin thinking from it and in the space it denotes; it must be liberated from the scandalous or subversive, that is, from anything aroused by negative associations.[11] Transgression does not seek to oppose one thing to another, nor does it achieve its purpose through mockery or by upsetting the solidity of foundations; it does not transform the other side of the mirror, beyond an invisible and uncrossable line, into a glittering expanse. Transgression is neither violence in a divided world (in an ethical world) nor a victory over limits (in a dialectical or revolutionary world); and, exactly for this reason, its role is to measure the excessive distance that it opens at the heart of the limit and to trace the flashing line that causes the limit to arise. Transgression contains nothing negative, but affirms limited being – affirms the limitlessness into which it leaps as it opens this zone to existence for the first time. But correspondingly, this affirmation contains nothing positive: no content can bind it, since, by definition, no limit can possibly restrict it. Perhaps it is simply an affirmation of division; but only in so far as division is not understood to mean a cutting gesture, or the establishment of a separation or the measuring of a distance, retaining in it only that which may designate the existence of difference.[12]

Perhaps when contemporary philosophy discovered the possibility of non-positive affirmation, it began a process of reorientation whose only equivalent is the shift instituted by Kant when he distinguished the nihil negativum and the nihil privatium – a distinction known to have opened the way for the advance of critical thought. This philosophy of non-positive affirmation is, I believe, what Blanchot was defining through his principle of 'contestation'.[13] Contestation does not imply a generalised negation, but an affirmation that affirms nothing, a radical break of transitivity. Rather

---

[11] [The Order of Things, pp. 327–8.]

[12] [See The Archaeology of Knowledge, Pantheon Books, New York, 1972, pp. 130–1 (British edition: Routledge, London, 1989); and 'Theatrum philosophicum' in Language, Counter-Memory, Practice, ed. Donald F. Bouchard, Cornell, Ithaca, New York, 1977, pp. 181–7. See also Mark Seems, 'Liberation of difference: towards a theory of antiliterature', New Literary History, vol. 5 (1973), pp. 121–34.]

[13] [For a discussion of this term, see Bataille's L'expérience intérieure in Oeuvres, V, 24, 143, 221; and Foucault's study of Blanchot, 'La pensée du dehors', Critique, no. 229, 1966: 'We must transform reflexive language. It should not point to an inner confirmation, a central certainty where it is impossible to dislodge it, but to the extreme where it is always contested' (p. 528).]

than being a process of thought for denying existences or values, contestation is the act which carries them all to their limits and, from there, to the Limit where an ontological decision achieves its end; to contest is to proceed until one reaches the empty core where being achieves its limit and where the limit defines being. There, at the transgressed limit, the 'yes' of contestation reverberates, leaving without echo the hee-haw of Nietzsche's braying ass.[14]

Thus, contestation shapes an experience that Bataille wanted to circumscribe through every detour and repetition of his work, an experience that has the power 'to implicate (and to question) everything without possible respite'[15] and to indicate, in the place where it occurs and in its most essential form, 'the immediacy of being'.[16] Nothing is more alien to this experience than the demonic character who, true to his nature, 'denies everything'. Transgression opens on to a scintillating and constantly affirmed world, a world without shadow or twilight, without that serpentine 'no' that bites into fruits and lodges their contradictions at their core. It is the solar inversion of satanic denial. It was originally linked to the divine, or rather, from this limit marked by the sacred it opens the space where the divine functions. The discovery of such a category by a philosophy which questions itself upon the existence of the limit is evidently one of the countless signs that our path is circular and that, with each day, we are becoming more Greek.[17] Yet, this motion should not be understood as the promised return to a homeland or the recovery of an original soil which produced and which will naturally resolve every opposition. In reintroducing the experience of the divine at the centre of thought, philosophy has been well aware since Nietzsche (or it should undoubtedly know by now) that it questions an origin without positivity and an opening indifferent to the patience of the negative.[18] No form of dialectical movement, no analysis of constitutions and of their transcendental ground can serve as support for thinking about such an experience or even as access to this experience. In our day, would not the instantaneous play of the limit and of transgression be the essential test for a thought which centres on the 'origin', for that form of thought to which Nietzsche dedicated us from the beginning of his works and one which would be, absolutely and in the same motion, a Critique and an Ontology, an understanding that comprehends both finitude and being?

What possibilities generated this thought from which everything, up until our time, has seemingly diverted us, but as if to lead us to the point of its returning? From what impossibilities does it derive its hold on us? Undoubtedly, it can be said that it comes to us through that opening made by Kant in Western philosophy when he articulated, in a manner which is still enigmatic, metaphysical discourse and his reflection on the limits of reason. However, Kant ended by closing this opening when

---

[14] [Nietzsche, *Thus Spoke Zarathustra*, Part Four, 'The awakening'.]

[15] [*L'expérience intérieure* in *Oeuvres*, V, 16, and also 347.]

[16] [*L'expérience intérieure*, p. 60: 'A project is not only a mode of existence implied by action, necessary to action; it is rather existence within a paradoxical form of time – the postponement of life to a later of time ... The inner experience denounces this intermission; it is being without delay.']

[17] [Cf. *The Order of Things*, p. 342.]

[18] [For an extended discussion of the 'origin', see 'Nietzsche, genealogy, history' in *Language, Counter-Memory, Practice*, pp. 139–64; and, on contradiction, see *The Archaeology of Knowledge*, pp. 151–5.]

he ultimately relegated all critical investigations to an anthropological question; and, undoubtedly, we have subsequently interpreted Kant's action as the granting of an indefinite respite to metaphysics, because dialectics took the place of the questioning of being and limits the play of contradiction and totality.[19] To awaken us from the confused sleep of dialectics and of anthropology, we required the Nietzschean figures of tragedy, of Dionysus, of the death of God, of the philosopher's hammer, of the Superman approaching with the steps of a dove, of the Return. But why, in our day, is discursive language so ineffectual when asked to maintain the presence of these figures and to maintain itself through them? Why is it so nearly silent before them, as if it were forced to yield its voice so that they may continue to find their words, to yield to these extreme forms of language in which Bataille, Blanchot and Klossowski have made their home, which they have made the summits of thought?[20]

The sovereignty of these experiences must surely be recognised some day, and we must try to assimilate them: not to reveal their truth − a ridiculous pretension with respect to words that form our limits − but to serve as the basis for finally liberating our language. But our task for today is to direct our attention to this non-discursive language, this language which, for almost two centuries, has stubbornly maintained its disruptive existence in our culture; it will be enough to examine its nature, to explore the source of this language that is neither complete nor fully in control of itself, even though it is sovereign for us and hangs above us, this language that is sometimes immobilised in scenes we customarily call 'erotic' and suddenly volatised in a philosophical turbulence, when it seems to lose its very basis.

The parcelling out of philosophical discourse and descriptive scenes in Sade's books is undoubtedly the product of complex architectural laws. It is quite probable that the simple rules of alternation, of continuity or of thematic contrast are inadequate for defining a linguistic space where descriptions and demonstrations are articulated, where a rational order is linked to an order of pleasures, and where, especially, subjects are located both in the movement of various discourses and in a constellation of bodies. Let us simply say that this space is completely covered by a language that is discursive (even when it involves a narrative), explicit (even when it denotes nothing), and continuous (especially at the moment that the thread passes from one character to another): a language that nevertheless does not have an absolute subject, that never discovers the one who ultimately speaks and incessantly maintains its hold on speech from the announcement of the 'triumph of philosophy' in Justine's first adventure to Juliette's corpseless disappearance into eternity.[21] Bataille's language, on the other hand, continually breaks down at the centre of its space, exposing in his nakedness, in the inertia of ecstasy, a visible and insistent subject who had tried to keep language at arm's length, but who now finds himself thrown by it, exhausted, upon the sands of that which he can no longer say.

[19] [For Bataille's analysis of Hegel, see Oeuvres, I, 177−90. Cf. Karl Popper's 'What is dialectics' in Conjectures and Refutations, Routledge and Kegan Paul, London, 1975, pp. 312−35.]
[20] [In connection with this passage, see 'La pensée du dehors', p. 524; and Foucault's essay on Klossowski 'The prose of Actaeon' in this volume, pp. 75−84.]
[21] [See Eroticism, pp. 185−96.]

How is it possible to discover, under all these different figures, that form of thought we carelessly call 'the philosophy of eroticism', but in which it is important to recognise (a less ambitious goal, but also more central to our understanding) an essential experience for our culture since Kant and Sade – the experience of finitude and being, of the limit and transgression? What natural space can this form of thought possess and what language can it adopt? Undoubtedly, no form of reflection yet developed, no established discourse, can supply its model, its foundation, or even the riches of its vocabulary. Would it be of help, in any case, to argue by analogy that we must find a language for the transgressive which would be what dialectics was, in an earlier time, for contradiction? Our efforts are undoubtedly better spent in trying to speak of this experience and in making it speak from the depths where its language fails, from precisely the place where words escape it, where the subject who speaks has just vanished, where the spectacle topples over before an upturned eye – from where Bataille's death has recently placed his language. We can only hope, now that his death has sent us to the pure transgression of his texts, that they will protect those who seek a language for the thought of the limit, that they will serve as a dwelling place for what may already be a ruined project.

In effect, do we not grasp the possibility of such thought in a language which necessarily strips it of any semblance of thought and leads it to the very impossibility of language? Right to this limit where the existence of language becomes problematic? The reason is that philosophical language is linked beyond all memory (or nearly so) to dialectics; and the dialectic was able to become the form and interior movement of philosophy from the time of Kant only through a redoubling of the millenary space from which philosophy had always spoken. We know full well that reference to Kant has invariably addressed us to the most formative elements of Greek thought: not to recapture a lost experience, but to bring us closer to the possibility of a non-dialectical language. This age of commentary in which we live, this historical redoubling from which there seems no escape, does not indicate the velocity of our language in a field now devoid of new philosophical objects, which must be constantly recrossed in a forgetful and always rejuvenated glance. But far more to the point, it indicates the inadequacy, the profound silence, of a philosophical language that has been chased from its natural element, from its original dialectics, by the novelties found in its domain. If philosophy is now experienced as a multiple desert, it is not because it has lost its proper object or the freshness of its experience, but because it has been suddenly divested of that language which is historically 'natural' to it. We do not experience the end of philosophy, but a philosophy which regains its speech and finds itself again only in the marginal region which borders its limits: that is, which finds itself either in a purified metalanguage or in the thickness of words enclosed by their darkness, by their blind truth. The prodigious distance that separates these alternatives and that manifests our philosophical dispersion marks, more than a disarray, a profound coherence. This separation and real incompatibility is the actual distance from whose depths philosophy addresses us. It is here that we must focus our attention.

But what language can arise from such an absence? And above all, who is the philosopher who will now begin to speak? 'What of us when, having become sobered, we learn what we are? Lost among idlers in the night, where we can only hate the semblance of light coming from their small talk.'[22] In a language stripped of dialectics, at the heart of what it says but also at the root of its possibilities, the philosopher is aware that 'we are not everything'; he learns as well that even the philosopher does not inhabit the whole of his language like a secret and perfectly fluent god. Next to himself, he discovers the existence of another language that also speaks and that he is unable to dominate, one that strives, fails, and falls silent and that he cannot manipulate, the language he spoke at one time and that has now separated itself from him, now gravitating in a space increasingly silent. Most of all, he discovers that he is not always lodged in his language in the same fashion and that in the location from which a subject had traditionally spoken in philosophy – one whose obvious and garrulous identity has remained unexamined from Plato to Nietzsche – a void has been hollowed out in which a multiplicity of speaking subjects are joined and severed, combined and excluded.[23] From the lessons on Homer to the cries of a madman in the streets of Turin,[24] who can be said to have spoken this continuous language, so obstinately the same? Was it the Wanderer or his shadow? The philosopher or the first of the non-philosophers? Zarathustra, his monkey or already the Superman? Dionysus, Christ, their reconciled figures, or finally this man right here? The breakdown of philosophical subjectivity and its dispersion in a language that dispossesses it while multiplying it within the space created by its absence is probably one of the fundamental structures of contemporary thought. Again, this is not the end of philosophy, but, rather, the end of the philosopher as the sovereign and primary form of philosophical language. And perhaps to all those who strive above all to maintain the unity of the philosopher's grammatical function – at the price of the coherence, even of the existence of philosophical language – we could oppose Bataille's exemplary enterprise: his desperate and relentless attack on the pre-eminence of the philosophical subject as it confronted him in his own work, in his experience and his language which became his private torment, in the first reflected torture of that which speaks in philosophical language – in the dispersion of stars that encircle a median night, allowing voiceless words to be born. 'Like a flock chased by an infinite shepherd, we, the bleating wave, would flee, endlessly flee from the horror of reducing being to totality.'[25]

It is not only the juxtaposition of reflective texts and novels in the language of thought that makes us aware of the shattering of the philosophical subject. The works of Bataille define the situation in far greater detail: in the constant movement to different levels of speech and a systematic disengagement from the 'I' who has begun

[22] [This passage is taken from the Preface to *L'expérience intérieure* in Oeuvres, V, 10.]
[23] [Cf. *Eroticism*, pp. 274–6.]
[24] [The reference is, of course, to the beginning of Nietzsche's madness in Turin in the late autumn of 1888.]
[25] [*L'expérience intérieure*, in Oeuvres, V, 48. 'Median' is a mathematical term: perhaps Foucault is indicating a space where points of dispersion meet to form a new position or voice.]

to speak and is already on the verge of deploying his language and installing himself in it: temporal disengagements ('I was writing this', or similarly 'in retrospect, if I return to this matter'), shifts in the distance separating a speaker from his words (in a diary, notebooks, poems, stories, meditations, or discourses intended for demonstration), an inner detachment from the assumed sovereignty of thought or writing (through books, anonymous texts, prefaces to his books, footnotes). And it is at the centre of the subject's disappearance that philosophical language proceeds as if through a labyrinth, not to recapture him, but to test (and through language itself) the extremity of its loss. That is, it proceeds to the limit and to this opening where its being surges forth, but where it is already completely lost, completely overflowing itself, emptied of itself to the point where it becomes an absolute void – an opening which is communication: 'at this point there is no need to elaborate; as my rapture escapes me, I immediately re-enter the night of a lost child, anguished in his desire to prolong his ravishment, with no other end than exhaustion, no way of stopping short of fainting. It is such excruciating bliss.'[26]

This experience forms the exact reversal of the movement which has sustained the wisdom of the West at least since the time of Socrates, that is, the wisdom to which philosophical language promised the serene unity of a subjectivity which would triumph in it, having been fully constituted by it and through it. But if the language of philosophy is one in which the philosopher's torments are tirelessly repeated and his subjectivity is discarded, then not only is wisdom meaningless as the philosopher's form of composition and reward, but in the expiration of philosophical language a possibility inevitably arises (that upon which it falls – the face of the die; and the place into which it falls – the void into which the die is cast): the possibility of the mad philosopher. In short, the experience of the philosopher who finds, not outside his language (the result of an external accident or imaginary exercise), but at the inner core of its possibilities, the transgression of his philosophical being; and thus, the non-dialectical language of the limit which only arises in transgressing the one who speaks. This play of transgression and being is fundamental for the constitution of philosophical language, which reproduces and undoubtedly produces it.

Essentially the product of fissures, abrupt descents and broken contours, this misshapen and craglike language describes a circle; it refers to itself and is folded back on a questioning of its limits – as if it were nothing more than a small night lamp that flashes with a strange light, signalling the void from which it arises and to which it addresses everything it illuminates and touches. Perhaps, it is this curious configuration which explains why Bataille attributed such obstinate prestige to the Eye.[27] Throughout his career (from his first novel to *Larmes d'Eros*), the eye was to keep its value as a figure of inner experience: 'When at the height of anguish, I gently solicit a strange absurdity, an eye opens at the summit, in the middle of my skull.'[28] This is

[26] [*L'expérience intérieure*, in Oeuvres, V, 68.]
[27] [Cf. Roland Barthes, 'La métaphor de l'oeil', *Essais critique*, Editions du Seuil, Paris, 1964, pp. 238–44.]
[28] [*L'expérience intérieure*, in Oeuvres, V, 92.]

because the eye, a small white globe that encloses its darkness, traces a limiting circle that only sight can cross. And the darkness within, the sombre core of the eye, pours out into the world like a fountain which sees, that is, which lights up the world; but the eye also gathers up all the light of the world in the iris, that small black spot, where it is transformed into the bright night of an image. The eye is mirror and lamp: it discharges its light into the world around it, while in a movement that is not necessarily contradictory, it precipitates this same light into the transparency of its well. Its globe has the expansive quality of a marvellous seed – like an egg imploding towards the centre of night and extreme light, which it is and which it has just ceased to be. It is the figure of being in the act of transgressing its own limit.

The eye, in a philosophy of reflection, derives from its capacity to observe the power of becoming always more interior to itself. Lying behind each eye that sees, there exists a more tenuous one, an eye so discreet and yet so agile that its all-powerful glance can be said to eat away at the flesh of its white globe; behind this particular eye, there exists another and, then, still others, each progressively more subtle until we arrive at an eye whose entire substance is nothing but the transparency of its vision. This inner movement is finally resolved in a non-material centre where the intangible forms of truth are created and combined, in this heart of things which is the sovereign subject.[29] Bataille reverses this entire direction: sight, crossing the globular limit of the eye, constitutes the eye in its instantaneous being; sight carries it away in this luminous stream (an outpouring fountain, streaming tears and, shortly, blood), hurls the eye outside of itself, conducts it to the limit where it bursts out in the immediately extinguished flash of its being. Only a small white ball, veined with blood, is left behind, only an exorbitated eye to which all sight is now denied. And in the place from which sight had once passed, only a cranial cavity remains, only this black globe which the uprooted eye has made to close upon its sphere, depriving it of vision, but offering to this absence the spectacle of that indestructible core which now imprisons the dead glance. In the distance created by this violence and uprooting, the eye is seen absolutely, but denied any possibility of sight: the philosophising subject has been dispossessed and pursued to its limit; and the sovereignty of philosophical language can now be heard from the distance, in the measureless void left behind by the exorbitated subject.

But perhaps the eye accomplishes the most essential aspect of its play when, forced from its ordinary position, it is made to turn upwards in a movement that leads it back to the nocturnal and starred interior of the skull and it is made to show us its usually concealed surface, white and unseeing: it shuts out the day in a movement that manifests its own whiteness (whiteness being undoubtedly the image of clarity, its surface reflection, but for this very reason, it cannot communicate with it, nor communicate it); and the circular night of the iris is made to address the central absence which it illuminates with a flash, revealing it as night The upturned orb suggests both the most open and the most impenetrable eye: causing its sphere to pivot, while remaining exactly the same and in the same place, it overturns day and

[29] [Cf. *The Birth of the Clinic*, pp. 107–8.]

night, crosses their limit, but only to find it again on the same line and from the other side; and the white hemisphere that appears momentarily at the place where the pupil once opened is like the being of the eye as it crosses the limit of its vision – when it transgresses this opening to the light of day which defined the transgression of every sight. 'If man did not imperiously close his eyes, he would finally be unable to see the things worth seeing.'[30]

But what we need to see does not involve any interior secret or the discovery of a more nocturnal world. Torn from its ordinary position and made to turn inwards in its orbit, the eye now pours its light only into a bony cavern. This turning up of its globe may seem a betrayal of 'la petite mort',[31] but, more exactly, it simply indicates the death that it experiences in its natural location, in this springing up in place which causes the eye to rotate. Death, for the eye, is not the always elevated line of the horizon, but the limit it ceaselessly transgresses in its natural location, in the hollow where every vision originates, and where this limit is elevated into an absolute limit by an ecstatic movement which allows the eye to spring up from the other side. The upturned eye discovers the bond that links language and death at the moment that it acts out this relationship of the limit and being; and it is perhaps from this that it derives its prestige, in permitting the possibility of a language for this play. Thus, the great scenes that interrupt Bataille's stories invariably concern the spectacle of erotic deaths, where upturned eyes display their white limits and rotate inwards in gigantic and empty orbits. Bleu du ciel gives a singularly precise outline of this movement: early in November, when the earth of a German cemetery is alive with the twinkling light of candles and candle stubs, the narrator is lying with Dorothy among the tombstones; making love among the dead, the earth around him appears like the sky on a bright night. And the sky above forms a great hollow orbit, a death mask, in which he recognises his inevitable end at the moment that pleasure overturns the four globes of flesh, causing the revolution of his sight.

The earth under Dorothy's body was open like a tomb, her belly opened itself to me like a fresh grave. We were struck with stupor, making love on a starred cemetery. Each light marked a skeleton in a grave and formed a wavering sky as perturbed as our mingled bodies. I unfastened Dorothy's dress, I dirtied her clothes and her breast with the fresh earth which was stuck to my fingers. Our bodies trembled like two rows of clattering teeth.[32]

But what might this mean at the heart of a system of thought? What significance has this insistent eye which appears to encompass what Bataille successively designated the inner experience, the extreme possibility, the comic process, or simply meditation?[33] It is certainly no more metaphoric than Descartes's phrasing of the 'clear perception of sight' or this sharp point of the mind which he called acies mentis.[34] In point of fact, the

[30] [An aphorism (from René Char) used at the beginning of Méthode de méditation in Oeuvres, V, 192.]
[31] [Eroticism, p. 170: 'Pleasure is so close to ruinous waste that we refer to the moment of climax as a "little death".']
[32] [Oeuvres, III, 481.]
[33] [These concepts are opposed to Hegel's philosophy of work and encourage 'non-discursive existence, laughter, ecstasy' (Oeuvres, V, 96).]
[34] [With respect to this reference to Descartes's 'Third meditation', see Oeuvres, V, 123–6.]

upturned eye has no meaning in Bataille's language, can have no meaning since it marks its limit. It indicates the moment when language, arriving at its confines, overleaps itself, explodes and radically challenges itself in laughter, tears, the overturned eyes of ecstasy, the mute and exorbitated horror of sacrifice, and where it remains fixed in this way at the limit of its void, speaking of itself in a second language in which the absence of a sovereign subject outlines its essential emptiness and incessantly fractures the unity of its discourse. The enucleated or upturned eye marks the zone of Bataille's philosophical language, the void into which it pours and loses itself, but in which it never stops talking – somewhat like the interior, diaphanous and illuminated eye of mystics and spiritualists that marks the point at which the secret language of prayer is embedded and choked by a marvellous communication which silences it. Similarly, but in an inverted manner, the eye in Bataille delineates the zone shared by language and death, the place where language discovers its being in the crossing of its limits: the non-dialectical form of philosophical language.

This eye, as the fundamental figure of the place from which Bataille speaks and in which his broken language finds its uninterrupted domain, establishes the connection, prior to any form of discourse, that exists between the death of God (a sun that rotates and the great eyelid that closes upon the world), the experience of finitude (springing up in death, twisting the light which is extinguished as it discovers that the interior is an empty skull, a central absence), and the turning back of language upon itself at the moment that it fails – a conjunction which undoubtedly has no other equivalent than the association, well known in other philosophies, of sight to truth or of contemplation to the absolute. Revealed to this eye, which in its pivoting conceals itself for all time, is the being of the limit: 'I will never forget the violent and marvellous experience that comes from the will to open one's eyes, facing what exists, what happens.'[35]

Perhaps in the movement which carries it to a total night, the experience of transgression brings to light this relationship of finitude to being, this moment of the limit which anthropological thought, since Kant, could only designate from the distance and from the exterior through the language of dialectics.

The twentieth century will undoubtedly have discovered the related categories of exhaustion, excess, the limit and transgression – the strange and unyielding form of these irrevocable movements which consume and consummate us. In a form of thought that considers man as worker and producer – that of European culture since the end of the eighteenth century – consumption was based entirely on need, and need based itself exclusively on the model of hunger. When this element was introduced into an investigation of profit (the appetite of those who have satisfied their hunger), it inserted man into a dialectic of production which had a simple anthropological meaning: if man was alienated from his real nature and immediate needs through his labour and the production of objects with his hands, it was nevertheless through its agency that he recaptured his essence and achieved the

---

[35] [Eroticism, p. 266.]

indefinite gratification of his needs. But it would undoubtedly be misguided to conceive of hunger as that irreducible anthropological factor in the definition of work, production and profit; and similarly, need has an altogether different status, or it responds at the very least to a code whose laws cannot be confined to a dialectic of production. The discovery of sexuality – the discovery of that firmament of indefinite unreality where Sade placed it from the beginning, the discovery of those systematic forms of prohibition which we now know imprison it, the discovery of the universal nature of transgression in which it is both object and instrument – indicates in a sufficiently forceful way the impossibility of attributing the millenary language of dialectics to the major experience that sexuality forms for us.[36]

Perhaps the emergence of sexuality in our culture is an 'event' of multiple values: it is tied to the death of God and to the ontological void which his death fixed at the limit of our thought; it is also tied to the still silent and groping apparition of a form of thought in which the interrogation of the limit replaces the search for totality and the act of transgression replaces the movement of contradictions. Finally, it involves the questioning of language by language in a circularity which the 'scandalous' violence of erotic literature, far from ending, displays from its first use of words. Sexuality is only decisive for our culture as spoken, and to the degree it is spoken: not that it is our language which has been eroticised now for nearly two centuries. Rather, since Sade and the death of God, the universe of language has absorbed our sexuality, denatured it, placed it in a void where it establishes its sovereignty and where it incessantly sets up as the Law the limits it transgresses. In this sense, the appearance of sexuality as a fundamental problem marks the transformation of a philosophy of man as worker to a philosophy based on a being who speaks; and, in so far as philosophy has traditionally maintained a secondary role to knowledge and work, it must be admitted, not as a sign of crisis but of essential structure, that it is now secondary to language. Not that philosophy is now fated to a role of repetition or commentary, but that it experiences itself and its limits in language and in this transgression of language which carries it, as it did Bataille, to the faltering of the speaking subject. On the day that sexuality began to speak and to be spoken, language no longer served as a veil for the infinite; and in the thickness it acquired on that day, we now experience finitude and being. In its dark domain, we now encounter the absence of God, our death, limits and their transgression. But perhaps it is also a source of light for those who have liberated their thought from all forms of dialectical language, as it became for Bataille, on more than one occasion, when he experienced the loss of his language in the dead of night. 'What I call night differs from the darkness of thoughts: night possesses the violence of light. Yes, night: the youth and the intoxication of thinking.'[37]

Perhaps this 'difficulty with words' that now hampers philosophy, a condition fully explored by Bataille, should not be identified with the loss of language that the closure of dialectics seemed to indicate. Rather, it follows from the actual penetration

[36] [Eroticism, pp. 275–6; cf. The Order of Things, pp. 221–6.]
[37] [Le coupable, in Oeuvres, V, 354; cf. pp. 326–7, 349.]

of philosophical experience in language and the discovery that the experience of the limit, and the manner in which philosophy must now understand it, is realised in language and in the movement where it says what cannot be said.

Perhaps this 'difficulty with words' also defines the space given over to an experience in which the speaking subject, instead of expressing himself, is exposed, goes to encounter his finitude and, under each of his words, is brought back to the reality of his own death: that zone, in short, which transforms every work into the sort of 'tauromachy' suggested by Leiris, who was thinking of his own action as a writer, but undoubtedly also of Bataille.[38] In any event, it is on the white beach of an arena (a gigantic eye) where Bataille experienced the fact – crucial for his thought and characteristic of all his language – that death *communicated with communication* and that the uprooted eye, a white and silent sphere, could become a violent seed in the night of the body, that it could give substance to this absence of which sexuality has never stopped speaking and from which it is made to speak incessantly. When the horn of the bull (a glittering knife that carries the threat of night, and an exact reversal of the image of light that emerges from the night of the eye) penetrates the eyeball of the toreador, who is blinded and killed, Simone performs an act we have come to expect: she swallows a pale and skinless seed and returns to its original night the luminous virility which has just committed murder. The eye is returned back to its night, the globe of the arena turns upwards and rotates; but it is the moment when being necessarily appears in its immediacy and where *the act which crosses the limit touches absence itself*: 'Two globes of the same colour and consistency were simultaneously activated in opposite directions. A bull's white testicle had penetrated Simone's black and pink flesh; an eye had emerged from the head of the young man. This coincidence, linked until death to a sort of urinary liquefaction of the sky, gave me Marcelle for a moment. I seemed, in this ungraspable instant, to touch her.'[39]

---

[38] [See M. Leiris, *Manhood*, trans. Richard Howard, Jonathan Cape, London, 1968): 'The bull's keen horn ... gives the torero's art a human reality, prevents it from becoming no more than the vain grace of a ballerina.']

[39] [*Histoire de l'oeil*, in *Oeuvres*, I, 57.]

CHAPTER THREE

The debate on the novel (1964)

Part translation of a discussion led by Michel Foucault (with G. Amy, J.-L. Baudry, M.-J. Durry, J. P. Faye, M. de Gandillac, C. Ollier, M. Pleynet, E. Sanuineti, P. Sollers, J. Thibaudeau, J. Tortel) at a conference on 'The new novel?' organised by the *Tel Quel* group, in Cerisy-la-Salle, September 1963. Originally published in full as 'Débat sur le roman' in *Tel Quel*, no. 17, Spring 1964, pp. 12–54. It was subsequently reprinted (with these footnotes) in *Dits et écrits*, vol. I, Gallimard, Paris, 1994, pp. 338–90.

Translated by Elizabeth Ezra

M. Foucault: Guided solely by my naivety, I would like to say a few words that have nothing in common other than my curiosity. What I would like to do is to say how I understood Sollers's text[1] yesterday, and the real reason why I read *Tel Quel* and all of the novels written by this group, whose coherence, if difficult to express in the explicit form of a presentation such as this, is none the less incontestable. Just what is it that could interest a naive man like myself, who stomps around in his big philosopher's workboots? I was struck by the fact that, in Sollers's reading yesterday and in the novels of his that I've read, reference is constantly made to a certain number of experiences – experiences, if you like, that I will call, in quotation marks, 'spiritual experiences' (although 'spiritual' is not quite the right word) – such as dreams, madness, folly, repetition, doubling [le double], the disruption of time, return [le retour], etc. These experiences form a constellation that is doubtless quite coherent. I was also struck by the fact that this constellation was already mapped out in surrealism. Because, ultimately, I think that the allusions Sollers makes to Breton are no accident. There seems to be something like a kinship, or isomorphism, between what is currently going on at *Tel Quel* and what the surrealists were doing. The question, then, is: what is the difference between them? When Sollers speaks of return or reminiscence, or when these texts speak of day and night and of the progression by which the light of day fades into night, etc., how is this different from experiences we can find in surrealism? ... It seems to me – although I am not certain about this – that the surrealists had situated these experiences in a space that could be called psychological, or at least within the realm

[1] 'Logique de la fiction', *Tel Quel*, no. 15, autumn 1963, pp. 3–29.

of the psyche: in doing these experiments, they discovered this inner realm, beyond or beneath the outside world, which for them was the basis of all reason. They recognised there a kind of unconscious, collective or otherwise. I think that this is definitely not something that we see with Sollers or in the Tel Quel group; it seems to me that Sollers does not situate the experiences he spoke of yesterday in the realm of the psyche, but rather in the realm of thought. People who do philosophy are perplexed by this effort to reinstate certain tests of the limits [épreuves-limites] like reason, dreams and waking life, to the level of thought, an enigmatic and not easily accessible level of experience that the surrealists had relegated to the psychological dimension. In this sense, I believe that people like Sollers are continuing a project that has often been interrupted or disrupted, a project that can be traced back to Bataille and Blanchot. Why else would Bataille have been such an important figure for the Tel Quel group, if he had not uncovered within the psychological dimensions of surrealism what he called 'limit', 'transgression', 'laughter' or 'madness', and which he relocated within the realm of thought? I would say that this raises the following question: what does it mean to think – what is this extraordinary experience known as thought? Literature is currently rediscovering this question, which is close to but distinct from the one raised recently by the work of Roussel and Robbe-Grillet: what does it mean to see and to speak?

I think that there is also a second point: for the surrealists, language was ultimately nothing more than a means of access or a reflecting surface for their experiments. Wordplays, the opacity of words, were simply a door leading to a psychological and cosmic area beyond; automatic writing was the surface on which these experiments were reflected. I have the feeling that, for Sollers, language is instead the thick space within – and between – whose layers these experiments are conducted; it is in the element of language – as in the elements of water or air – that all of these experiments take place, which accounts for the influence of someone like Ponge on Sollers's work. And the double heritage of Ponge and Bataille that might seem a bit odd and inexplicable would thus make sense: both men took a series of experiences born from and belonging to language out of the psychological realm and reinstated them in the realm of thought. For this reason, the philosophical references cited by Philippe Sollers made sense to me. Philippe Sollers belongs to the contemporary philosophical tradition of anti-psychologism.

This, then, is the question that I would like to ask in this doubtless somewhat convoluted intervention, a question that is also my cross-examination [audition] of Sollers's reading yesterday, and of his novels: isn't a literary work, a book, the trajectory within language that both surpasses language and reveals within it a unique space, at once empty and full, that is the place of thought? Since you made the important observation that every work of art has a double, were you not referring to precisely this gap opened up in the positivity of language? Ultimately, your challenge – which is shared by contemporary philosophy – is to think and speak, and your work is located exactly in the dimension of that little linking word or conjunction, the 'and' between thinking and speaking; and that might be the thing that you call the intermediary. All of your work comprises this intermediary, the space at once empty and full of the thought that speaks, the thinking utterance [parole].

P. Sollers: Yes, I think I could not have said it better myself, and, indeed, that is what I tried to define when I said that, from a single point of view, the mind exposed to language and the language exposed to the mind – i.e., thought – had to end up finding common ground.

M. Foucault: That is why the categories of spirituality, mysticism etc., do not appear to hold up.[2] There is an ongoing effort, fraught with difficulty (even, and especially, in philosophy), to determine what thought is without applying the old categories, by attempting to bypass this dialectic of mind once defined by Hegel. Using dialectic thought to conceive of something that is newer than dialectics seems to me to be a completely inadequate analytical approach for what you are doing.

P. Sollers: Which is to say that I work wholly intuitively, and in perhaps what a philosopher would consider to be a state of confusion.

M. Foucault: Maybe we have already spent too much time speaking about philosophy, and I have only made matters worse, for which I apologise. What I have just said is far too abstract, not at all clear, and a bit muddled in relation to the beautiful text that you read to us yesterday. But I felt obliged, since you were kind enough to invite me, to tell you how I understood it, why I was there, why it interested me. Out of a sense of great curiosity, I am going to try to steer the discussion toward much more important topics, topics found within your work, while leaving aside philosophy and conceptual peripheries. It is the works themselves that we must examine. [...]

[2] The objection is clearly Marxist in nature and was presented by Edoardo Sanguineti later in the discussion.

CHAPTER FOUR

The prose of Actaeon (1964)

Originally published as 'La prose d'Actéon' in La Nouvelle Revue Française, no. 135, March 1964, pp. 444–59. It was subsequently reprinted in Dits et écrits, vol. I, Gallimard, Paris, 1994, pp. 326–37. This translation originally appeared in Pierre Klossowski, The Baphomet, Eridanos Press, Hygiene, Colorado, 1988, pp. xxi–xxxviii.

Translated by Stephen Sartarelli

Klossowski revives a long-lost experience. Of this experience hardly any vestiges remain that might call our attention to it; and those that do survive would no doubt remain enigmatic if they had not been given new vividness and prominence in Klossowski's language. And if, since then, they had not resumed speaking – saying that the Demon is not the Other, the opposite pole of God, the Antithesis without recourse (or almost), evil matter, but rather something strange and unsettling that leaves one baffled and motionless: the Same, the perfect Likeness.

Dualism and Gnosticism, despite all the denials and persecutions, have indeed borne heavily on the Christian conception of Evil: their binary mode of thought (God and Satan, Light and Darkness, Good and Heaviness, the great battle, and a certain radical, obstinate spitefulness) has organised, for our thought, the order of disorders. Western Christianity condemned Gnosticism, but from it retained a light, appealing form of reconciliation; for a long time, in its fantasies, it carried on the simplified duels of the Temptation: through the cracks in the world, a whole people of strange animals rises up before the half-open eyes of the kneeling anchorite – ageless figures of matter.

But what if, on the contrary, the Other were the Same? And the Temptation were not one episode of the great antagonism, but the meagre insinuation of the Double? What if the duel took place inside a mirror's space? What if eternal History (of which our own is but the visible form, soon to be effaced) were not simply always the same, but the identity of this Same – at once the imperceptible displacement and the grip of the non-dissociable? There is a vast range of Christian experience well familiar with this danger: the temptation to experience the temptation in the mode of the indiscernible.

The quarrels of demonology are devoted to this profound danger; and consumed, or rather animated and multiplied, by it, they are forever resuming an endless discussion: to go to the Sabbath is to surrender to the Devil, or perhaps also to devote oneself to the Devil's simulacrum which God has sent to tempt men of little faith – or men of too much faith, the credulous who imagine that there is another god than God. And the judges who burn the possessed are themselves victims of this temptation, this trap in which their justice becomes entangled: for those possessed are but a vain image of the false power of demons, an image by means of which the Demon takes possession not of the bodies of the sorcerers but of the souls of their executioners. Unless of course God himself has donned the face of Satan in order to becloud the spirits of those who do not believe in the uniqueness of his omnipotence; in which case God, in simulating the Devil, would bring about the odd espousal of the two condemned figures, the witch and her persecutor – both thereby consigned to Hell, to the reality of the Devil, to the true simulacrum of God's simulation of the Devil. In all these twists and turns the perilous games of extreme similitude multiply: God so closely resembling Satan who imitates God so well …

It took no less than Descartes's Evil Genius to put an end to this great peril of Identities, over which seventeenth-century thought had 'subtilised' to no end. The Evil Genius of the Third Meditation is not a lightly seasoned compendium of the powers of deception residing within man, but he who most resembles God, who can imitate every one of His powers, can pronounce eternal verities like Him, and can, if he wishes, make two plus two equal five. He is His marvellous twin, except for a malignance that expels him immediately from all possible existence. Ever since then, the concern over simulacra has fallen into silence. We have even forgotten that until the beginning of the Neoclassical age (observe the literature and especially the theatre of the Baroque era) such simulacra constituted one of the great causes of vertigo for Western thought. We continued to worry about evil, about the reality of images and representation, and about the synthesis of the different. We no longer thought that the Same could still get the better of one's reason.

Incipit Klossowski, like Zarathustra. In this somewhat obscure and secret side of the Christian experience, he suddenly discovers (as if it were the latter's double, perhaps its simulacrum) the resplendent theophany of the Greek gods. Between the ignoble Goat who presents himself at the Sabbath and the virgin goddess who steals away into the water's coolness, the game is reversed: during Diana's bath, the simulacrum occurs in the flight from extreme proximity and not in the insistent intrusion of the other world. But the doubt is the same, as well as the risk of splitting in two: 'Diana makes a pact with an intermediary demon between the gods and humanity to appear to Actaeon. By means of his airy form, the Demon simulates Diana in her theophany and inspires in Actaeon the desire and mad hope of possessing the goddess. He becomes the imagination and mirror of Diana.' And Actaeon's final metamorphosis transforms him not into a hounded stag but into an impure, frantic and delightfully desecrating goat. As if, in the complicity of the divine in sacrilege, something of the light of Greece streaked with lightning the dark background of the Christian night.

Klossowski finds himself situated at the intersection of two very divergent and yet very similar paths, both originating in the Same, and both perhaps leading there as well: that of the theologians and that of the Greek gods, whose glorious return Nietzsche proclaimed to be imminent. The return of the gods, which is also, without any possible dissociation, the insinuation of the Demon into the unsavoury, tepid night:

What, if some day or night a *demon* were to steal after you into your loneliest loneliness and say to you: 'This life as you now live it and have lived it, you will have to live once more and innumerable times more; and there will be nothing new in it, but every pain and joy and every thought and sigh and everything unutterably small or great in your life will return to you, all in the same succession and sequence – even this spider and this moonlight between the trees, and even this moment and I *myself*. The eternal hourglass of existence is turned upside down again and again, and you with it, speck of dust!' Would you not throw yourself down and gnash your teeth and curse the demon who spoke thus? Or have you once experienced a tremendous moment when you could reply to him: 'You are a *god*, and never have I heard anything more divine.'[1]

Klossowski's experience lies here, more or less: in a world where reigns an evil genius who has not found his god, or who might just as well pass himself off as God, or who might even be God himself. Such a world is neither Heaven nor Hell, nor limbo; it is, quite simply, our own world. That is, a world that would be the same as ours except for the fact that, indeed, it is the same. In this imperceptible divergence of the Same, an endless movement finds its place of birth. This movement is utterly foreign to dialectics; for it concerns not the test of contradiction, nor the game of identity at first affirmed then denied. The equation $A = A$ is animated by an internal, unending movement which separates each of the two terms from its own identity and refers the one to the other by the game (the force and treachery) of this very separation. With the result that no truth can be engendered by this affirmation; however, a space of danger here begins to open up, in which the arguments, fables and booby-trapped, alluring ruses of Klossowski will find their language. A language which for us is as essential as that of Blanchot and Bataille, since in its turn it teaches us how the gravest of thought must find its enlightened lightness outside of dialectics.

In reality, neither God nor Satan ever appear, in this space – a strict absence which is also their interweaving. But neither of the two is ever named, perhaps because it is they who invoke, rather than being invoked. This is a narrow, numinous region where all figures are the sign of something. Here one passes through the paradoxical space of real presence – a presence which is only real in so much as God has absented himself from the world, leaving behind only a trace and a void, so that the reality of this presence is the absence in which it resides, and in which it unrealises itself through transubstantiation. *Numen quod habitat simulacro*.

This is why Klossowski hardly approves of Claudel's and Du Bos's summoning Gide to convert; he well knows that those who put God at one end and the Devil at the other (a god of bone against a devil of flesh) were mistaken, and that Gide was closer

---

[1] Italics are mine (*demon, I myself* and *God*). The text is from Nietzsche's *Gay Science* (trans. W. Kaufmann), as quoted in *Un si funeste désir*, an important collection which contains some very profound pages on Nietzsche and makes possible an entire rereading of Klossowski's work ('Sur quelques thèmes foundamenteaux de la "Gaya Scienza" de Nietzsche' in *Un si funeste désir*, Gallimard, Paris, 1962, pp. 21–2).

to being right when by turns he would come near and steal away, playing the Devil's simulacrum at the behest of others, but not knowing, in so doing, whether he was serving as the Devil's toy, object and tool, or whether he was not as well the chosen man of an attentive, crafty god. It is perhaps of salvation's essence that it is not announced by signs but takes place in the profound depths of simulacra.

And since all the figures that Klossowski sketches and sets in motion inside his language are simulacra, it is necessary that we understand this word in terms of the resonance that we may now confer upon it: vain image (as opposed to reality); the representation of something (in which this thing delegates itself and is manifested, but also withdraws and in a sense is hidden); a lie which leads one to take one sign for another;[2] a sign of the presence of a deity (and the reciprocal possibility of taking this sign as its opposite); the simultaneous irruption of the Same and the Other ('to simulate' originally meant 'to come together'). Thus is formed the wondrously rich constellation so characteristic of Klossowski: simulacrum, similitude, simultaneity, simulation and dissimulation.

For linguists, a sign possesses its meaning only by virtue of the play and sovereignty of all other signs. It has no autonomous, natural and immediate relationship with what it signifies. It is valid not only through its context, but also by means of a virtual reach which extends like a dotted line on the same plane as it: by virtue of this ensemble of all the signifiers which define a language at a given moment, it is forced to mean what it says. In the religious domain one often finds a sign entirely different in structure; what it says, it says by virtue of a profound belonging to an origin, by virtue of a consecration. There is not a single tree in the Scriptures, not a single living or dissicated plant which does not refer back to the tree of the Cross – or to the wood cut from the First Tree at the foot of which Adam succumbed. Such a figure breaks down into stages through moving forms, which gives it that strange, twofold property of designating no meaning in particular but of referring back to a model (to a simple of which it is supposed to be the double, but which takes it back within itself as its own diffraction and transitory duplication) and being bound to the history of a manifestation that is never completed; within this history the sign may always be deferred to some new episode where a simpler simple, an earlier model (though later in Revelations) will appear, giving it an entirely opposite meaning; thus the tree of the Fall one day becomes what it has always been, the tree of the Reconciliation. A sign of this sort is at once prophetic and ironic: hanging entirely from a future that it repeats in advance, and which will repeat it in turn, in broad daylight. It says this, then that, or rather it already said, without our knowing, both this and that. In its essence it is a simulacrum, saying everything simultaneously and ceaselessly simulating something other than that which it says. It presents an image that depends on a forever receding truth – *Fabula*; and it binds in its form, as in an enigma, the avatars of the light that will come to it – *Fatum*. Fabula and Fatum, both sending us back to the first utterance from

[2] Marmontel said adirably: 'Simulating would express the lies of feeling and thought' (*Oeuvres*, Verdier, Paris, 1819, vol. X, p. 431).

which they spring, that root which the Latins understood as word, and in which the Greeks saw the greatest essence of luminous visibility.

Clearly it is necessary to make a rigorous distinction between signs and simulacra. They do not at all involve the same experience, even though they may happen at times to overlap. For the simulacrum does not determine a meaning; it belongs to the realm of appearance, in the explosion of time: Noontide illumination and eternal recurrence. Perhaps the Greek religion knew nothing but simulacra. First the Sophists, then the Stoics and the Epicureans wanted to read these simulacra as signs – a rather belated reading, in which the Greek gods were effaced. Christian exegesis, which is of Alexandrian birth, has inherited this mode of interpretation.

In the great detour that is our own current experience, whereby we attempt to sidestep all the Alexandrianism of our culture, Klossowski is the one who, from the bottom of the Christian experience, has rediscovered the marvels and depths of the simulacrum, beyond the games of yesterday: those of sense and non-sense, of signifier and signified, of symbol and sign. It is this, no doubt, which gives his work its religious, solar aspect once one grasps in it the Nietzschean interplay of Dionysius and Christ (since they are each, as Nietzsche saw, a simulacrum of the other).

The realm of simulacra, in Klossowski's oeuvre, conforms to a precise set of rules. The reversal of situations takes place in the moment, the inversion of for and against being effected in an almost detective-genre fashion (the good become bad, the dead come back to life, rivals turn out to be accomplices, executioners are subtle saviours, encounters are prepared long beforehand, the most banal statements are endowed with double meanings). Each reversal seems to be on the road to an epiphany; but in fact each discovery only makes the enigma more profound, increases the uncertainty and never reveals an element except to conceal the relationship existing among all the other elements. But what is most unusual and difficult in all this, is that the simulacra are neither things nor clues, nor those beautiful motionless forms that were the Greek statues. Here the simulacra are human beings.

Klossowski's world is sparing of objects; moreover, they form only meagre connections between the men whose doubles and as it were precarious intervals they constitute: portraits, photographs, stereoscopic views, signatures on cheques, open corsets that are like the empty but still rigid shells of a figure. On the other hand, the Simulacra-Men abound: still few in number in *Roberte*, they multiply in *La révocation* and especially in *Le souffleur*, so much so, in fact, that this latter text, nearly stripped of all setting and materiality that might bring fixed signs to bear on interpretation, no longer consists of much more than a sequential joining of dialogues. The point is that humans are simulacra much more vertiginous than the painted faces of deities. They are perfectly ambiguous beings because they speak, make gestures, communicate by winks of the eyes, move their fingers and appear suddenly in windows like semaphores (is it to send signs or to give the impression of doing so while in fact they are only making simulacra of signs?).

With such characters as these, one is dealing not with the profound, continuous beings of reminiscence, but with beings consigned, like those of Nietzsche, to a profound forgetfulness, to that oblivion which makes possible, in 're-collection', the

sudden appearance of the Same. Everything in them is breaking apart, bursting, presenting itself and then withdrawing in the same instant; they might well be living or dead,
it matters little; oblivion in them oversees the Identical. They signify nothing; they
simulate themselves: Vittorio and von A., Uncle Florence and the monstrous husband,
Théodore who is K., and especially Roberte who simulates Roberte in the minute, in-
superable distance through which Roberte is such as she is, this evening (cf. *Roberte ce soir*).

All these simulacra-figures pivot in place: rakes become inquisitors, seminarians
become Nazi officers, the confused persecutors of Théodore Lacase find themselves in
a friendly semicircle around the bed of K. These sudden twists only come about by
means of the play of 'alternators' of experience. These alternators are, in Klossowski's
novels, the sole peripeties – but in the literal sense of the word: that which ensures the
detour and return. Thus: the test-provocation (the stone of truth which is at the same
time the temptation of the worst: the fresco of the *Vocation*, or the sacrilegious task
assigned by von A.); the specious inquisition (censors who present themselves as
former rakes, like Malagrida or the psychiatrist with dubious intentions); the two-
sided conspiracy (the 'resistance' network which executes Dr Rodin). But most of all
the two great configurations which cause appearance to alternated are hospitality and
the theatre: two structures which stand face to face with each other in reverse
symmetry.

The host (a word which in French – *hôte* – already whirls about its interior axis,
meaning both the thing and its complement, host and guest), the host offers what he
possesses, for he can only possess what he proposes – which is there before his eyes
and is for everyone. He is, to use the wonderfully ambiguous word, *regardant*.[3]
Surreptitiously and with avarice, this giving regard sets aside its own portion of
pleasure and confiscates by sovereign authority one aspect of things which *regards* only
it. But this regard has the power to absent itself, to leave the place it occupies empty
and to offer instead what it envelops with its avidity. Thus its gift is the simulacrum of
an offering, as soon as it only preserves the feeble, distant silhouette, the visible
simulacrum of what it gives. In *Le souffleur* the theatre takes the place of this giving
'regard', such as it reigned in *Roberte* and *La révocation*. The theatre imposes on Roberte
the role of Roberte; that is, it tends to reduce the interior distance which opened up in
the simulacrum (under the effect of the giving regard), and to make the double of
Roberte, separated from Roberte by Théodore (perhaps K.), be inhabited by Roberte
herself. But if Roberte plays her role with natural ease (which comes to her at least as
if on cue), it is no longer but a simulacrum of theatre; and if Roberte on the other
hand stumbles through her text, it is Roberte-Roberte who slips away beneath a
pseudo-actress (and who is a poor actress inasmuch as she is not an actress but
Roberte). That is why this role can only be played by a simulacrum of Roberte who
resembles her so much that Roberte herself might well be this simulacrum herself. It
is thus necessary that Roberte should have two existences, or that there should be two

---

[3] [The French *regardant*, as discussed here by the author, means 'particular, careful, punctilious' as well
as 'stingy, close-fisted'; it also, as a noun, means 'onlooker', and, since Foucault is playing on all these
meanings, I have left it in the original French.]

Robertes with one existence; she must be a pure simulacrum of herself. In the *regard*, it is the *Regardant* who is made double (and until death); on the stage of the false theatre, it is the *la Regardée* (the woman seen) who undergoes an irreparable ontological split.[4]

Yet behind this whole game of alternating experiences in which the simulatra flicker, is there some absolute Operator who is thereby sending out enigmatic signs? In *La vocation suspendue* it seems that all the simulacra and their alternations are organised around a greater invocation which makes itself heard within them or which, perhaps, just as well remains mute. In the subsequent texts, this imperceptible but 'invoking' God has been replaced by two visible figures, or rather two series of figures who are, in their relation to the simulacra, at once with both feet on the ground and in perfect disequilibrium – both dividing, and divided, in two. At one end, the dynasty of monstrous characters, at the borderline of life and death: the Professor Octave, or that 'old master' that one finds at the beginning of *Le souffleur* controlling the shuntings at a suburban train station, in a vast, glazed hall before or after life. But does this 'operator' really intervene? How does he tie the plot together? Who is he, really? Is he the Master, Roberte's uncle (the one with two faces), Dr Rodin (the one who dies and is resuscitated), the lover of stereoscopic spectacles, the chiropractor (who massages and works on bodies), K. (who steals the works and perhaps the wives of others when he's not giving away his own wife), or Théodore Lacase (who makes Roberte act)? Or is he Roberte's husband? A vast genealogy runs from the Almighty to the one crucified in the simulacrum that he is (since he, who is K., says 'I' when Théodore speaks). But at the other end, Roberte herself is the great operatrix of the simulacra. Tirelessly, with her hands, her long, beautiful hands, she caresses shoulders and heads of hair, arouses desires, recalls former lovers, gives herself to soldiers or seeks out hidden miseries. It is without question she who diffracts her husband in all the monstrous or lamentable characters in which he scatters himself. She is legion. Not the one who always says no, but, inversely, the one who forever says yes. A forked yes which gives rise to that interspace where everyone stands beside himself. Let us not say Roberte-the-Devil and Théodore-God; let us say, rather, that the one is the simulacrum of God (the same as God, hence the Devil), and that the other is the simulacrum of Satan (the same as the Evil One, hence God). But the one is the Insulted-Inquisitor (laughable seeker of signs, obstinate and always disappointed interpreter – for there are no signs, only simulacra), while the other is the Holy-Sorceress (forever on her way to a Sabbath where her desire invokes human beings in vain, for there are never any humans, only simulacra). It is in the nature of simulacra not to tolerate either that exegesis which believes in signs or that virtue which loves humanity.

Catholics scrutinise signs. Calvinists have no trust at all in them, because they believe only in the election of souls. But what if we were neither signs nor souls, but merely the same as ourselves (neither visible sons of our works, nor predestined), and thereby torn apart in the discrete distance of the simulacrum? Well, the point is that the signs and destiny of man supposedly no longer have a common ground; the point is that the Edict of Nantes supposedly was revoked; that we are henceforth in the void

[4] Here one encounters again – though as a pure form, in the stripped-down game of the simulacrum – the problem of real presence and of transubstantiation.

left behind by the division of Christian theology;[5] and that on this deserted earth (which might indeed be rich from this abandonment) we can turn our ears to the words of Hölderlin: 'Zeichen sind wir, bedeutungslos', and perhaps still beyond, to all those great and fleeting simulacra that made the gods sparkle in the rising sun or shine like great silver arches in the heart of the night.

This is why Le bain de Diane is probably, of all of Klossowski's texts, the one closest to this dazzling – but to us gloomy – light, from which the simulacra come to us. In this exegesis of a legend we find a configuration similar to the one that gives order to his other narratives, as though they all had their great mythical model therein: a proclamatory fresco as in La vocation; Actaeon is Artemis's nephew, as is Antoine to Roberte; Dionysius is Actaeon's uncle and the old master of drunkenness, of anarchy, of death forever revived, of perpetual theophany; Diana is divided in two by her own desire, Actaeon metamorphosed at once by his desire and by that of Artemis. And yet, in this text devoted to an interpretation of a remote legend and a myth of distance (man chastised for having attempted to approach the naked goddess) the offering is as close as can be. There the bodies are young, beautiful, whole; they flee toward one another with all certainty. The simulacrum still presents itself in its sparkling fresh-ness, without resorting to the enigma of signs. There, phantasms are the welcome of appearance in the light of origin. But this origin is one that by its own movement recedes into an inaccessible remoteness. Diana at her bath, the goddess stealing away into the water at the moment in which she offers herself to the gaze, is not only the turning away of the Greek gods; it is the moment in which the intact unity of the divine 'reflects its divinity in a virgin body', and thereby doubles into a demon who makes her, at a distance from herself, appear chaste and at the same time offers her to the violence of the Goat. And when divinity ceases to shine in the clearings only to split in two in the appearance where it succumbs while vindicating itself, it leaves the space of myth and enters the time of theologians. The desirable trace of the gods withdraws (and perhaps is lost) in the tabernacle and the ambiguous play of signs.

At this point the pure word of myth ceases to be possible. How can one henceforth transcribe into a language such as ours the lost but insistent order of simulacra? The word perforce must be impure, which draws such shades toward the light and wants to give back to all simulacra, beyond the river, something like a visible body, a sign or a being. Tam dira cupido. It is this desire which the goddess placed in Actaeon's heart at the moment of metamorphosis and death: if you can describe the nudity of Diana, you are welcome to do so.

Klossowski's language is the prose of Actaeon: the transgressive word. Is not every word so, when it must deal with silence? Gide and many others with him wanted to transcribe an impure silence into a pure language, no doubt not seeing that such a word only possesses its silence from a much deeper silence that it does not name and which speaks in it and in spite of it – thus rendering it confused and impure.[6] We now

---

[5] When Roberte the Calvinist, in order to save a man, violates a tabernacle in which real presence is not hidden, she is suddenly seized, through that miniscule temple, by two hands, which are her own: in the void of the sign and of the artwork, the simulacrum of the doubled Roberte triumphs.

[6] On the word and purity, cf. Un si funeste désir, pp. 123–5.

know, thanks to Bataille and Blanchot, that language owes its power of transgression to an inverse relationship, that existing between an impure word and a pure silence, and that it is in the indefinitely travelled space of this impurity that the word may address such a silence. For Bataille, writing is a consecration undone: a transubstantiation ritualised in reverse where real presence becomes again a recumbent body and finds itself led back to silence in an act of vomiting. Blanchot's language addresses death: not in order to triumph over it in words of glory, but so as to remain in that orphic dimension where song, made possible and necessary by death, can never look at death face to face nor render it visible: thus he speaks to it and of it in an impossibility that relegates him to an infinity of murmurs.

Klossowski knows these forms of transgression well. But he recaptures them in a movement that is entirely his own: he treats his own language like a simulacrum. *La vocation suspendue* is a simulated commentary on a story that is itself a simulacrum, since it does not exist or rather it lies entirely within the commentary made on it. As a result, in a single layer of language there opens up that inner distance of identity that enables the commentary on an inaccessible work to exist in the very presence of the work and enables the work to slip away inside this commentary, which is nevertheless its only form of existence: the mystery of real presence and the enigma of the Same. The Roberte trilogy is treated differently, at least in appearance — journal fragments, scenes with dialogues, long exchanges that seem to tilt the word towards the currency of an immediate language without overview. But among these three texts a complex relationship is established. *Roberte ce soir* already exists inside the text itself, since the text recounts Roberte's decision of reproof against one of the novel's episodes. But this first narrative also exists in the second, which contests it from within through Roberte's journal, and later in the third, where one sees its theatrical representation being prepared, a representation which escapes into the very text of the *Souffleur*, where Roberte, called upon to give life to Roberte through her identical presence, splits apart into an irreducible gap. At the same time, the narrator of the first story, Antoine, breaks up, in the second, between Roberte and Octave, then is scattered in the multiplicity of the *Souffleur*, where the one speaking is, without one's being able to determine for certain, either Théodore Lacase or K., his double — who passes himself off as him, wants to take credit for his books and finally finds himself in his place — or even the Old Man, who presides over the shuntings and remains the invisible 'breather' (*Souffleur*) of all this language. A breather already dead, breather and breathed — perhaps Octave speaking yet again beyond death?

It's neither the ones nor the others, probably, but rather this overlapping of voices that 'breathe' one another, insinuating their words into the other's speech and animating him with a movement, a 'pneuma' that is not his own — but also breathing in the sense of a breath, an *expiration* that extinguishes the light of a candle; and lastly breathing (*soufflant*) in the specifically French sense of cheating or trickery, where one seizes upon something destined for another (taking his place, his role, his situation, his wife). Thus, as Klossowski's language recuperates itself, looming over what it has just said in the swirl of a new narration (and there are three, just as there are three turns in the spiral staircase adorning the cover of *Le souffleur*), the speaking subject is dispersed into various voices that 'breathe' and 'trick' one another, suggest, extinguish and replace one another – scattering the act of writing and the writer himself into the distance of the simulacrum in which he loses himself, breathes and lives.

As a rule, when an author speaks of himself as an author, it is in the vein of the 'diaristic' confession that tells of everyday truths – an impure truth in a spare, pure language. In this recovery of his own language, this retreat that inclines towards no intimacy, Klossowski invents a space of the simulacrum that is without doubt the contemporary, but still hidden, place of literature. Klossowski writes a work, one of those rare works which discover: in it, one sees that the existence of literature concerns neither humans nor signs, but this space of the double, this hollow of the simulacrum where Christianity has fallen under the spell of Demon, and where the Greeks once feared the gleaming presence of the gods with their arrows. It is the distance and proximity of the Same where the rest of us, now, encounter our only language.

CHAPTER FIVE

Philosophy and the death of God (1966)

Interview with M.-G. Foy. Originally published as 'Qu'est-ce'un philosophe?' in *Connaissance des hommes*, no. 22, autumn 1966, p. 9. Subsequently reprinted as 'Qu'est-ce'un philosophe?' in *Dits et écrits*, vol. I, Gallimard, Paris, 1994, pp. 552–3.

Translated by Elizabeth Ezra

What is the philosopher's role in society?

Philosophers don't have a role in society. Their thought cannot be situated in relation to the current [*actual*] movement of a group. Socrates is an excellent example: Athenian society could see in him only a subversive, because the questions he raised were not acceptable to the established order. In reality, a philosopher's role is acknowledged only after a certain period of time; it is, in short, a retrospective role.

But then, how do you integrate yourself into society?

Integrate myself …? You know, until the nineteenth century, philosophers were not recognised. Descartes was a mathematician, and Kant did not teach philosophy, he taught anthropology and geography; you learned rhetoric, not philosophy, and so there was no need for philosophers to be 'integrated'. It was not until the nineteenth century that chairs in philosophy were finally established; Hegel was a professor of philosophy. But, at the time, everyone agreed that philosophy was coming to an end.

A time that coincides roughly with the death of God?

To a certain extent, but we must be careful, because the notion of the death of God does not have the same meaning in Hegel, Feuerbach and Nietzsche. For Hegel, Reason takes the place of God, and it is the human spirit that develops little by little; for Feuerbach, God is the illusion that alienates Man, but once rid of this illusion, it is Man who comes to realise his liberty; finally, for Nietzsche, the death of God signifies the end of metaphysics, but God is not replaced by man, and the space remains empty.

Yes, the last man and superman.

We are indeed the last man in the Nietzschean sense of the term, and the superman will be whoever can overcome the absence of God and the absence of man in the same gesture of overtaking. But with regard to Nietzsche, we can return to your question: for him, the philosopher was someone who diagnosed the state of thought. We can envisage, moreover, two kinds of philosopher: the kind who opens up new avenues of thought, such as Heidegger, and the kind who in a sense plays the role of an archaeologist, studying the space in which thought unfolds, as well as the conditions of that thought, its mode of constitution.

CHAPTER SIX

Who are you, Professor Foucault? (1967)

Interview with P. Caruso. Originally appeared as 'Che cos'è Lei Professor Foucault?' (translated into Italian by C. Lazzeri),[1] *La fiera letteraria*, year XLII, no. 39, 28 September 1967, pp. 11–15. A different version was published in P. Caruso, *Conversazioni con Claude Lévi-Strauss, Michel Foucault, Jacques Lacan*, Mursia, Milan, 1969, pp. 91–131. The interview was subsequently published as 'Qui êtes-vous, professeur Foucault?' in *Dits et écrits*, vol. I, Gallimard, Paris, 1994, pp. 601–23. This translation is taken from *Dits et écrits* and following this text the sections in square brackets appeared in the 1969 version.

Translated by Lucille Cairns

Caruso: Can you talk to me about your cultural education, and retrace the route you have taken to reach your current positions? I refer above all to the positions articulated in the book published last year, *The Order of Things*, thanks to which you became a public figure, and not just in France.

Foucault: It is rather difficult for me to describe the route that has led me to my current positions, for the very good reason that I hope, precisely, that I have not already got to the point of arrival. It is only at the end of the course that you can really establish the route you have followed. The book I published last year works out certain ideas; consequently, it is a transitional book, a book which enables me, which I hope will enable me, to go further.

Caruso: In which direction?

Foucault: I feel that I can see it already. But I cannot state firmly that the direction I see now will be the final direction, that which can only be discovered by somebody who, at the end of his life, turns around towards what he has achieved.

---

[1] [It is worth drawing attention to the fact that the following interview has been translated from a French text which was itself translated from an original Italian text. The present translator has encountered a very small number of obscurities and grammatical errors in the French version, and has attempted in these cases to make the most coherent construction available in English.]

Caruso: And what if you tried to reconstruct it despite everything, imagining that you were about to die?

Foucault: Well, I would then say to you that during the 1950s, like all those of my generation, I was preoccupied, faced with the great example of our new masters, and under their influence, with the issue of meaning. We were all educated within the school of phenomenology, all trained to analyse the meanings immanent in lived experience, the implicit meanings of perception and of history. In addition, I was preoccupied with the relationship that might exist between individual existence and the set of structures and historical conditions in which such an individual existence appears; with the question of the relations between meaning and history, or between the phenomenological and the Marxist method as well. And I believe that, as with all those of my generation, there took place within me between 1950 and 1955 a sort of conversion which initially seemed unimportant, but which in reality was profoundly to set us apart: the small discovery, or if you like the slight disquiet which was at its origin, was concern about the formal conditions which can cause meaning to appear. In other words, we re-examined the Husserlian idea that there exists everywhere meaning which already envelops and invests us even before we start to open our eyes and to speak. For those of my generation, meaning does not appear on its own, it is not 'already there', or rather, 'it is there already', yes, but under a certain number of conditions which are formal conditions. And, since 1955, we have mainly devoted ourselves to analysing the formal conditions for the appearance of meaning.

Caruso: How would you situate the four books you have written so far?

Foucault: In *Madness and Civilization* and *The Birth of the Clinic*, I sought to analyse the conditions according to which a scientific object could be constituted.

Caruso: The 'archaeology of the clinical gaze' and the 'archaeology of madness'.

Foucault: Exactly. That is the problem. There existed in all Western cultures certain individuals who were considered mad and certain individuals who were considered ill: it was a question, so to speak, of immediately lived meanings in society which for its part recognised ill people and mad people without hesitation. These meanings were abruptly modified with the appearance of new forms of knowledge, specific bodies of scientific knowledge, and with the appearance of something like psychiatric medicine or psychopathology, and something like clinical medicine at the end of the eighteenth century. My problem was to show how it could come about that meanings immediately lived within a society could appear as sufficient conditions for the constitution of a scientific object. [For madness and mental illness to cease having an immediate meaning and to become the object of a rational form of knowledge, a certain number of conditions had to be brought together, conditions that I sought to analyse. It was a question, so to speak, of the 'interruption' between meaning and scientific object, that is to say of the formal conditions for the appearance of an object in a meaningful context.

Caruso: But does that not contradict what you were saying at the outset?

Foucault: On the face of it, yes. I was talking to you about our generation and the way in which we were preoccupied with the conditions for the appearance of meaning. Conversely, I am now telling you that I was preoccupied with the way in which meaning disappeared, as though eclipsed, through the constitution of the object. Well, it is precisely to that extent that I cannot be assimilated to what has been defined as 'structuralism'. Structuralism poses the problem of the formal conditions for the appearance of meaning, starting above all from the privileged example of language – language being itself an extraordinarily complex object, full of potential for analysis. But, at the same time, it serves as a model to analyse the appearance of other meanings which are not exactly meanings of a linguistic or verbal order. Now, from that point of view, it cannot be said that I practise structuralism, since in fact I am concerned neither with meaning nor with the conditions in which meaning appears, but with the conditions for the modification or the interruption of meaning, with the conditions in which meaning disappears and in so doing gives rise to the appearance of something else.]

Caruso: How can we see in today's mentality the fact that illness and madness have become a special scientific object?

Foucault: Every society establishes a whole series of systems of opposition – between good and bad, allowed and forbidden, lawful and unlawful, criminal and uncriminal; all these oppositions, which are constitutive of every society, are reduced in the Europe of today to the simple opposition between normal and pathological. This opposition is not only simpler than the others, but it also presents the advantage of allowing us to believe that there exists a technique which allows the reduction of the pathological to the normal. [Thus, faced with offences, with sexual deviation etc., we say it is a pathological case. Now, this codification of all oppositions in the opposition between normal and pathological in fact occurs thanks to an alternative opposition, implicit in our culture, but very active even though virtually invisible: the opposition between madness and reason. To be able to say that a criminal is a pathological case, you have to start by saying that you are dealing with a madman; you will go on to say that every madman is a person suffering from mental illness, thus, a pathological case. This is how the criminal can enter the category of the pathological. In other words, the madness–reason opposition functions as an alternative opposition which allows all the old oppositions peculiar to our culture to be translated into the major, sovereign and monotonous opposition between normal and pathological.]

Caruso: And yet there are many phenomena, even in terms of customs, which do not fit this schema very well: one example among the most obvious is the rediscovery of drugs by our Western society.

Foucault: With the introduction of drugs in our society, we are indeed witnessing to some extent the inverse operation: that of seeking to restore to the madness–reason

89

opposition its autonomy, rather than considering it merely as a replacement code between two systems of opposition, depathologising this madness and proclaiming it as a non-pathological cultural opposition, that is to say, irreducible in terms of the normal–pathological opposition. And effectively, entirely healthy people who freely and voluntarily decide to take LSD, to enter into a state of 'non-reason' for a period of twelve hours, have an experience of madness while remaining outside the opposition between normal and pathological.

Caruso: Do you think, then, that drugs can take on another meaning within our very culture, that of an expansion of the horizons of our mentality to the point of including new forms of sensitivity? Do you think, for example, that it is possible to speak of an irruption of the thought and culture of certain Eastern civilisations within our Western civilisation?

Foucault: No, I think on the contrary that the opposite phenomenon is occurring. On the face of it, for the last one hundred and fifty years, since Schopenhauer, say, we have been orientalising; in reality, it is precisely because the whole world is Westernizing that the West is becoming relatively more permeable to Indian philosophy, to African art, to Japanese painting, to Arabic mysticism. Hindu philosophy, African art acquire a consciousness of self by virtue of those structures through which Western civilisation assimilates them. Consequently, the use of drugs does not at all seem to me a way for the Westerner to open up to the East. It seems to me that drugs as used in the East functioned essentially to tear man away from the mad illusion that the world exists and to reveal to him another reality which was the annihilation of the individual; the use made of them today turns out to be an individualistic one if ever there was one: it is all about refinding in oneself the internal possibilities of madness. Not, then, about dispelling the madness of the normal in order to recover true reality, according to the Eastern use of drugs, but about reclaiming through the reason of the world an individual madness which we all involuntarily possess.

Caruso: To come back to your work, it seems to me that, in the book on Raymond Roussel, you also analyse the case of this writer as an example of the current reappraisal of 'madness'.

Foucault: Certainly. This book constitutes a small piece of research, on the face of it marginal. Roussel was in fact treated by psychiatrists, by Pierre Janet in particular. The latter diagnosed in him a fine case of obsessional neurosis, a diagnosis which was, moreover, justified. Roussel's language, at the end of the last century and at the beginning of this one, could not be anything other than a mad language and identified as such. And now today this language has lost its signification of madness, of pure and simple neurosis, and has been assimilated to a literary mode of being. Suddenly, Roussel's texts have joined a mode of existence within literary discourse. It is precisely this modification which interested me and led me to undertake an analysis of Roussel. Not to find out if the pathological meanings were still present or if they

90

were in some way constitutive of Roussel's work. It was of no interest to me to establish whether Roussel's work was or was not the work of a neurotic. Conversely, I did want to see how the workings of Roussel's language could henceforth take their place within the general workings of contemporary literary language. [Thus, in this case too, it is not exactly a question of the problem of structuralism: what was important to me and what I sought to analyse was not so much the appearance of meaning in language as the way discourses function within a given culture: how a discourse could have functioned as pathological in one period and as literary in other. It was therefore the workings of the discourse which interested me, and not its mode of signification.]

Caruso: To which discipline do you think your research belongs? To philosophy? Are we dealing with a 'critique' which could serve as a support for certain human sciences?

Foucault: It is hard for me to classify a form of research like my own within philosophy or within the human sciences. I could define it as an analysis of the cultural facts characterising our culture. In that sense, it would be a question of something like an ethnology of the culture to which we belong. I do in fact seek to place myself outside the culture to which we belong, to analyse its formal conditions in order to make a critique of it, not in the sense of reducing its values, but in order to see how it was actually constituted. [In addition, through analysing the very conditions of our rationality, I call into question our language, my language, and analyse the way it was suddenly able to emerge.]

Caruso: In short, you are performing an ethnology of our culture?

Foucault: Or at the very least, of our rationality, of our 'discourse'.

Caruso: But what you say is also of immediate concern for contemporary philosophy, for every contemporary philosopher. Above all when you move from specific analyses bearing on precise themes to implications of a more general nature.

Foucault: It is very possible that my work has something to do with philosophy, above all in so far as, at least since Nietzsche, the task of philosophy has been to make diagnoses, and its aim is no longer to proclaim a truth which would be valid for all and for all time. I seek to diagnose, to carry out a diagnosis of the present: to say what we are today and what it means, today, to say what we do say. This work of excavation beneath our feet has characterised contemporary thought since Nietzsche, and in this sense I can declare myself a philosopher.

Caruso: But this work of excavation, this 'archaeology' is also a work of history.

Foucault: Indeed, and it is curious to see how certain individuals in France, and particularly the non-historians, failed to recognise a history book in my last book. And yet it really is a history book. The historians got it right, but the non-historians claimed that it was a book aimed at denying history, at evacuating history, at ending history. That probably depends on the rather simplistic conception they have of history. For them, history is essentially a set of analyses which must first of all follow a well-defined linearity proceeding from A to B, according to a misleading evolution (the myth of evolution as a pillar of history). [Second, they always conceive of history as a matter between the individual and the institution, the materiality of things, the past, in other words, as a dialectic between an individual free consciousness and the whole of the human world taken in all its weight and opacity. With these presuppositions, you can write very interesting history books, as has moreover been done since Michelet. But I think that there are other ways of making history, and in that I certainly cannot be considered as someone who has innovated, as many professional historians have for a long time been performing analyses of the type that figure in The Order of Things: thus, one of the most illustrious contemporary historians, Braudel, cannot be taken as a supporter of this ideal of evolutionary, linear history, in which consciousness plays a role.

All in all, we have to be wary about an overly simple linear conception of history. We consider the understanding of the way one event succeeds another as a specifically historical issue, and yet we do not consider as an historical issue one which is in fact equally so: understanding how two events can be contemporaneous. I would like to point out, moreover, that history is quite frequently considered as the privileged site of causality: all historical approaches should aim at highlighting relations of cause and effect. And yet it is several centuries ago now that the natural sciences – and several decades ago that the human sciences – realised that the causal relation is impossible to establish and to verify in terms of formal rationality: in fact, causality does not exist in logic. Now, work is nowadays being done on, precisely, introducing relations of a logical type into the field of history. As soon as relations of a logical type, like implication, exclusion, transformation, are introduced in historical analysis, it is obvious that causality disappears. But we have to rid ourselves of the prejudice that history without causality would no longer be history.]

Caruso: As well as 'causal history', your last book aims at other polemical objectives: I refer above all to ideologies which are said to be 'humanist'.

Foucault: In trying to make a diagnosis of the present in which we live, we can isolate as already belonging to the past certain tendencies which are still considered to be contemporary. That is precisely why a polemical value has been attributed to certain of my analyses, which for me were just analyses. You referred to my diagnosis on humanism. In The Order of Things, I sought to pursue the two lines of research about which I was talking to you: the idea was to see how an object for knowledge had come to be constituted, and how a certain type of discourse had functioned. I sought to analyse the following phenomenon: in the scientific discourses that man has formulated since the seventeenth century, a new object appeared in the course of the eighteenth century: 'man'. With man was given the possibility of constituting the human sciences. We also witnessed the emergence of a type of ideology or general philosophical theme which was that of man's imprescriptible value. When I say imprescriptible value, I say it in a very precise sense, that is to say that man appeared as a possible object of science – the human sciences – and at the same time as the being thanks to whom any knowledge is possible. Man thus belonged to the field of knowledge as a possible object and, on the other hand, he was placed in a radical manner as the point of origin of every type of knowledge.

Caruso: Object and subject, in short.

Foucault: Subject of all types of knowledge and object of a possible type of knowledge. Such an ambiguous situation characterises what could be called the anthropologico-humanist structure of nineteenth-century thought. It seems to me that this thought is coming apart, disintegrating before our very eyes. That is due in large measure to the structuralist development. As soon as it was realised that all human knowledge, all human existence, all human life, and perhaps even the biological heredity of man, are contained within structures, that is to say within a formal set of elements which obey relations anybody could describe, man ceased, so to speak, to be his own subject, to be simultaneously subject and object. [It is discovered that what makes man possible is in fact a set of structures, structures which he can, admittedly, conceive and describe, but of which he is not the subject, or the sovereign consciousness. This reduction of man to the structures within which he is contained seems to me characteristic of contemporary thought. This is why the ambiguity of man as both subject and object no longer now seems to me a fruitful hypothesis, a fruitful theme for research.]

Caruso: Consequently, you state for example that a thinker like Sartre, whatever his merits may be, belongs to the nineteenth century. And yet Sartre is sensitive to the demand for an anthropology which is not only historical but structural; he does not seek to deny structures in favour of the lived experience of temporality or of history: he seeks, on the contrary, to reconcile the two levels, horizontal and vertical, progressive and regressive, diachronic and synchronic, structural and historical. His whole endeavour aims at reconciling praxis, meaning, with what appears to be pure inertia from the perspective of intentionality.

Foucault: I shall answer by saying that, in my view, the real problem today is only apparently constituted by the relation between synchrony and diachrony, or between structure and history. Discussion does indeed seem to be developing on this theme. But, to tell the truth, no serious 'structuralist' would think of trying to deny or reduce the diachronic dimension, just as no serious historian ignores the synchronic dimension. Thus it is that Sartre undertakes analysis of the synchronic exactly as does Saussure, who leaves ample space for the possibility of a diachronic analysis, and all linguists can study the economy of linguistic transformations as for instance Martinet did in France. In short, if the problem boiled down merely to that, it would be fairly easy to reach agreement. Moreover it is not without good reason that we have seen

93

some very interesting discussions on this point, but never any serious controversies. Conversely, controversy has arisen and has quite recently reached a high degree of intensity when we have called something else into question: not diachrony in favour of synchrony, but the sovereignty of the subject, or of consciousness. It was at that point that some individuals indulged in passionate explosions. [It seems to me that all that is going on at the moment cannot be reduced to the discovery of synchronic relations between elements. Further, it should be borne in mind that these analyses, when taken to their extreme logical conclusions, reveal to us the impossibility of continuing to think about history and society in terms of the subject or human consciousness. It could then be said that Sartre does not reject so much synchrony as the unconscious.]

Caruso: But Sartre never maintains that the reflexive cogito constitutes the only starting point; he even says, in *Critique of Dialectical Reason*,[2] that we have at least two starting points: apart from a methodological starting point which initiates reflection on the basis of the cogito, there is another one, an anthropological one, which defines the concrete individual on the basis of his materiality. Moreover, the cogito opens up to us a world which already existed before reflection.

Foucault: Even if one were to admit the existence of a pre-reflexive cogito, the very fact that it is a cogito inevitably alters the result we aim at.

Caruso: And yet, phenomenologists could in turn reproach you with forgetting, or concealing, the genesis of your way of looking at things. In your analysis, there is a kind of methodological neglect of the subject who is carrying out the analysis itself, as if taking it into account necessarily implied a whole metaphysics. [But a correct interpretation of phenomenology in my opinion excludes all metaphysics. It is probable that everything you do on the level of real research can be done even if one starts out from a phenomenological point of view (provided of course that it is not too rigid and narrow).]

Foucault: Well, I shall answer by saying that it was in fact believed at one point that a method could be justified only to the extent that it could account for the 'totality'. I shall take a very precise example. [When historians of philology studied the history of a language, they claimed to give an account of the evolution of that language and of the result to which that evolution had given rise. In this sense, the historical method was more comprehensive than the structural method in so far as it wished to account simultaneously for the evolution and the result. After Saussure, we get the sudden appearance of methodologies which present themselves as deliberately incomplete methodologies. That is to say that recourse is made to the elimination of a certain number of existing areas, and it is thanks to such a concealment that, as if by contrast,

[2] J.-P. Sartre, *Critique of Dialectical Reason*, trans. Alan Sheridan Smith, ed. Jonathan Ree, New Left Books, London, 1976. First appeared in French as *Critique de la raison dialectique*, Gallimard, Paris, 1960.

phenomena can appear which otherwise would have remained buried beneath a set of overly complex relations. From this we must conclude that the phenomenological method certainly wants to account for everything, whether it be to do with the cogito or with what precedes reflection, with what 'is already there' when the cogito is activated; in this sense, it is clearly a totalising method. I believe however that from the moment one cannot describe everything, it is through concealing the cogito, in a way putting aside that first illusion of the cogito, that we can see emerging entire systems of relations that otherwise would not be describable. As a consequence, I do not deny the cogito, I confine myself to observing that its methodological potential is ultimately not as great as one might have believed and that, in any case, we can nowadays make descriptions which seem to me objective and positive, by dispensing with the cogito entirely. It is surely significant that I have been able to describe structures of knowledge as a whole without ever referring to the cogito, even though people were for several centuries convinced of the impossibility of analysing knowledge without starting from the cogito.

Caruso: Certainly, any kind of positive research can, and probably should, proceed without paying attention to its own types of intentionality, in the sense that it is essential, when observing a particular area, to in a way isolate it from the rest in order to avoid, as you were just saying, being engulfed by this 'rest'. But none the less, the fact remains that we still after all position ourselves on the level of totality and that the philosophical standpoint consists precisely in taking account of this level. Questions of 'context' cannot be ignored: we can limit a research field as much as we like but we cannot prevent it from having a context. As a result, one is, *nolens volens*, inevitably a philosopher too – unconsciously or naively, but a thing cannot be studied without the whole being implicated. You can very easily put aside these questions, because these are traditional philosophical questions, but, in one way or another, you are placing yourself from the point of view of the 'whole'. In fact, even nowadays, analysis presupposes a dialectic and each specific area presupposes a context and thus presupposes the 'whole'.

Foucault: These are observations I share to a large extent and to which it is not easy to respond. I consider myself to be as attentive as the next person, and perhaps even more so, to what we might call 'effects of context'. Indeed I have set out to understand, for example, how it was possible that, in a type of discourse as limited, as meticulous as that of grammatical or philological analysis, phenomena could be observed which point to a whole epistemological structure that we find in political economy, natural history, biology and also in modern philosophy. I really would be blind if I were to neglect with regard to my own situation what I have highlighted so many times. I am perfectly aware that I am situated in a context. The problem, then, lies in knowing how to attain consciousness of such a context and even, so to speak, in assimilating it, in letting it exert its effects on one's own discourse, on the very discourse one is currently employing. You say that one is inevitably a philosopher in the sense that one inevitably conceives the whole in some way, even though, in the limits within which a scientific activity takes place, it is perfectly possible to put the problem to one side. But are you quite sure that philosophy consists precisely in that? What I mean is that the philosophy which aims to conceive the whole could perfectly easily be only one of the possible forms of philosophy, one of the possible forms which was in fact the royal road of philosophical thought in the last century from Hegel; but, after all, we could very well think nowadays that philosophy no longer consists in that.] I would like to point out that before Hegel philosophy did not necessarily have this claim to totality: Descartes no more produced a form of politics than did Condillac and Malebranche, Hume's mathematical thought can be neglected without any great risk. So I believe that the idea of a philosophy which embraces the totality is a relatively recent idea; it seems to me that twentieth-century philosophy is again changing in nature, not only in the sense that it is becoming more limited and more narrowly defined, but also in the sense that it is being relativised. What does engaging in philosophy nowadays mean, in fact? It does not mean forming a discourse on totality, a discourse in which the totality of the world would be taken up again, but rather, engaging in a certain activity, a certain form of activity. I would say briefly that philosophy is today a form of activity which can be practised in different fields. When Saussure distinguished language from speech, and when he thus brought into being an object for linguistics, he carried out an operation of a philosophical type. When, in the field of logic, Russell highlighted the difficulty, the impossibility of considering 'existence' as an attribute, or the existential proposition as a proposition of the type subject–attribute, he was certainly engaging in a work of logic, but the activity which enabled him to make this discovery of a logical type was a philosophical activity. This is why I would say that, if philosophy is less a discourse than a type of activity internal to an objective domain, it can no longer be required to provide a totalising perspective. That is why Husserl, in so far as he sought to rethink the whole of our knowledge universe according to and in relation to a transcendental subject, is clearly the last philosopher to have had absolutely universalist claims. That claim seems to me to have disappeared nowadays. On that point, moreover, I would say that Sartre is a philosopher in the most modern sense of the term, as in fact, for him, philosophy essentially boils down to a form of political activity. For Sartre, to philosophise today is a political act. I do not believe that Sartre still thinks that philosophical discourse is a discourse about totality.

Caruso: If I am not mistaken, in this refusal of philosophy's claims to universality, you have links with Nietzsche.

Foucault: I believe that Nietzsche who, after all, was almost Husserl's contemporary, even if he stopped writing just at the moment when Husserl was about to begin, contested and destroyed Husserlian totalisation. For Nietzsche, philosophising consisted in a series of acts and operations falling within the province of various domains: describing a Greek tragedy was philosophising, engaging in philology or history was philosophising. Moreover, Nietzsche discovered that philosophy's distinctive activity consists in the work of diagnosis: What are we today? What is this 'today' in which we live? Such a diagnostic activity entailed a work of excavation beneath his own feet in order to establish how this world of thought, of discourse, of culture which was his world had been formed before him. It seems to me that Nietzsche had ascribed to philosophy a new objective which has been somewhat forgotten, even though Husserl in *The Crisis of European Sciences*[3] in his turn attempted a 'genealogy'. As for the actual influence Nietzsche has had on me, I would find it difficult to specify, because I am, precisely, aware just how deep it has been. I shall simply say that I remained ideologically 'historicist' and Hegelian until I read Nietzsche.

Caruso: And, beyond Nietzsche, which other factors have influenced you most in this sense?

Foucault: If I remember rightly, I owe the first great cultural jolt to French serial and dodecaphonic musicians – like Boulez and Barraqué – to whom I was linked through friendship. For me they represented the first 'breach' in that dialectical world I had been living in.

Caruso: Are you still interested in contemporary music, do you still listen to it?

Foucault: Yes, but it is not a special interest. However, I realise how important listening to it was for me at a certain time in my life. It had as great an importance as reading Nietzsche. In this connection, I can tell you a little story. I don't know if you've ever listened to Barraqué, if you've heard of him: in my opinion, he is one of the most brilliant and most neglected musicians of the current generation. Well, he wrote a cantata which was performed in 1955 and whose words came from a text by Nietzsche that I had obtained for him. Nowadays, though, I am more interested in painting than in music.

Caruso: That does not surprise me. I assure you that I very much admired, in *The Order of Things*, your analysis of Velázquez's *Las Meninas*. I wanted to ask you another question on this theme: in what sense do you consider Klee to be the most representative contemporary painter?

Foucault: On this point, you see, I do not know if I would want to state things so dogmatically today, since I have looked at the matter a little more closely and in particular at the whole issue of the relations between Klee and Kandinsky, which seems to me a prodigious story worthy of very serious analysis.

Caruso: But in *The Order of Things* you oppose the world of 'representation' symbolised by Velázquez and Klee's world corresponding to the modern sensibility.

[3] E. Husserl, *The Crisis of European Sciences and Transcendental Phenomenology: An Introduction to Phenomenological Philosophy*, trans. David Carr, Northwestern University Press, Evanston, 1970. First appeared in German as *Die Krisis der europäischen Wissenschaften und die transzendentalen Phänomenologie. Eninleitung in die Phänomenologie*, Philosophia, Belgrade, 1936.

Foucault: I still think that this opposition is valid. Klee is the one who took from the surface of the world a whole series of figures which had value as signs, and who orchestrated them within pictorial space while leaving them their form and structure as signs, in short, while preserving their mode of being as signs and making them function at the same time in such a way as no longer to have any meaning. And the non-structuralist, the non-linguist in me is enraptured at such a use of the sign: that is to say, of the sign in its mode of being as a sign, and not in its capacity to create meaning.

Caruso: And, to stay in the area of painting, have you anything to say on the new tendencies? Have you been interested, for example, in pop art? Do you see any new tendency emerging which interests you?

Foucault: I have to admit that I have not been very interested either in pop art or in op art,[4] precisely because of their immediate and conscious relationship, so to speak, with the social context from which they emerge: it is rather too easy a relationship. For me, the great contemporary painters are individuals like Arnal, Corneille, even if the influence exerted by op art on Arnal and Corneille is fairly insistent.

Caruso: What have the other important influences on you been? Could you indicate who your spiritual masters were?

Foucault: For a long time, there was a sort of unresolved conflict in me between a passion for Blanchot and Bataille, and on the other hand the interest I nurtured for certain positive studies, like those of Dumézil and Lévi-Strauss, for example. But in fact, these two directions, whose only common denominator was perhaps the religious question, contributed in equal measure to leading me to the theme of the disappearance of the subject. As for Bataille and Blanchot, I believe that the former's experience of eroticism and the latter's of language, understood as experiences of dissolution, disappearance, denial of the subject (of the speaking subject and the erotic subject), suggested to me, simplifying things a bit, the theme I transposed in the reflection on structural or 'functional' analyses like those of Dumézil or Lévi-Strauss. In other words, I consider that structure, the very possibility of a rigorous discourse on structure, leads to a negative discourse on the subject, in short, to a discourse similar to Bataille's and Blanchot's.

Caruso: Can your interest in Sade be interpreted in the same way?

Foucault: Yes, in so far as Sade constitutes an optimum example, be it to do with the denial of the subject in eroticism or with the absolute deployment of structures in their most arithmetic positivity. For after all, is Sade anything other than the development to the most extreme consequences of the whole combination of erotic

---

[4] ['Op art' (in full, optical art): a form of abstract art developed in the 1960s, in which optical effects are used to provide illusions of movement in the patterns produced, or designs in which conflicting patterns emerge and overlap.]

elements in its most logical form, through a sort of exaltation (at least in Juliette's case) of the subject itself, an exaltation leading to its complete explosion?

Caruso: At this point let us come back to a favourite theme of yours, the disappearance of the human subject and of all forms of humanism. I would like you to clarify the significance of your two theses. To start off, you have referred to 'soft forms of humanism' (Saint-Exupéry's, Camus's) to designate those humanists whom you find particularly repugnant: am I to infer from this that even for you there exist forms of humanism worthy of respect?

Foucault: I have indeed adopted the expression 'soft humanism', and for obvious linguistic reasons that implies that I am capable of thinking there are non-soft, hard humanisms, which might be promoted over others. But, on reflection, I would say that 'soft humanism' is a purely redundant expression, and that 'humanism' implies 'softness' in any case.

Caruso: You do realise that statements like these are often and even for the most part extremely provocative. So I would like you to explain a little more clearly what you mean in saying this.

Foucault: I shall answer by saying that, precisely, the use of humanism constitutes a provocation. In fact – and I refer here to a landscape that you too most probably know very well, since we probably passed through it together – you are aware that it was precisely this humanism which was used in 1948 to justify Stalinism and the hegemony of Christian democracy, that it is the self-same humanism which we find in Camus or in Sartre's existentialism. Ultimately, this humanism has in a certain sense been the little whore of all the thought, culture, morality and politics of the last twenty years. I consider that the wish to propose it nowadays as an example of virtue really is provocation, now.

Caruso: But it is not a question of taking a given form of humanism as an example of virtue. You have confined yourself to condemning a humanism which contradicts its own, ambiguous or outmoded premises; what I would like, on the contrary, is for you to tell me how it is possible today not to be humanist in any way whatsoever.

Foucault: I believe that the human sciences do not at all lead to the discovery of something which would be the 'human' – the truth about man, his nature, his birth, his destiny; in reality, what the various human sciences are dealing with is something very different from man: systems, structures, combinations, forms etc. Consequently, if we want to deal seriously with the human sciences, we will need above all to destroy those obsessive chimera constituted by the idea that we have to seek out man.

Caruso: On the scientific, cognitive level, yes. But on the moral level …

Foucault: Let us say on the political level: I in fact consider that from now on morality
may be reduced entirely to politics and to sexuality, which itself may be reduced to
politics: this is why the moral is the political. The experience of the last fifty years (and
not only of the last fifty) proves just how far this humanist idea not only is completely
sterile, but happens to be noxious, harmful, since it has allowed the most diverse and
the most dangerous political operations; in reality, the problems faced by those in
politics are problems like knowing whether the rate of demographic growth should
be left to increase, whether it is better to encourage heavy or light industry, whether
consumption, the growth of consumption can in a given situation present economic
advantages or not. These are political problems. And at this level, we never encounter
'men'.

Caruso: But are you not yourself now proposing a form of humanism? Why support
one economic direction rather than another, why regulate the rate of demographic
growth? Through all these political operations, are we not in fact aiming at human
well-being?

What is at the base of the economy if not man, not only as a source of labour but
also as an end in himself? How can you not retract here, at least partially, the nihilistic
assertion of the 'disappearance' of man, of the 'dissolution' of man? In short, I do not
believe that you accord an absolute value to these assertions. But if you were to give
them one, I would like you to say so clearly and if possible to justify doing so. Unless
you interpret it simply as a slogan designed to demystify.

Foucault: I would not want this to be considered as a slogan. It has now become
something of a slogan, it is true, but against my will. We are talking about one of my
deep convictions due to all the disservice this idea of man has done us for many years.

Caruso: Disservice . . . to man. You see that even your demands are humanist demands.
In short, to what degree do you think that you can deny humanism, in view of the fact
that in practical terms you confine yourself to denouncing forms of humanism that
contradict their own premises, either outmoded, or else too limited (which implies
the existence of a human ideology that is more modern, more appropriate to the
current situation, more flexible)?

Foucault: I would not want to appear as the promoter of a technocratic humanism or
of a type of humanism which does not declare itself as such. It is true that nobody is
more humanist than the technocrats. Moreover, it must surely be possible to engage in
a left-wing politics which does not exploit all these confused humanist myths. I
believe that one can define the best conditions for the functioning of society through
obtaining them, thanks to a certain relationship between demographic growth,
consumption, individual freedom and the possibility of pleasure for all, without ever
relying on the concept of man. The best conditions for this functioning may be
defined internally, without one being able to say 'for whom' it is best that things be
like that. The technocrats, now, *are* humanists, technocracy is a form of humanism.

They in fact consider that they are the only ones in possession of the card game which would allow a definition of what the 'happiness of man' is and its realisation.

Caruso: But do you not ask yourself the same question?

Foucault: No, why? On the contrary, I bring technocracy back to humanism and I refute both.

Caruso: Yes, but that is because you see in this technocratic humanism a bad form of humanism which you contrast with another, more valid way of being humanist.

Foucault: But why 'being humanist'? I simply say that we can seek to define, politically, the best conditions for the functioning of society which are possible today.

Caruso: But the functioning of society is the functioning of men who form a given society.

Foucault: It is obvious that in saying to you that man has ceased to exist I absolutely did not mean that man, as a living or social species, has disappeared from the planet. The functioning of society will of course be the functioning of individuals in their relationships with one another.

Caruso: You simply think that it is in no way necessary to link these humanist myths to the issue of the functioning of men in their relationships with one another.

Foucault: We are apparently discussing the issue of humanism, but I wonder if in reality we are not referring to a simpler issue, that of happiness. I consider that humanism, at least on a political level, could be defined as any kind of attitude that considers the aim of politics as being to produce happiness. Now, I do not believe that the notion of happiness is really thinkable. Happiness does not exist, the happiness of men even less so.

Caruso: With what do you contrast the notion of happiness?

Foucault: You cannot contrast anything with the notion of happiness: you can contrast B with A, but only when A exists.

Caruso: So you think that instead of posing problems in terms of happiness we should pose them in terms of functioning?

Foucault: Certainly.

Caruso: Does that seem to you satisfactory? Is this fetishism for smooth functioning not a little masochistic?

Foucault: We have to resign ourselves to taking, faced with mankind, a position similar to the one taken towards the end of the eighteenth century with regard to other living species, when it was realised that they did not function for someone – neither for themselves, nor for man, nor for God – but that they quite simply functioned. Organisms function. Why do they function? In order to reproduce? Not at all. To keep alive? No more for this reason. They function. They function in a very ambiguous way, in order to live but also in order to die, since it is well known that the functioning which makes life possible is a functioning which constantly wears matter out, in such a way that it is precisely that which makes possible life which at the same time produces death. Species do not function for themselves, nor for man, nor for the greater glory of God; they confine themselves to functioning. The same thing may be said of the human species. Mankind is a species endowed with a nervous system such that to a certain point it can control its own functioning. And it is plain that this possibility of control continuously raises the idea that mankind must have a purpose. We discover that purpose in so far as we have the possibility of controlling our own functioning. But this is to turn things round. We tell ourselves: as we have a purpose, we must control our functioning; whereas in reality it is only on the basis of this possibility of control that ideologies, philosophies, systems of metaphysics, religions can appear, which provide a certain image able to focus this possibility of controlling functioning. Do you understand what I mean? It is the possibility of control which gives rise to the idea of a purpose. But mankind has in reality no purpose, it functions, it controls its own functioning, and it continually creates justifications for this control. We have to resign ourselves to admitting that these are *only* justifications. Humanism is one of them, the last one.

Caruso: But how about if one were to say to you: no doubt justifications are *needed* for the smooth functioning of this system. Humanism could constitute one of the conditions facilitating the smooth functioning of society, without claiming to ascribe an absolute value either to the meaning or to the purposes of mankind.

Foucault: I would say that your hypothesis confirms the idea I have had for some time, that is to say that man, the idea of man, functioned in the nineteenth century somewhat similarly to the way in which the idea of God had functioned in the course of the preceding centuries. People believed, and people still believed in the last century, that it was practically impossible for man to be able to tolerate the idea that God does not exist (it used frequently to be said that 'If God does not exist, everything would be allowed'). People were appalled by the idea of a mankind able to function without God, hence the conviction that the idea of God had to be maintained for mankind to be able to continue functioning. Now you are saying to me: perhaps the idea of mankind has to exist even if it is only a myth for mankind to function. I'll reply by saying: perhaps, but perhaps not. No more and no less than the idea of God.

Caruso: But there is first and foremost a difference, for I am not saying that mankind should acquire a transcendent or metaphysical value. I am merely saying to you that, since men exist, these men have from inside their own functioning to presuppose themselves in one way or another. Not to mention that there is perhaps nothing more mythical than this absence of totalising myth: today at least, for we certainly can't exclude *a priori* the possibility that one day or another mankind may be able to function without myths (something which seems to me at any rate improbable).

Foucault: The philosopher's role, which is to say 'what is happening', perhaps today consists in demonstrating that mankind is starting to discover that it can function without myths. No doubt the disappearance of philosophies and religions would correspond to something of that kind.

Caruso: But if the philosopher's role is really what you say it is, why do you speak of the disappearance of philosophies? If the philosopher has a role, why must he disappear?

Foucault: I have talked to you about a disappearance of philosophies, and not about a disappearance of the philosopher. I believe that in specific areas there exists a certain type of 'philosophical' activities which consist generally in making a diagnosis of the present of a culture: this is the true function that individuals we call philosophers may have today.

Religion, politics and the East

On religion (1978)

Originally published as 'La religion', a section from Thierry Voeltzel's *Vingt ans et après*, Grasset, Paris, 1978 pp. 155–9. *Vingt ans et après* is a collection of transcripts from a series of taped discussions between a young hitch-hiker, Thierry Voeltzel, and Foucault.[1] In the original publication the names are not given in the text and Foucault remained anonymous.

Translation by Richard Townsend

Voeltzel: We can talk about religion, but it really makes me laugh [*laughs*] I am sorry. Really, it depends on what you call religion. Well, yes, talk about faith that is perhaps more serious, more interesting, but religion, it is a sinister and terrible piece of theatre which, for me, has never had any real interest. I was brought up in that. When I saw how that worked, how it was, and when I look at it now, it is a permanent burst of laughter at hypocrisy.

Foucault: What distinction do you make between faith and religion? Do you mean faith verses the church, for example?

Voeltzel: I've known some very nice people who believed. That is their problem: they felt like believing, they have got the faith. In any case, they are always coming a cropper [*ils se ramassent tout le temps des gamelles*]. Those are more or less honest, that is all right. But the priests, the nuns, the church, the bonzes, the pope, that is a sinister piece of theatre, that makes me laugh.

Foucault: C will be happy with that, because me, my position is exactly the opposite. I think the church is wonderful.

Voeltzel: Yes, okay, the show. Everything you read in the papers, the repercussions of the Lefèvre[2] business.

---

[1] [The taped discussion is casual, relaxed and often light-hearted. The present translator has sought to capture this feature as much as possible in the translation.]

[2] [A priest who resisted strongly the modernisation of the Mass, including the abandoning of the Latin.]

Foucault: Historically, what exists is the church. Faith, what is that? Religion is a political force.

Voeltzel: It is a political force and that is why it has to be fought. In Latin America, in Spain for example, where it is completely at the service of the right. The church is cash, it is power. But it can be an instrument in struggles through the trends of the left which are developing in certain parts of the church. Liberation theology?

Foucault: Absolutely, it is a superb instrument of power for itself. Entirely woven through with elements that are imaginary, erotic, effective, corporal, sensual, and so on, it is superb!

Voeltzel: Oh yes, it's superb! I've seen what happens in church schools, this continual hypocrisy, those daily lies, this malice that you find in most people of the church. It is detestable, it is something I hate.

Foucault: Would you like to be cardinal?

Voeltzel: Oh! No, no. I don't know, perhaps the vestments ...

Foucault: Admit that it is a dream.

Voeltzel: Oh, it can't be bad, but in the end they get by pretty badly. When you look at the French, to be a French cardinal, that wouldn't please me too much. When you look at that other priest from Paris, the ... Marty, well that is pitiable.

Foucault: Intellectually, I believe that it has become extraordinarily weak. When you hear them talk now. Whereas they were all the same, the big apparatus of knowledge in the West for centuries, particularly from the eighteenth century. It is admirable all the same! And I've seen what it is like in Brazil when that Jewish journalist was killed by the police.

Voeltzel: Herzog.

Foucault: Yes, Herzog. And the Jewish community didn't dare hold a funeral service. It was the Archbishop of São Paulo, Dom Evariste, who organised the ceremony, which was moreover inter-denominational, in memory of the journalist in the cathedral of St Paul. It drew thousands and thousands of people into the church, on to the square and so on, and the cardinal in red robes presided over the ceremony, and he came forward at the end of the ceremony, in front of the faithful, and he greeted them shouting: 'Shalom, shalom.' And there was all around the square armed police and there were plain clothes policemen in the church. The police pulled back; there was nothing the police could do against that. I have to say, that had a grandeur of strength, there was a gigantic historical weight there.

Voeltzel: I understand that. If we come on to faith, it is something that I understand. It's a bit like the visionary school master. There is a sort of parallel with nurses who have faith in medicine. It's less funny than the church, and it's less detestable.

Foucault: There, less funny, less detestable.

Voeltzel: It's smaller, I believe. There are some that I can't stomach, those people who say they have faith. Those who write in *Le Nouvel Observateur*. I believe. His name is ... 'God is God name of God' or something like that, it is ... Clavel?

Foucault: Perhaps, I don't know.

Voeltzel: Well, anyway, him. Really, I don't like him. And then, there is a whole pile of others like that.

Foucault: But then, all this current of neo-Catholicism, what do you think about it? I was going to say neo-Catholicism of the left or Christianity of the left, but that is exactly what Clavel would reject. It is none the less true that at present, in a political region which is not of the right, there is a very strong current of Catholicism.

Voeltzel: I don't know much about it, apart from *Hebdo* T.C.[3] which is more or less their mouthpiece, I believe. But, in fact, I believe that it is a movement which, in any case, is destined to fail like the rest.

Foucault: In your life, in your group, have you met Catholics?

Voeltzel: Yeah, there are some.

Foucault: Does that not present any problems?

Voeltzel: I believe, like I said just now, that they're always coming a cropper and it is their problem [*laughs*].

Foucault: I don't know really what you mean by the expression 'come a cropper'?

Voeltzel: They fall. They are failures. At bottom it is not really laughable; there are some that are moved to tears by that, others that are interested in that. The worker priest who was with Renault and went into the PC [Communist Party] afterwards.

Foucault: Yes that is really sad. It makes me think about the former Jesuit who became a psychoanalyst [*laughs*].

[3] [*Hebdo Témoignage Chrétien*, a weekly Christian periodical.]

Voeltzel: It has got to be said that, religion, is something which interests me at the level of a glance. It is funny because sometimes it is beautiful. I liked it fine, when I was a choir boy, singing beautiful things. Churches are beautiful. It is calm in a church. When I go into a big town, I always go into the church to see what it is like. But, the rest, simulacrum really. Above all the French church, parish priests, hypocrites. In any case I don't believe there are many people who take an interest in all that.

Foucault: No, no, doubtless not. There is only me left [*laughs*]. I don't know any more ... I think the tape has almost run out, hasn't it?

CHAPTER EIGHT

Michel Foucault and Zen:
a stay in a Zen temple (1978)

Originally published in the Japanese Buddhist Review *Shunjû* and translated by Christian Polac in *Umi*, no. 197, August–September 1978, pp. 1–6, as 'Michel Foucault et le zen: un séjour dans un temple zen'. The interview was reprinted (with footnotes) in *Dits et écrits*, vol. III, Gallimard, Paris, 1994, pp. 618–24. The following English translation is based on the text from *Dits et écrits*, which contained the following introductory note: 'Working on the history of the Christian discipline, M. Foucault wished to understand better the practice of Zen and was invited to spend some time at the temple of Seionji at Uenohara, in the area of Yamanashi, where Master Omori Sogen led the meditation room. An editor of the Buddhist review *Shunjû* recorded a number of interviews with the bonze which are translated by Christian Polac.'

Translation by Richard Townsend

Foucault: I don't know if I am able to follow correctly the rigorous rules of a Zen temple, but I'll do my best. I am very interested in Buddhist philosophy. But, this time, I didn't come for this. What interests me most, is life itself in a Zen temple, that is to say the practice of Zen, its exercises and its rules. For I believe that a totally different mentality to our own is formed through the practice and exercises of a Zen temple. Just now, you told us this is a living temple which is different from traditional temples. Do you have different rules to other temples?

Priest:[1] I want to say that this is not a temple that is representative of Zen culture. In this sense, the temple is perhaps not sufficient enough. There is an expression which says that 'Zen represents man'. We have here a number of monks who follow with ardour Zen in itself. Living Zen means that.

Foucault: As concerns memories of my first visit to Japan, I have rather a feeling of regret to have seen nothing and to have understood nothing. That absolutely doesn't mean that I wasn't shown anything but that during and also after I had made my tour to observe many things I felt I hadn't grasped anything. For me, from the point of view of technology, a way of life, the appearance of social structure, Japan is extremely close to the Western world. At the same time the inhabitants of this country seem in every

[1] [A bonze or Japanese priest.]

way a lot more mysterious compared with those of all other countries in the world. What impressed me, was the mixture of proximity and distancing and I couldn't get any clearer impression.

Priest: I am told that almost all your works are translated into Japanese. Do you think that your thoughts are understood enough?

Foucault: I have no way of knowing how people interpret the work that I have done. It is always a great surprise to me that my works have been translated abroad and even that my works are read in France. To speak frankly, I hope that my work interests ten or a hundred people; and, if it is a question of a larger number, I am always a bit surprised. From my point of view, it's that my name, Foucault, is easy to pronounce in Japanese; for example, much easier than Heidegger. That is a joke of course. I believe that somebody who writes has not got the right to demand to be understood as he had wished to be when he was writing; that is to say from the moment when he writes he is no longer the owner of what he says, except in a legal sense. Obviously, if someone criticises you and says that you're wrong, interpreting badly your arguments, you can emphasise what you wanted to express. But, apart from that case, I believe that the freedom of the reader must be absolutely respected. A discourse is a reality which can be transformed infinitely. Thus, he who writes has not the right to give orders as to the use of his writings.

I don't believe that I write an oeuvre in the original and classical sense of the word. I write things which seem usable. In a word, usable in a different way, by different people, in different countries in certain cases. Thus, if I analyse something such as madness or power and that serves some purpose, then that's enough, that's why I write. If someone uses what I write differently then that's not disagreeable to me, and even if he uses it in another context for something else, then I am quite happy. In this way, I do not believe that I am the author of an oeuvre and the thought and the intention of the author should be respected.

Priest: Your interest in Japan is it deep or superficial?

Foucault: Honestly, I am not constantly interested by Japan. What interests me is the Western history of rationality and its limit. On this point, Japan poses a problem that we can't avoid, and it's an illustration of this problem. Because Japan is an enigma, very difficult to decode. That doesn't mean to say that it is that which opposes itself to Western reality. In reality, that rationality constructs colonies everywhere else, whereas Japan is far from building one, it is, on the contrary, colonised by Japan.

Priest: I have been told you are interested in mysticism. In your opinion, do mysticism and esotericism mean the same thing?

Foucault: No.

Priest: Do you think that Zen is Japanese mysticism?

Foucault: As you know, Zen was born in India, developed in China and arrived in Japan in the thirteenth century. I don't believe therefore that it is totally Japanese. Rinzai is a Zen priest whom I like a lot and he's not Japanese.[2] He is neither a translator of sutra nor a founder of Chinese Zen, but for me I find he is a great Zen philosopher. He is from the nineteenth century, isn't he? I read the French translation by Professor Demiéville, who is an excellent French specialist on Buddhism.

Priest: It seems that most Chinese specialists believe that Zen Buddhism came from China rather than from India.

Foucault: The Zen which came from India is perhaps a little mythological. It's probably to link Zen to the Buddha himself. Zen in India isn't very important, and certainly it developed strongly in China in the seventh century and in Japan from the thirteenth, isn't that so?

Priest: What do you think of the relationship between Zen and mysticism?

Foucault: I believe that Zen is totally different from Christian mysticism, but I think that Zen is a mysticism. That said, I don't know Zen well enough to defend this conviction. It might be said in any case that there is virtually no point in common with Christian mysticism, whose tradition goes back to St Bernard, St Teresa of Avila, to St John of the Cross. It is completely different. When I say mysticism, I use the term in the Christian sense. What is very impressive concerning Christian spirituality and its technique is that we always search for more individualisation. We try to seize what's at the bottom of the soul of the individual. 'Tell me who you are', there is the spirituality of Christianity. As for Zen, it seems that all the techniques linked to spirituality are, conversely, tending to attenuate the individual. Zen and Christian mysticism are two things you can't compare, whereas the technique of Christian spirituality and that of Zen are comparable. And, here, there exists a great opposition. In Christian mysticism, even when it preaches the union of God and the individual, there is something that is individual; because it is a question of the relations of love between God and the individual. The one is he who loves and the other is he who is loved. In a word, Christian mysticism concentrates on individualisation.

On Zen meditation

Foucault: With so little experience, I can't say precisely. Despite that, if I have been able to feel something through the body's posture in Zen meditation, namely the correct position of the body, then that something has been new relationships which can exist between the mind and the body and, moreover, new relationships between

[2] [Lin Chi Rinzai, died in 867. One of the greatest Zen Masters of the Tang dynasty.]

the body and the external world. We haven't got a lot of time. I'd like to ask you just one question. It is about the universality of Zen. Is it possible to separate the practice of Zen from the totality of the religion and the practice of Buddhism?

Omori: Zen is born out of Buddhism. Therefore, there exist tight relationships between Zen and Buddhism. That said, Zen does not necessarily require the form of Zen. You can even abandon the name 'Zen'. Zen is a lot freer.

You've just said that you felt new relationships between the mind and the body, and between the body and the outside world. I find you are admirable to have felt this with so little experience of Zen. Don't you agree that it is these universal experiences of feeling that the mind and the body join together and that oneself and the outside world join together? That shows well that Zen possess a universal and international character. Zen is small if we think that it is only part of Buddhism, but we don't consider it as part of Buddhism. If you could understand Zen in this sense with your experience, I think you would be convinced of the universality of Zen.

Priest: I am very happy to welcome into my little Japanese town, Uenohara, a great philosopher like yourself.

Foucault: I am not a great philosopher as you say. I'm the one who is happy to be able to join in this celebration.[3] I didn't expect to be able to take part in such an event.

Priest: On the subject of the crisis of Western thought which at present dominates Europe, do you think that Eastern thought could help a reconsideration of Western thought? What I mean, is do you think that Eastern thought would allow, in a certain way, Western thought to find a new way?

Foucault: Re-examinations of these subjects are carried out in diverse ways, through psychoanalysis, anthropology and the analysis of history. And I think also that re-examinations can be followed by confronting Western thought with Eastern thought.

It is true, European thought finds itself at a turning point. This turning point, on an historical scale, is nothing other than the end of imperialism. The crisis of Western thought is identical to the end of imperialism. This crisis has produced no supreme philosopher who excels in signifying that crisis. For Western thought in crisis expresses itself by discourses which can be very interesting, but which are neither specific nor extraordinary. There is no philosopher who marks out this period. For it is the end of the era of Western philosophy. Thus, if philosophy of the future exists, it must be born outside of Europe or equally born in consequence of meetings and impacts between Europe and non-Europe.

Priest: What do you think of the spread of Western thought and its universality?

---

[3] [A memorial service for children who died before birth.]

Foucault: Europe finds itself in a defined region of the world and in a defined period. That said, it presents the specificity of creating a universal category which categorises the modern world. Europe is the birth place of universality. In this sense, the crisis of European thought concerns the whole world. It is a crisis which influences different thoughts in all the countries of the world, as well as the general thought of the world. For example, Marxism is born at a defined period and in a defined area: it was founded by a Jew through contacts with a handful of workers. It has become not only an ideological form but a vision of the world, a social organisation. Marxism claims universality and moreover, as you know, in spite of a little refraction, it is reflected in the entire world.

Thus Marxism at present finds itself in an undeniable crisis: the crisis of Western thought, the crisis of the Western concept which is revolution, the crisis of the Western concept which is man and society. It is a crisis which concerns the entire world and which concerns just as much the Soviet Union as Brazil, Czechoslovakia, Cuba etc.

Priest: As far as Marxism is concerned, what thoughts do you have on its future and what do you think of Euro-Communism?

Foucault: In my opinion, one of the most important things that is called the crisis of Marxism, is the fact that Marxism is no longer useful as theoretical guarantee to the Communist Party. The Communist party is no longer Marxist. It is the same in the Soviet Union, in the countries of popular democracy, in France and in Cuba.

Concerning Euro-Communism, the important question today is not so much its future, but the idea and the theme of the revolution. Since 1789, Europe has changed depending on the idea of revolution. European history has been dominated by this idea. It is exactly this idea that's in the process of disappearing at the moment.

Priest: Here is my last question. According to you, how do you think Japan should be in the future?

Foucault: My answer is simple. I think the role of the intellectual, in reality, does not consist in playing prophets or legislators. For two thousand years, philosophers have always spoken of what we must do. But that's always translated itself into a tragic end. What's important, is that philosophers speak of what is going on at the present, and not of what might happen.

[...]

Foucault: I have already visited several Zen temples. I've had the impression that they were closed, cold and cut off from the world. But yours gave me the impression very clearly of an open temple which is integrated into its environment.

I thank you very much for having given me this experience of Zen, which I find very precious. But it's a modest experience. I hope to be able to come back in a year or two to gain more experience.

CHAPTER NINE

Sexuality and power (1978)

Conference paper at the University of Tokyo, 20 April 1978. Originally published as 'Sei to kenryoku', *Gendai-shisô*, July 1978, pp. 58–77. It was subsequently published as 'Sexualité et pouvoir' in *Dits et écrits*, vol. III, Gallimard, Paris, 1994, pp. 552–70.

Translated by Richard A. Lynch

I would like first of all to thank those officials of the University of Tokyo who have allowed me to come here and hold this meeting with you; I would have liked it to be a seminar in the course of which we could each argue, ask questions, try to answer them, and more often, moreover, pose questions in response. I would most especially like to thank Mr Watanabe,[1] who has been very willing, for so many years now, to remain in contact with me, to keep me aware of things Japanese, to meet with me when he comes to France, to attend to me with such paternal – or maternal – care when I am in Japan, and I truly do not know how to express to him all of my gratitude for what he has done and what he is doing even now.

This afternoon I had thought that we would have the occasion for a small group discussion, around what is called a 'round table', even if it happened to be square, I mean a table that would allow relations of continuous exchange and equality. The large number of participants – I am complimented by this, of course – has the disadvantage of obliging me to take this position of the master, this distanced position, and obliges me to speak to you in a manner which will be somewhat sustained, even

[1] [Moriaki Watanabe, professor of French literature and translator into Japanese of Foucault's *La volonté de savoir* (*The History of Sexuality Volume one: an Introduction*) was one of Foucault's hosts during this 1978 trip and had also invited Foucault to Japan in 1970. For further background about Foucault's 1978 trip to Japan, see David Macey, *The Lives of Michel Foucault*, Vintage, New York, 1995, pp. 237–8 and 399–401 (British edition: Hutchinson, London, 1993), and the chronology in *Dits et écrits*, Gallimard, Paris, vol. I, 1994, pp. 36 and 53–4. For photographs from this trip, see *Michel Foucault: une histoire de la vérité*, Syros, Paris, 1985, pp. 20–1, 115, 118. The five interviews and two lectures published from this trip, as well as a lecture from the 1970 trip, are available in *Dits et écrits*, vol. III, pp. 477–99 and 522–624. Two lectures and an interview from the 1970 trip are also available in vol. II, pp. 104–35 and 268–81. While in Japan, Foucault briefly returned to the theme of pastoral power in a lecture he gave a week later (27 April 1978). See 'La philosophie analytique de la politique', *Dits et écrits*, vol. III, pp. 534–51, especially pp. 547–51.]

if I try to make it as little dogmatic as possible. In any case, I want to present to you neither a theory, nor a doctrine, nor even the results of some research, since, as Mr Watanabe has reminded me, I have the luck to see most of my books and articles translated into Japanese. It would be indecent on my part, and ill-mannered, to go over them again and to thrust them upon you as a dogma. I would rather explain to you where I stand now and what kinds of problems concern me, and submit to you a few of the hypotheses which are useful to me in supporting my work at this time. Of course, I would be very pleased if, after this presentation (which I expect will last about thirty or forty-five minutes), we could discuss, and perhaps at that moment the atmosphere will be – how to say this? – more relaxed, and it will be easier to exchange questions and answers. It is understood, of course, that you may ask your questions in Japanese – not that I will understand them, but someone [on][2] will translate them for me; you may ask questions in English as well. I will respond in plain language, and, there again, it will sort itself out. I will try – since you have so kindly come to hear a lecture in French – I will try to speak as clearly as possible. I know that with the capable professors that you have, I do not have to worry much about your linguistic level, but in the end, politeness demands all the same that I try to make myself understandable. Thus, if there are any problems or difficulties, if you do not understand something, or even, very simply, if you have a question that comes to mind, by all means, interrupt me, ask your question. We are here, essentially, in order to make contacts, to discuss, and to try to disrupt as much as possible the typical form of the lecture.

I would like to present to you today the state, not even of my work, but of the hypotheses of my work. I am currently working on a sort of history of sexuality, which, I promised with the greatest imprudence, would have six volumes. I well expect that I will not arrive at the very end [of this project], but I believe all the same, it continues to appear to me that around these problems of the history of sexuality there are a certain number of questions which are important or which could be important if they were treated in an appropriate way. I am not sure that I will treat them in an appropriate way, but perhaps it is worth posing them despite all the difficulties.

Why undertake a history of sexuality? For me, it meant this: a thing had struck me, that Freud and psychoanalysis took the historical point of their departure – their point of departure – in a phenomenon which, at the end of the nineteenth century, had a very great importance in psychiatry, and even in a general way in society, and it can be said, in Western culture. This singular phenomenon – almost marginal – fascinated doctors, and fascinated in a general way, let us say, the researchers who were interested in one manner or another in the very broad problems of psychology. This phenomenon was hysteria. Let us, if you will, set aside the properly medical problems of hysteria; hysteria was essentially characterised by a phenomenon of forgetfulness, of massive misunderstanding [méconnaissance][3] of oneself by the subject who was able,

---

[2] [This 'on' could be a direct reference to Mr Watanabe or another particular individual (if, for example, he was sitting on stage and Foucault gestured to him at this point), or it could be, as translated here, an impersonal reference.]

[3] [Méconnaissance, literally 'failure to recognise', or 'misrecognition' is a psychoanalytic technical term.]

through the increase of his hysterical syndrome, to ignore an entire fragment of his past or an entire part of his body. Freud showed that the subject's misunderstanding of himself was the point of anchorage for psychoanalysis; that it was, in fact, a misunderstanding by the subject, not of himself generally, but of his desire or of his sexuality, to use a word that is perhaps not very good. Misunderstanding, thus, of his desire by the subject, at the beginning. There we have the point of departure of psychoanalysis, and from there, the subject's misunderstanding of his own desire was located and used by Freud as a general means at once of theoretical analysis and practical investigation of these illnesses.

What is the significance of misunderstanding one's own desires? This is a question that Freud never stopped asking. Now, however great the fecundity of this problem and the richness of the results to which it leads, it seems to me that there is all the same another phenomenon which is almost the inverse of the latter, a phenomenon which, it struck me, one could call – well now, I ask the professors of French to please close their ears, lest they banish me from their club and demand that I never set foot in here again, for I will use a word that does not exist – a phenomenon of 'over-knowledge' [sur-savoir]. I mean a somehow excessive knowledge, a geared-down knowledge, at the same time an intensive and extensive knowledge of sexuality, not according to an individual's plan, but according to a cultural, social plan, in theoretical or simplified forms. It seems to me that Western culture was struck by a sort of development, of hyper-development of discourse about sexuality, theory of sexuality, science of sexuality and knowledge of sexuality.

One could perhaps say that there was a very important double phenomenon in Western societies at the end of the nineteenth century. There was on the one hand a general phenomenon, located only at the level of the individual, of the subject's misunderstanding of his own desire; this manifested itself particularly in hysteria. At the same time, on the other hand, there was a phenomenon of cultural, social, scientific and theoretical over-knowledge of sexuality. These two phenomena, the subject's misunderstanding of his own sexuality and the over-knowledge of sexuality in society, are not contradictory. They effectively co-exist in the West, and one of the problems is without doubt knowing how it is possible, in a society like ours, that there exists simultaneously this theoretical production, this speculative production, this analytical production about sexuality according to the general cultural plan, and, at the same time, a misunderstanding of one's sexuality by the subject.

You know that psychoanalysis has not answered this question directly. I do not believe one could legitimately say that psychoanalysis grappled with precisely this problem, but it did not completely ignore it either; and the tendency of psycho-analysis would be to say, at the beginning, that this production, this theoretical and discursive overproduction regarding sexuality in Western societies was only in fact the product, the result of a misunderstanding of sexuality which appeared at the level of the individual and in the subject himself. Better, I think psychoanalysis would say it is even in order that the subjects continue to ignore their sexuality and their desire that there is a whole social production of discourse on sexuality, which was also a production of erroneous discourses, of irrational discourses, of emotional and mythological discourses. Let us say that psychoanalysts have grappled with knowledge of sexuality only in two ways: namely, in taking the famous theories that children develop regarding their birth, regarding the fact that they have or do not have a masculine sex, regarding the difference between boy and girl, as a point of departure, as an example, as a matrix as it were, of knowledge of sexuality. Freud tried to think about knowledge of sexuality starting with this phantasmatic production found in children; he also tried to grapple with the psychoanalyst's knowledge of sexuality starting with the great myths of Western religion, but I believe that psychoanalysts have never taken very seriously the problem of the production of theories of sexuality in Western society.

For this massive production, which goes back a great distance, at least since St Augustine, since the first Christian centuries, is a phenomenon to be taken seriously which cannot be simply reduced to models of myth or mythology or, even less, of phantasmatic theory. So although my project, in doing the history of sexuality, is the reverse of that perspective, this is not at all to say that psychoanalysis is mistaken, not at all to say that there is not in our societies a misunderstanding by the subject of his own desire, but to say that, on the one hand, we must try to study this overproduction of socio-cultural knowledge of sexuality in itself, in its origins and in its own forms, and, on the other hand, we must try to see to what extent psychoanalysis itself, which justly presents itself as a rational foundation of a knowledge of desire, how psychoanalysis itself takes part, without doubt, in this grand economy of the overproduction of critical knowledge regarding sexuality. Here we have the stakes of the work that I want to do, which is not at all an anti-psychoanalytic work, but which tries to take up the problem of sexuality or rather of the knowledge of sexuality, starting not with the subject's misunderstanding of his own desire but with the over-production of social and cultural knowledge, of collective knowledge of sexuality.

If we want to study this overproduction of theoretical knowledge of sexuality, it seems to me that the first thing to be taken up, the first striking trait in the discourse that Western culture has held on sexuality, is that this discourse very quickly and very early took a form that could be called scientific. By this I do not mean that this discourse was always rational; I do not mean that it always obeyed criteria of what we now call scientific truth. Well before psychoanalysis, in the psychiatry of the nineteenth century, but equally in what could be called the psychology of the eighteenth century, and, even more, in the moral theology of the seventeenth century and even the Middle Ages, one found quite a speculation over what was sexuality, on what was desire, on what at that time was concupiscence – each a discourse that was maintained as a rational discourse and a scientific discourse. And it is there, it seems to me, that we can perceive, between Western societies and at least a certain number of Eastern societies, a fundamental difference.

I refer here to an analysis that I sketched in the first volume of my *History of Sexuality*, which Mr Watanabe was willing to translate and comment upon, I believe, in a journal.[4] It is the opposition between societies that try to hold a scientific discourse

---

[4] [*La Volonté de Savoir* – a part of the Japanese translation was published as 'Sei no kokogaku', in Umi, vol. 9, no. 3 (March 1977), pp. 266–96. The complete translation was published as *Sei no rekishi* (Shinchosha, Tokyo, 1986).]

on sexuality, as we do in the West, and those societies in which the discourse on sexuality is also very large, very proliferating, and very multiplied, but does not try to found a science, but on the contrary, to define an art – an art which would be an art of producing, through sexual relations or with the sexual organs, a type of pleasure that one seeks to make the most intense, the strongest, or as long-lasting as possible. One finds in many Eastern societies, one finds also in Rome and in ancient Greece, quite a series of very numerous discourses on this possibility, searching, in any case, for the methods by which one will be able to intensify sexual pleasure. The discourse that one finds in the West, at least since the Middle Ages, is completely different.

In the West, we do not have an erotic art. Put differently, one does not learn how to make love, one does not learn to devote oneself to pleasure, one does not learn how to produce pleasure in others, one does not learn to maximise, to intensify one's own pleasure through the pleasure of others. None of that is easy to learn in the West, and our only discourse on and initiation to this erotic art is covert and purely private. On the other hand, one has, or one tries to have, a sexual science – *scientia sexualis* – about the sexuality of people and not about their pleasure; its subject will not be how to make pleasure the most intense possible, but the truth of this thing, in the individual, that is his sex or his sexuality: the truth of sex and not the intensity of pleasure. I believe that we have two types of analysis, two types of research, two completely different types of discourse, and that they will be found in two equally different kinds of society. I am again making a small digression – this is evidently something which I would very much like to discuss with people whose cultural and historical background is different from mine and, because there is very little about this in the West, I would especially like to know what an erotic art consisted of in societies like yours and the Chinese, how it developed, starting with what knowledge. I believe it would be very interesting in any case to undertake a comparative study of erotic art in Eastern societies and the birth of a sexual science in the West ...

Let's return, if you will, to the West itself. What I would like to do in this work on the history of sexuality is precisely the history of this sexual science, of this *scientia sexualis*, not to say exactly what were its different concepts, its different theories or its different affirmations – that would be a veritable encyclopaedia. But what I wonder about is why Western societies, let us say European societies, had such a great need for a sexual science, or, in any case, for what reason they have tried for so many centuries up until now to set up a science of sexuality. Put differently, why do we Europeans want, and why have we wanted, for millennia, to know the truth of our sex rather than to achieve intensity of pleasure? To resolve this question, it is evident that we encounter a habitual schema, a hypothesis that comes immediately to mind and which consists in saying this: in the West, certainly now thanks to Freud – since Freud – and just as much since quite a series of political, social, and diverse cultural movements, we begin a little bit to liberate sexuality from the shackles in which it had been placed, we begin to permit speech about sexuality, when during so many centuries we had consecrated it to silence. We are in the process at the same time of liberating sexuality itself and unbinding our capacity to become aware of it; whereas in the preceding centuries, the gravity, on the one hand, of a bourgeoisie moral and, on the other hand, of a Christian moral (the former taking over for and continuing, as it were, the latter) had prevented the West from really interrogating itself about sexuality. Put differently, the historical schema that is frequently used developed in three times, three terms, and three periods.

The first movement: Greek and Roman antiquity, where sexuality was free, expressed itself without difficulties, and developed effectively, was devoted, in any case, to a discourse in the form of an erotic art. Then Christianity intervened, Christianity which, for the first time in the history of the West, would pose a great prohibition on sexuality, which said 'no' to pleasure and, by the same token, to sex. This 'no', this prohibition lead to a silence on sexuality, a silence on sexuality essentially founded on these moral prohibitions. But the bourgeoisie, starting in the sixteenth century, finding themselves in a hegemonic situation, a situation of economic dominance and cultural hegemony, somehow recaptured for themselves, in order to reapply – more severely and with more rigorous means – this Christian asceticism, this Christian refusal of sexuality; and in consequence, prolonged it until the nineteenth century, where, finally, in the very last years, we began to lift the veil with Freud.

Thus we see the historical schema that is ordinarily used in the history of sexuality in the West; that is to say, this history is done first of all by essentially studying the mechanisms of repression, of prohibition, of that which rejects, excludes and refuses, and then in placing the responsibility for this great Western refusal of sexuality on Christianity. It was Christianity, according to this schema, that said 'no' to sexuality.

I believe that this traditionally accepted historical schema is incorrect and cannot be held for many reasons. In the book of which Mr Watanabe has translated a chapter, I especially concerned myself with problems of method and with the privilege that interdiction and negation are granted when the history of sexuality is done. I tried to show that it would certainly be more interesting and richer to do the history of sexuality starting with what motivated and incited it rather than what had prohibited it. Well, let us leave that. I believe that we can make a second objection to the traditional schema of which I have just spoken, and it is the latter objection that I would rather speak to you about. It is an objection, not about method, but about the facts. It is not I who makes this objection of fact – it is the historians, or rather, a historian of Roman antiquity currently working in France, Paul Veyne, who is in the course of doing a series of studies on sexuality in the Roman world before Christianity.[5] He has discovered a number of important things of which we must take account.

You know that in general, when one wants to characterise Christian morals regarding sexuality, and when one wants to oppose them to a pagan moral, to Greek or Roman morals, one puts forward the following traits. First of all, it is Christianity that would impose on ancient societies the rule of monogamy. Second, it is Christianity that would give reproduction as the function – not the privileged or principal, but the exclusive function – as the sole and unique function of sexuality: do

---

[5] [Paul Veyne, *Roman Erotic Elegy: Love, Poetry, and the West* (University of Chicago, Chicago, 1988), originally published 1983.]

not make love except to have children. Third and finally, moreover, one would be able to begin with a general disqualification of sexual pleasure. Sexual pleasure is an evil – an evil which must be avoided and which must, in consequence, be accorded the smallest possible place. To give sexual pleasure only the smallest possible place; to use sexual pleasure somehow in spite of itself only in order to have children; and to have these children (and, in consequence, to have sexual relations and to find pleasure) only within marriage, within legitimate and monogamous marriage: these three characteristics would define Christianity. But Paul Veyne's work shows that these three great principles of sexual morality existed in the Roman world before the appearance of Christianity; and that a whole way of life, in large part of Stoic origin and supported by the social and ideological structures of the Roman Empire, had begun, well before Christianity, to inculcate these principles in the inhabitants of the Roman world, that is to say from the Europeans' point of view, in the inhabitants of the world. To marry and to take care of one's wife, to make love with her in order to have children, to free oneself as much as possible from the tyrannies of sexual desire: these precepts were already acquired by the citizens, the inhabitants, of the Roman Empire in that period, before the appearance of Christianity. Christianity is thus not responsible for this series of prohibitions, disqualifications and limitations of sexuality for which it was often said to be responsible. Polygamy, pleasure outside of marriage, valorisation of pleasure, and indifference toward children had already essentially disappeared from the Roman world before Christianity, and there was no longer any but a very small elite, a very small strata, a small social caste of privilege, of rich (and thus libertine) people who did not practise these principles: for the most part, they had already been acquired.

Must we say then that Christianity did not play any role in this history of sexuality? I believe that in fact Christianity indeed played a role, but its role was not so much in the introduction of new moral ideas. It was not in the introduction, the contribution or the injunction of new prohibitions. It seems to me that what Christianity brought to this history of sexual morality were new techniques: new techniques for imposing this moral, or, to speak precisely, a new mechanism or an ensemble of new mechanisms of power for inculcating these new moral imperatives, or rather, these moral imperatives which had already ceased to be new at the moment when Christianity entered the Roman Empire and very rapidly became the state religion. It is thus to the side of these mechanisms of power, much more than to the side of the moral ideas and ethical prohibitions, it is to the mechanisms of power that we would have to turn to do the history of sexuality in the Western world since Christianity.

A question, then: what are these new mechanisms of power that Christianity introduced into the Roman world, affirming those prohibitions which were already recognised or accepted?

This power I would call – no, is called – the pastorate. That is the existence within society of a category of individuals absolutely specific and singular, who do not define themselves absolutely by their status, nor absolutely by their profession, nor absolutely by their individual, intellectual or moral qualifications, but who in the Christian society play the role of pastor [pasteur], shepherd [berger] in relation to others who are their sheep or their flock. The introduction of this type of power, of this type

121

of dependence, of this type of domination within Roman society, within ancient society, is, I believe, a very important phenomenon.

In effect, the first thing that must be noted about this subject is that never in Greek and Roman antiquity did one have the idea that certain individuals could play the role of shepherd in relation to others, guiding them along their entire lives, from birth until death. Politicians had never been defined in Greek and Roman literature as pastors or as shepherds. When Plato asked himself in *The Statesman*[6] what is a king, a patrician, who governs a city, he did not speak of a shepherd, but of a weaver who arranges the different individuals of the society as threads which he weaves together to form a beautiful cloth. The state, the city, is a cloth, the citizens are the threads of the cloth. There was no idea of a flock, nor of a shepherd.

On the other hand, one finds the idea that a leader is to those whom he commands as a shepherd is to his flock not in the Roman world but in the eastern Mediterranean world. One finds this idea in Egypt; it has also been found in Mesopotamia and in Assyria. One finds this idea particularly in Hebrew society, where the theme of the flock and the shepherd is an absolutely fundamental theme: a religious, political, moral and social theme. God is the shepherd of his people. The people of Jehovah are the flock of sheep. David, the first king of Israel, received from the hands of God the task of becoming the shepherd of a people who will be his flock; and the salvation of the Jewish people will be established and guaranteed on the day when the flock will finally be returned to the fold and returned to the bosom of God.[7] Consequently, the pastoral theme has had a very great importance in each of a series of societies of the eastern Mediterranean, when it did not exist with the Greeks nor with the Romans.

Of what does this pastoral power – found so developed in Egypt, in Assyria and with the Hebrews – consist, and how is it defined? One can quickly characterise it by saying that pastoral power is opposed to a customary, traditional political power, in that it does not essentially extend over a territory: the shepherd does not rule over a territory, he rules over a multiplicity of individuals, he reigns over sheep, cows, animals. He rules over a flock, and over a travelling flock. To rule over a roving multiplicity: this is the role of the shepherd [*pasteur*].[8] And it is this power which is the distinctive pastoral power. Its principle function is not so much the assurance of a victory, since it does not extend over a territory. Its essential manifestation is not conquest, nor furthermore the quantity of riches or slaves that one can bring back

[6] [The discussion of weaving begins at 279a, and statecraft is compared to weaving at 305e and 308c–311c. Earlier in the dialogue, Plato had compared statecraft to shepherding, but that definition was found inadequate. Foucault perhaps overstates the point in this paragraph, for another ancient comparison of kings and shepherds – which Foucault himself will later cite (for example, in the 1983 course given at the University of California at Berkeley, *Discourse and Truth*, ed. J. Pearson (unpublished typescript, 1985), pp. 82–8) – is found in Dio Chrysostom, *The Fourth Discourse on Kingship* (c.AD 103).]

[7] [David, a shepherd, is chosen by God to be the first king of united Judah and Israel at 1 Samuel 16, becomes king at 2 Samuel 5, and receives God's promise for the eternal salvation of the people of Israel at 2 Samuel 7. See also Psalm 23. 2 Samuel 5:2 (NRSV): 'The Lord said to you [David]: It is you who shall be shepherd of my people Israel, you who shall be ruler over Israel.']

[8] [Foucault has been referring to the shepherd as *le berger*, he here shifts to *le pasteur*, also translated as pastor. As Foucault exploits the double meaning of this term throughout the lecture, I generally indicate in brackets which French term is being used.]

from war. Put differently, pastoral power does not have as its principle function doing harm to one's enemies; its principle function is doing well for those over whom one watches. That is to say, 'to do well for' in the most material sense of the term: to nourish, to give subsistence, to provide fodder and pasture, to lead to water, to allow to drink, to find good meadows. Consequently, pastoral power is a power that ensures at the same time the subsistence of individuals and the subsistence of the group, unlike traditional power which is manifested essentially in triumph over one's subjects. It is not a triumphant power, it is a beneficial power.

We find a third characteristic of pastoral power in the civilisations that I was speaking of: having as its principle function the provision of subsistence for the flock, it is at bottom a responsibility; the shepherd has the moral characteristic of being essentially devoted, of sacrificing himself, if necessary, for his sheep. This is what is found in several famous Biblical texts often taken up by commentators: the Good Shepherd [pasteur], the good shepherd [berger] is he who agrees to sacrifice his life for his sheep.[9] In traditional power, this mechanism is reversed: what makes a good citizen is the power to sacrifice oneself for the civil order or to accept death for one's king. With pastoral power, it is the opposite: it is the king, the shepherd [pasteur] who accepts death in order to sacrifice himself.

Finally – and this is perhaps the most important feature – pastoral power is an individualistic power. That is to say that, while the king or the magistrate has for his essential function the protection of the totality of the state, the territory, the city, the citizens as a body; the good shepherd [berger], the good pastor [pasteur] is qualified as the one who watches over the individuals in particular, over the individuals taken one by one. This is not a global power. Of course, the shepherd [berger] must ensure the salvation of the flock, but he must ensure the salvation of each individual. This thematic of the shepherd is easily found in the Hebrew texts and in a certain number of Egyptian and Assyrian texts. Power, then, extends over a multiplicity – over a multiplicity of moving individuals, going from one point to another: it is an oblative, sacrificial power, an individualistic power.

It seems to me that Christianity, from the moment that it became a force of political and social organisation within the Roman Empire, brought this type of power into a world which still totally ignored it. I will pass over the manner in which these things concretely happened: how Christianity developed as a church; how, within the church, the priests took a position and a particular status; how they received the obligation to ensure a certain number of responsibilities; how, effectively, they became the shepherds [pasteurs] of the Christian community. I believe that, through the organisation of the pastorate in Christian society, from the fourth century AD, and even from the third century, a mechanism of power developed which was very important for the entire history of the Christian West, and, in a particular way, for the history of sexuality.

Generally, for Western man, what is the meaning of life in a society where this type of pastoral power exists?

[9] [John 10:7–18; At John 10:11 (NRSV), Jesus says, 'I am the good shepherd: the good shepherd lays down his life for the sheep.']

First of all, the existence of a pastor [pasteur] would imply that, for each individual, there is an obligation to seek one's salvation. Put differently, salvation is at once, in the Christian West, an individual matter – each person seeks his salvation – but it is not a matter of choice. The Christian society, the Christian societies, did not allow individuals the freedom to say, 'Well, myself, I do not want to seek my salvation.' Each individual was required to seek his salvation: 'You will be saved, or rather, you must do everything that is required in order for you to be saved and we will punish you here in this world if you will not do what is necessary to be saved.' The power of the pastor consists precisely in that he has the authority to require the people to do everything necessary for their salvation: obligatory salvation.

Second, one does not seek this obligatory salvation by oneself. One seeks salvation for oneself, certainly, but one can do this only if one accepts the authority of another. To accept the authority of another means that each of the actions that one will be able to perform will have to be known or, in any case, will have to be able to be known by the pastor [pasteur], who has authority over the individual and over several individuals, and who, in consequence, will be able to say 'yes' or 'no': 'a thing is well done like that, we know that it must not be done differently'. That is to say that to the old juridical structures which every society has known for a very long time – that is, a certain number of common laws whose infractions are punished – there has come to be added another form of analysis of comportment, another form of culpability, another type of condemnation, much more subtle, much tighter, much finer. This new form is ensured by the pastor, who can require the people to do everything that they must for their salvation, and who is in a position to watch over them and to exercise with respect to them, in any case, a surveillance and continuous control.

Third, in a Christian society, the pastor [pasteur] is he who can demand of others an absolute obedience; this phenomenon is still very important, and very new. The Gallo-Roman societies, certainly, knew law and magistrates. They knew an imperial power which was an absolutely autocratic power. But at bottom, never in Greek or Roman antiquity would one have had the idea to demand of someone a total, absolute and unconditional obedience in relation to someone else. But that is effectively what happened with the appearance of the pastor and the pastorate in Christian society. The pastor can impose his will upon individuals – as a function of his own ruling, without even the existence of general rules or a law – because the important thing in Christianity is that one does not obey to reach a certain result, one does not obey, for example, simply to acquire a habit, an aptitude or even an honour. In Christianity, the absolute honour is precisely to be obedient. Obedience must lead to a state of obedience. To remain obedient is the fundamental condition for all the other virtues. To be obedient with respect to whom? To be obedient with respect to the pastor [pasteur]. One is in a system of generalised obedience, and the famous Christian humility is nothing other than the form, somehow internalised, of this obedience. I am humble: this means that I accept the orders of whomever, seeing that he will give the orders to me and that I – myself, who am the last – would be able to recognise in this will of the other the very will of God.

Finally – and we have here, I believe, something that will bring us back to our initial problem, i.e., the history of sexuality – the pastorate brought with it an entire series of techniques and procedures concerned with the truth and the production of truth. The Christian pastor [pasteur] teaches – in this he is, certainly, in the tradition of teachers of wisdom or masters of truth who could be for example, the ancient philosophers, the [Stoic] pedagogues. He teaches truth, he teaches writing, he teaches morality, he teaches the commandments of God and the commandments of the church. In this he is thus a master, but the Christian pastor is also a master of truth in another sense: The Christian pastor, on the one hand, in order to carry out his responsibility as pastor [pasteur], must know, certainly, everything that his sheep do, everything done by the flock and by each member of the flock at each moment; but he must also know [connaître] what goes on inside the soul, the heart, the most profound secrets of the individual. This knowledge of the interior of individuals is absolutely required for the practice of the Christian pastorate.

What does this knowledge of the interior of individuals mean? It means that the pastor [pasteur] will have at his disposal means of analysis, of reflection, of detection of what happens; but also that the Christian will be obliged to tell his pastor everything that occurs in the secrets of his soul – in particular, he will be obliged to have recourse, in relation to his pastor, to a practice specific, I believe, to Christianity: exhaustive and permanent confession. The Christian must confess without cease everything that occurs within himself to someone who will be charged to direct his conscience, and this exhaustive confession will somehow produce a truth, which certainly was not known by the pastor but was not known either by the subject himself. This truth, obtained by the examination of the conscience, the confession, this production of truth extends throughout the guidance of the conscience, throughout the guidance of the soul; this truth will, in some way, constitute the bond between the shepherd [berger] and his flock, and each member of his flock. Truth, the production of interior truth, the production of subjective truth, is a fundamental element in the practice of the pastor [pasteur].

We have now arrived precisely at the problem of sexuality. With what was Christianity concerned, as it developed from the second and third centuries forward? It was concerned with a Roman society which had already accepted, for the most part, its morality – this morality of monogamy, of sexuality, of reproduction of which I have spoken to you. In other respects, Christianity had before it, or rather beside it, behind it, a model of an intensely religious life, which was the Hindu monasticism, Buddhist monasticism and the Christian monks who spread out throughout the Mediterranean East and brought back, in large measure, ascetic practices. Between a civil society which had accepted a certain number of moral imperatives and this ideal of complete asceticism, Christianity has always wavered. It tried, on the one hand, to master and to interiorise this model of Buddhist asceticism, by controlling it; on the other hand, it tried to take back in hand, in order to be able to direct from inside, this civil society of the Roman Empire.

By what means did this happen? I believe that a very difficult, and moreover very obscure, conception of the flesh served to permit the establishment of this sort of balance between an asceticism which refused the world and a civil society that was a secular society. I believe that Christianity found the means to establish a type of power that controlled individuals by their sexuality, conceived as something of which one had to be suspicious, as something which always introduced possibilities of temptation and fall in the individual. But at the same time, it was absolutely not a matter – otherwise one fell into a radical asceticism – of refusing everything that could come from the body, as being noxious or evil. One had to be able to make the body, its pleasures, its sexuality, function within a society that had its [own] needs and requirements, familial organisation and requirements for reproduction. Thus, a basically relatively moderate attitude regarding sexuality meant that Christian flesh was never conceived as an absolute evil which had to be got rid of, but as a perpetual source within subjectivity, within individuals, of temptation which risked leading the individual beyond the limits posed by the common morality: marriage, monogamy, the sexuality of reproduction, and the limitation and disqualification of pleasure.

Christianity thus established a moderate morality between asceticism and civil society, which was made to function throughout the machinery of the pastorate; the essential pieces of this morality rested on a knowledge [connaissance], at the same time exterior and interior, a meticulous and detailed knowledge of individuals by themselves, and by others. Put differently, it is by the constitution of a subjectivity, of a self-consciousness perpetually alert to its own weaknesses, to its own temptations, to its own flesh; it is by the constitution of this subjectivity that Christianity came to make this basically average, ordinary, relatively uninteresting morality function between asceticism and civil society. The technique of interiorisation, the technique of taking conscience, the technique of alerting oneself to oneself, with respect to one's weaknesses, with respect to one's body, with respect to one's sexuality, with respect to one's flesh – this is, it seems to me, the essential contribution of Christianity in the history of sexuality. Flesh, the subjectivity itself of the body, Christian flesh, sexuality taken inside this subjectivity, inside this subjection of the individual to himself, is the premier effect of the introduction of pastoral power within Roman society. And it is in this way, it seems to me, that one can – all of this is a series of hypotheses, of course – that one can understand the actual role of Christianity in the history of sexuality. So it did not prohibit and refuse [sexuality], but put in place a mechanism of power and control that was, at the same time, a mechanism of knowledge [savoir], of knowledge of individuals, of knowledge over individuals, but also of knowledge by individuals over themselves and with respect to themselves. All of this constitutes the specific mark of Christianity, and it is in this measure, it seems to me, that one can do a history of sexuality in Western societies starting with mechanisms of power.

There you have, very schematically drawn, an outline of the work that I have begun. These are the hypotheses – nothing is certain – it is, very simply, a framework. You can throw them back at me as if they were so many unanswered questions that you challenge me to answer. Of course, if you have questions to ask – objections, suggestions, critiques, confirmations – I would be delighted.

Discussion

S. Hasumi: Asking questions of Mr Foucault seems to me to be no easy task, but it is not so much caused by my ignorance, nor by my timidity. The difficulty comes precisely in the very clarity of your presentation. We are very accustomed to this clarity thanks to your writings. Each of your books, in effect, announces in a precise manner, what problem will be treated and by which means it will be analysed, in trying to define the conditions and circumstances in which its work becomes necessary. We have just heard this clarity and precision confirmed. One more time, the precaution has been taken to answer in advance all the questions and even to annul all the objections that we could formulate. Thus, I have practically nothing to ask you, but in order to begin the discussions that will follow, I would like to ask you only this:

In the inaugural lecture at the Collège de France,[10] I believe I remember that you treated sexuality from the angle of repression or of exclusion: the discourse of sexuality was marked by prohibitions, and characterised by rarity. But, starting with *Volume One* of *The History of Sexuality*, you treat the discourse of sexuality no longer as an object of repression, but rather as something that proliferates in the scientific arena. In connection with that, one often speaks of the transformation of Michel Foucault, and some people feel a certain joy in these transformations …

M. Foucault: … and there are those others who are very dissatisfied.

S. Hasumi: I do not personally think things happen like that. You have not changed, you have not abandoned the hypothesis of repression, but you have called it into question in order to formulate the problem of power differently …

M. Foucault: I thank you for this question which, in fact, is important and merits being asked. You have asked it, I believe, in the best terms possible.

It is true that, in my most recent texts, I have especially referred to a conception of power and the mechanisms of power which was, as it were, a juridical conception. The analyses that I try to do – and I am not the only one, far from it, who is trying to do them – it is well known that these are partial analyses, fragmentary analyses. It is not at all a question of founding a theory of power, a general theory of power, nor of saying what power is, nor of saying where it comes from. Through the centuries, and even the millennia, in the West, this question has been asked, and it is not certain that the answers that were given were satisfying. In any case, what I try to do is, at an empirical level, to take things, as it were, in their environment. I do not ask, 'Where does power come from, where is it going?' but rather, 'In what way does it happen and how does it happen, what are all the relations of power, how can one describe certain of the principal relations of power which are exercised in our society?'

I do not mean, then, power in the sense of government, in the sense of the state. I

[10] [Published in English as 'The discourse on language', pp. 215–37 in *The Archaeology of Knowledge* (Routledge, London, 1989) (American edition: Pantheon, New York, 1972; also Harper Colophon, New York, 1976.)]

---

say: between different persons, in a family, in a university, in an army barracks, in a hospital, in a medical consultation there are relations of power which occur. What are they, what do they control, how do they bind individuals, why are they maintained, why, in other cases, are they not? That is the first thing.

A second point: I am not the first – far from it – to have tried. The psychoanalysts, Freud and many of his successors, in particular each of a series of people like Marcuse, Reich etc., have, at bottom, tried – they, too – not so much to ask the question of the origins of power, or of the foundations of power, or of its legitimacy, but to see how relations of power have occurred in the psyche of the individual, or in the unconscious of the individual, or in the economy of his desire. What role does the father come to play, for example, in the desire of the individual? What role does the prohibition, for example, of masturbation come to play, or how, again, do the relations between father and mother, the distribution of roles etc., come to be inscribed in the psyche of the infant? So the psychoanalysts, too, have certainly analysed mechanisms of power, relations of power within an environment, empirically.

But it strikes me that these analyses always thought the function and role of power was to say no, to prohibit, to prevent, to trace a limit, and, consequently, they thought that the principle effects of power were all these phenomena of exclusion, of hysterisisation, of obliteration, of masks, of forgetting, or, if you like, the constitution of the unconscious. The unconscious emerges – the psychoanalysts will tell you that I go too fast, well … – starting with a relation of power. This conception or idea that the mechanisms of power are always mechanisms of prohibition was, I believe, a widespread idea. It was an idea that had, if you will, an immediate advantage politically, but for the same reason was a bit dangerous, because it allows one to say, 'Lift the prohibitions and thereafter, power will have disappeared; we will be free on the day that we will lift the prohibitions.' Perhaps there is something there, that goes a bit too fast.

In any case, I have indeed changed on this point. I have indeed changed starting with a precise study that I tried to do, that I tried to make as precise as possible, on the prison and the systems of surveillance and punishment in Western societies in the eighteenth and nineteenth centuries, especially at the end of the eighteenth century.[11] It seemed to me that one saw developing in Western societies (at the same time as capitalism, moreover) an entire series of procedures, an entire series of techniques for taking charge, for observing, for controlling the behaviour of individuals, their gestures, their manner of acting, their positions, their residences, their aptitudes; but that these mechanisms did not have prohibition as their essential function.

Certainly, they prohibited and punished, but the essential objective of these forms of power – which made them efficient and strong – was to permit and require individuals to increase their efficiency, their strength, their aptitudes, in brief, everything that permitted them to be used in the social machinery of production: training individuals, placing them where they will be best utilised, forming them so

---

[11] [Discipline and Punish (Penguin, London, 1991), originally published in 1975 (American edition: Pantheon, New York, 1977.)]

that they would have this or that capacities. This is what was attempted in the army, starting in the seventeenth century, when the great, formerly unknown disciplines were imposed. Western armies had not been disciplined; they were disciplined, soldiers were called to drill, to march in rank, to fire weapons, to manipulate the weapons in such and such manner, in a way that the army would be best utilisable. In the same fashion, you had a complete disciplining of the working class, or rather of what was not yet the working class but the workers capable of working in the great workshops, or simply in the small domestic and crafts workshops, where one was accustomed to living in a particular household and managing one's family. You had a production of individuals, a production of individuals' capacities, of individuals' productivity; all this was acquired through mechanisms of power in which prohibitions existed, but existed simply as instruments. The essence of all this disciplinarisation of individuals was not negative.

You can think that this was catastrophic, you may use all the negative moral and political adjectives that you would like, but I mean that this was not a mechanism essentially of prohibition, but of production – on the contrary, of intensification, of reduction. Starting there, I asked myself, 'But at bottom, in the societies in which we live, is power essentially a thing with the form and purpose of prohibiting, of saying "no"?' Are the mechanisms of power no longer strongly inscribed in our societies, do they not come to produce something, to multiply, to intensify? It is this hypothesis that I presently tried to apply to sexuality, telling myself: at bottom, sexuality is quite apparently the most prohibited thing one could imagine, we spend our time prohibiting children from masturbation, adolescents from having sex before marriage, adults from having sex in this or that manner with this or that person. The world of sexuality is a world filled with prohibitions.

But it seemed to me that, in Western societies, these prohibitions were accompanied by a very intense, very large production of discourse – of scientific discourses, of institutional discourses – and, at the same time, of a concern, a veritable obsession with sexuality, which appeared very clearly in the Christian morality of the sixteenth and seventeenth centuries, during the Reformation and Counter-Reformation – an obsession which has not ended even now.

Western man – I do not know if he exists in your [Japanese] society – always thought that the essential thing in life was his sexuality, and thinks this more and more. In the sixteenth century, the greatest sin was the sin of the flesh. Well, if sexuality was simply barred, prohibited, dedicated to be forgotten, dismissed, denied, how was there such a discourse, such a proliferation, such a dread of sexuality? My analysis proceeds from the hypothesis – which I may not take to its end because it may not be correct – that at base the West is not really denying sexuality (it does not exclude it); but the West introduces to sexuality, it develops, starting with sexuality, an entire complex mechanism in which it is a question of the constitution of individuality, of subjectivity; in brief, of the manner in which we behave and in which we become conscious of ourselves. Put differently, in the West, men, people individualise themselves through a certain number of methods; and I believe that sexuality, much more than an element of the individual which could be discarded as external to himself, is constitutive of the bond that requires people to be tied to their identity under the form of subjectivity.

There, perhaps, is the famous clarity of which Mr Hasumi spoke, and I said that it was the ransom for wanting to be clear ... I do not like obscurity because I consider it to be a form of despotism; one must put oneself in danger of making mistakes; one must be willing to risk coming to say things that, probably, will be difficult to express and which, evidently, can be a bit confused. There, I am afraid that I have given you the impression of confusion. If you had that impression, then I have, effectively, confused things!

CHAPTER TEN

Is it useless to revolt? (1979)

Originally published as 'Inutile de se soulever?' in *Le Monde*, 11 May 1979, and reprinted in *Dits et écrits*, vol. III, Gallimard, Paris, 1994, pp. 790–4. Translated with an introduction by James Bernauer as 'Is it useless to revolt?', *Philosophy and Social Criticism*, vol. 8, no. 1, spring 1981, pp. 1–9.

Translated by James Bernauer

Last summer the Iranians said: 'We are ready to die by the thousands in order to get the Shah to go.' Today, it is the Ayatollah who says: 'Let Iran bleed so that the revolution may be strong.' There is a strange echo between these phrases which link them to one another. Does the horror of the second condemn the ecstasy of the first? While revolts take place in history, they also escape it in a certain manner. Some movements are irreducible: those in which a single man, a group, a minority or a complete people asserts that it will no longer obey and risks its life before a power which is considered unjust. There is no power which is capable of making such a movement impossible. Warsaw will always have the ghetto which revolted and those insurgents who filled its sewers. In the end, there is no explanation for the man who revolts. His action is necessarily a tearing that breaks the thread of history and its long chains of reasons so that a man can genuinely give preference to the risk of death over the certitude of having to obey.

All the forms of liberty, acquired or claimed, all the rights which one values, even those involving the least important of matters, doubtlessly find in revolt a last point on which to anchor themselves, one that is more solid and near than 'natural rights'. If there are societies which hold firm and live, that is to say, if there are powers that are not 'absolutely absolute', it is due to the fact that behind all the submissions and the coercions, and beyond the menace, the violence, the persuasion, there is the possibility of that moment when life will no longer barter itself, when the powers can no longer do anything, and when, before the gallows and the machine guns, men revolt. Since the man who revolts is, thus, 'outside of history' as well as in it, and since life and death are at stake, we can understand why revolts have easily been able to find their expression and their mode of performance in religious themes: the promises of the beyond, the return of time, the waiting for the saviour or the empire of the last days, the indisputable reign of good. When the particular religion has permitted, these themes have furnished throughout the centuries not an ideological cloak but the very way to live revolts.

The age of revolution has arrived. That realisation has hung over history for two centuries, organising our perception of time and polarising our hopes. It has shaped a colossal effort to become accustomed to revolt as interior to a history that is regarded as both rational and controllable. It has granted revolt a legitimacy, while sorting out its good from its bad forms. It has fixed its preliminary conditions, established its objectives and the ways in which they will be realised. Even the profession of the revolutionary has been defined. In repatriating revolt, one has claimed to have manifested its truth and to have brought it to its real issue. A marvellous and formidable promise. Certain people will say that revolt has found itself colonised in Realpolitik. Others will claim that the dimension of rational history has opened for it. I prefer the question that Horkheimer posed at another time, a question which is both naive and a little feverish: 'But is this revolution so desirable?'

The enigma of revolt. There was a striking discovery for the person who searched in Iran not for the profound reasons behind the movement but for the manner in which it was being lived, and who tried to comprehend what went on in the minds of the men and women who were risking their lives. Their hunger, their humiliations, their hatred of the regime and their will to overthrow it were registered on the borders of heaven and earth in a history which was dreamt of as being as much religious as political. They met the Pahlavis[1] face to face in a conflict where it was a matter of life and death for each, but where it was also a question of sacrifice and the promises of the millennium. The famous demonstrations, which played such an important role, could genuinely respond to the menace of the army (to the point of paralysing it), and proceed with the rhythm of religious ceremony and, finally, return to a timeless mode of performance where power is always cursed. It was in this striking superimposition that there appeared at the height of the twentieth century a movement so strong that it could overthrow a regime which seemed to be among the best armed in the world. It did this while staying so close to those old dreams which the West had known at another time, when it wanted to inscribe the figures of spirituality on the earth of politics.

After years of censorship and persecution, years of marginality for the political class and of prohibition against parties, years of decimation for revolutionary groups, what else but religion could provide support for the distress and then the revolt of a population which had been traumatised by 'development', 'reform', 'urbanisation', and all the other failures of the regime? It is true. Is it, however, to be expected that this religious element will fade away quickly for the sake of more realistic forces and less archaic ideologies? Certainly not, and this for many reasons.

There was first of all the rapid success of the movement, confirming it in the form that it had taken. It had the institutional solidity of a clergy whose hold on the people

[1] [The dynasty of the Shahs of Iran.]

was strong and whose political ambitions were intense. It took place completely in the context of an Islamic movement. Surrounding Iran, this Islamic movement constituted an intense and complex reality as a result of its strategic position, the economic keys held by the Muslim countries and its expansive force on two continents. The consequence was that the imaginative content of the revolt did not dissipate itself on the great day of the revolution. That content immediately transposed itself on to a political stage which seemed completely disposed to accept it, but which was, in fact, of an entirely different nature. On this stage the most important realities mingled with the most atrocious: on this stage met the formidable hope to make Islam once again a great, living civilisation with types of virulent xenophobia; world stakes mingled with regional rivalries. And then there was the problem of imperialism and that of the subjugation of women.

The Iranian movement has not submitted to this 'law' of revolutions according to which the tyranny, already dwelling secretly within them, is brought forth by blind enthusiasm. The most interior and intensely experienced element in the revolt directly touches a politically charged chessboard. But this contact is not an identity. The spirituality appealed to by those who went to die lacks a common measure with the bloody government of a reactionary clergy. Religious Iranians want to authenticate their regime with meanings that the revolt possessed. This is something completely different from those who disqualify the revolt because there is a government of mullahs. In one case as in the other, there is a fear: fear of that which took place last autumn in Iran,[2] an example which the world has not given for a long time. It is exactly due to this that there is the necessity to bring out the irreducible element in such a movement. It is an element that is profoundly threatening for every despotism, today's as it was for yesterday's. There is certainly no disgrace involved in changing one's opinion; but there is no reason to say that one's opinion is changing when one is against the punishments today, when one was against the tortures of the Savak[3] yesterday.

There is no right to say: 'Revolt for me, there is a final liberation coming for every man.' But I am not in agreement with someone who would say: 'It is useless to revolt; it will always be the same thing.' One does not make the law for the person who risks his life before power. Is there or is there not a reason to revolt? Let's leave the question open. There are revolts and that is a fact. It is through revolt that subjectivity (not that of great men but that of whomever) introduces itself into history and gives it the breath of life. A delinquent puts his life into the balance against absurd punishments; a madman can no longer accept confinement and the forfeiture of his rights; a people refuses the regime which oppresses it. This does not make the rebel in the first case innocent, nor does it cure in the second, and it does not assure the third rebel of the promised tomorrow. One does not have to be in solidarity with them. One does not have to maintain that these confused voices sound better than the others and express the ultimate truth. For there to be a sense in listening to them and in searching for

[2] [The events of September 1978, particularly 'Black Friday', 8 September 1978, the massacre at Jaleh Square in Tehran.]
[3] [The Iranian intelligence service.]

what they want to say, it is sufficient that they exist and that they have against them so much, which is set up to silence them. A question of morality? Perhaps. A question of reality? Certainly. All the disenchantments of history amount to nothing: it is due to such voices that the time of men does not have the form of an evolution, but precisely that of a history.

This perspective is inseparable from another principle: the power that one man exercises over another is always perilous. I am not saying that power is evil by nature; I am saying that, owing to its mechanisms, power is infinite (which does not mean to say that it is all powerful; quite to the contrary). In order to limit power, the rules are never sufficiently rigorous. In order to displace it from all the opportunities which it fails upon, universal principles are never strict enough. Against power it is always necessary to oppose unbreakable law and unabridgeable rights.

These days intellectuals do not have a very good 'press'. I believe that I can employ the word in a rather precise sense. Thus, this is not the time to say that one is not an intellectual. If I were to do so, I would provoke smiles. I am an intellectual. If someone asked me how I conceive what I am doing, I would respond with a contrast. The strategist is the man who says: 'What does it matter? Such death, such a cry, such a revolt in the context of the great necessity of the whole? Or, on the other hand, what difference does such a general principle make for the particular situation in which we find ourselves?' I am totally indifferent to whether the strategist is a politician, an historian, a revolutionary, a partisan of the Shah or of the Ayatollah. My ethic is the inverse of the one suggested by these questions. It is 'anti-strategic': to be respectful when something singular arises, to be intransigent when power offends against the universal. A simple choice, but a difficult work. It is always necessary to watch out for something, a little beneath history, that breaks with it, that agitates it; it is necessary to look, a little behind politics, for that which ought to limit it, unconditionally. After all, it is my work. I am neither the first nor the only one to be doing it. But I have chosen to do it.

CHAPTER ELEVEN

Pastoral power and political reason (1979)

Originally delivered as 'Omnes et singulatim: towards a criticism of political reason', the Tanner Lectures on Human Values, at Stanford University, California, USA, on 10 and 16 October. The lectures were originally published in English in *The Tanner Lectures on Human Values*, ed. Sterling M. McMurrin, vol. 2, Cambridge University Press, Cambridge, 1981. The Latin phrase means 'Everyone together and each individually'.

Lecture I

The title sounds pretentious, I know. But the reason for that is precisely its own excuse. Since the nineteenth century, Western thought has never stopped labouring at the task of critising the role of reason – or the lack of reason – in political structures. It's therefore perfectly unfitting to undertake such a vast project once again. However, so many previous attempts are a warrant that every new venture will be just about as successful as the former ones – and in any case, probably just as fortunate.

Under such a banner, mine is the embarrassment of one who has only sketches and uncompletable drafts to propose. Philosophy gave up trying to offset the impotence of scientific reason long ago; it no longer tries to complete its edifice.

One of the Enlightenment's tasks was to multiply reason's political powers. But the men of the nineteenth century soon started wondering whether reason weren't getting too powerful in our societies. They began to worry about a relationship they confusedly suspected between a rationalisation-prone society and certain threats to the individual and his liberties, to the species and its survival.

In other words, since Kant, the role of philosophy has been to prevent reason going beyond the limits of what is given in experience; but from the same moment – that is, from the development of modern states and political management of society – the role of philosophy has also been to keep watch over the excessive powers of political rationality – which is rather a promising life expectancy.

Everybody is aware of such banal facts. But that they are banal does not mean they don't exist. What we have to do with banal facts is to discover – or try to discover – which specific and perhaps original problems are connected with them.

The relationship between rationalisation and the excesses of political power is

135

evident. And we should not need to wait for bureaucracy or concentration camps to recognise the existence of such relations. But the problem is: what to do with such an evident fact?

Shall we 'try' reason? To my mind, nothing would be more sterile. First, because the field has nothing to do with guilt or innocence. Second, because it's senseless to refer to 'reason' as the contrary entity to non-reason. Last, because such a trial would trap us into playing the arbitrary and boring part of either the rationalist or the irrationalist.

Shall we investigate this kind of rationalism which seems to be specific to our modern culture and which originates in [the] Enlightenment? I think that that was the way of some of the members of the Frankfurt School. My purpose is not to begin a discussion of their works – they are most important and valuable. I would suggest another way of investigating the links between rationalisation and power:

First: it may be wise not to take as a whole the rationalisation of society or of culture, but to analyse this process in several fields, each of them grounded in a fundamental experience: madness, illness, death, crime, sexuality etc.

Second, I think that the word 'rationalisation' is a dangerous one. The main problem when people try to rationalise something is not to investigate whether or not they conform to principles of rationality, but to discover which kind of rationality they are using.

Third, even if the Enlightenment has been a very important phase in our history, and in the development of political technology, I think we have to refer to much more remote processes if we want to understand how we have been trapped in our own history.

This was my *ligne de conduite* in my previous work: analyse the relations between experiences like madness, death, crime, sexuality, and several technologies of power. What I am working on now is the problem of individuality – or, I should say, self-identity as referred to the problem of 'individualising power'.

Everyone knows that in European societies political power has evolved towards more and more centralised forms. Historians have been studying this organisation of the state, with its administration and bureaucracy, for dozens of years.

I'd like to suggest in these two lectures the possibility of analysing another kind of transformation in such power relationships. This transformation is, perhaps, less celebrated. But I think that it is also important, mainly for modern societies. Apparently this evolution seems antagonistic to the evolution towards a centralised state. What I mean in fact is the development of power techniques oriented towards individuals and intended to rule them in a continuous and permanent way. If the state is the political form of a centralised and centralising power, let us call pastorship the individualising power.

My purpose this evening is to outline the origin of this pastoral modality of power, or at least some aspects of its ancient history. And in the next lecture, I'll try to show how this pastorship happened to combine with its opposite, the state.

The idea of the deity, or the king, or the leader, as a shepherd followed by a flock of sheep wasn't familiar to the Greeks and Romans. There were exceptions, I know –

early ones in Homeric literature, later ones in certain texts of the Later Roman Empire. I'll come back to them later. Roughly speaking, we can say that the metaphor of the flock didn't occur in great Greek or Roman political literature.

This is not the case in ancient Oriental societies: Egypt, Assyria, Judaea. Pharaoh was an Egyptian shepherd. Indeed, he ritually received the herdsman's crook on his coronation day; and the term 'shepherd of men' was one of the Babylonian monarch's titles. But God was also a shepherd leading men to their grazing ground and ensuring them food. An Egyptian hymn invoked Ra this way: 'O Ra that keepest watch when all men sleep, Thou who seekest what is good for thy cattle ...' The association between God and King is easily made, since both assume the same role: the flock they watch over is the same; the shepherd–king is entrusted with the great divine shepherd's creatures. An Assyrian invocation to the king ran like this: 'Illustrious companion of pastures, Thou who carest for thy land and feedest it, shepherd of all abundance.'

But, as we know, it was the Hebrews who developed and intensified the pastoral theme – with nevertheless a highly peculiar characteristic: God, and God only, is his people's shepherd. With just one positive exception: David, as the founder of the monarchy, is the only one to be referred to as a shepherd. God gave him the task of assembling a flock.

There are negative exceptions, too: wicked kings are consistently compared to bad shepherds; they disperse the flock, let it die of thirst, shear it solely for profit's sake. Jahweh is the one and only true shepherd. He guides his own people in person, aided only by his prophets. As the Psalms say: 'Like a flock / hast Thou led Thy people, by Moses' and by Aaron's hand.' Of course I can treat neither the historical problems pertaining to the origin of this comparison nor its evolution throughout Jewish thought. I just want to show a few themes typical of pastoral power. I'd like to point out the contrast with Greek political thought, and to show how important these themes became in Christian thought and institutions later on.

First, the shepherd wields power over a flock rather than over a land. It's probably much more complex than that, but, broadly speaking, the relation between the deity, the land, and men differs from that of the Greeks. Their gods owned the land, and this primary possession determined the relationship between men and gods. On the contrary, it's the Shepherd–God's relationship with his flock that is primary and fundamental here. God gives, or promises, his flock a land.

Second, the shepherd gathers together, guides and leads his flock. The idea that the political leader was to quiet any hostilities within the city and make unity reign over conflict is undoubtedly present in Greek thought. But what the shepherd gathers together is dispersed individuals. They gather together on hearing his voice: 'I'll whistle and will gather them together.' Conversely, the shepherd has only to disappear for the flock to be scattered. In other words, the shepherd's immediate presence and direct action cause the flock to exist. Once the good Greek lawgiver, like Solon, has resolved any conflicts, what he leaves behind him is a strong city with laws enabling it to endure without him.

Third, the shepherd's role is to ensure the salvation of his flock. The Greeks said also that the deity saved the city; they never stopped declaring that the competent leader is a helmsman warding his ship away from the rocks. But the way the shepherd saves his flock is quite different. It's not only a matter of saving them all, all together, when danger comes nigh. It's a matter of constant, individualised and final kindness. Constant kindness, for the shepherd ensures his flock's food; every day he attends to their thirst and hunger. The Greek god was asked to provide a fruitful land and abundant crops. He wasn't asked to foster a flock day by day. And individualised kindness, too, for the shepherd sees that all the sheep, each and every one of them, is fed and saved. Later Hebrew literature, especially, laid the emphasis on such individually kindly power: a rabbinical commentary on Exodus explains why Jahweh chose Moses to shepherd his people: he had left his flock to go and search for one lost sheep.

Last and not least, it's final kindness. The shepherd has a target for his flock. It must either be led to good grazing ground or brought back to the fold.

Yet, fourth, another difference lies in the idea that wielding power is a 'duty'. The Greek leader had naturally to make decisions in the interest of all; he would have been a bad leader had he preferred his personal interest. But his duty was a glorious one: even if in war he had to give up his life, such a sacrifice was offset by something extremely precious: immortality. He never lost. By way of contrast, shepherdly kindness is much closer to 'devotedness'. Everything the shepherd does is geared to the good of his flock. That's his constant concern. When they sleep, he keeps watch.

The theme of keeping watch is important. It brings out two aspects of the shepherd's devotedness. First, he acts, he works, he puts himself out, for those he nourishes and who are asleep. Second, he watches over them. He pays attention to them all and scans each one of them. He's got to know his flock as a whole, and in detail. Not only must he know where good pastures are, the seasons' laws and the order of things; he must also know each one's particular needs. Once again, a rabbinical commentary on Exodus describes Moses' qualities as a shepherd this way: he would send each sheep in turn to graze – first, the youngest, for them to browse on the tenderest sward; then the older ones; and last the oldest, who were capable of browsing on the roughest grass. The shepherd's power implies individual attention paid to each member of the flock.

These are just themes that Hebraic texts associate with the metaphors of the Shepherd–God and his flock of people. In no way do I claim that that is effectively how political power was wielded in Hebrew society before the fall of Jerusalem. I do not even claim that such a conception of political power is in any way coherent.

They're just themes. Paradoxical, even contradictory, ones. Christianity was to give them considerable importance, both in the Middle Ages and in modern times. Among all the societies in history, ours – I mean, those that came into being at the end of antiquity on the Western side of the European continent – have perhaps been the most aggressive and the most conquering; they have been capable of the most stupefying violence, against themselves as well as against others. They invented a great many different political forms. They profoundly altered their legal structures several times. It must be kept in mind that they alone evolved a strange technology of power treating the vast majority of men as a flock with a few as shepherds. They thus established between them a series of complex, continuous, and paradoxical relationships.

This is undoubtedly something singular in the course of history. Clearly, the development of 'pastoral technology' in the management of men profoundly disrupted the structures of ancient society.

So as to better explain the importance of this disruption, I'd like to briefly return to what I was saying about the Greeks. I can see the objections liable to be made.

One is that the Homeric poems use the shepherd metaphor to refer to the kings. In the *Iliad* and the *Odyssey*, the expression *poimen laon* crops up several times. It qualifies the leaders, highlighting the grandeur of their power. Moreover, it's a ritual title, common in even late Indo-European literature. In *Beowulf* the king is still regarded as a shepherd. But there is nothing really surprising in the fact that the same title, as in the Assyrian texts, is to be found in archaic epic poems.

The problem arises rather as to Greek thought: There is at least one category of texts where references to shepherd models are made: the Pythagorean ones. The metaphor of the herdsman appears in the *Fragments* of Archytas, quoted by Stobeus. The word *nomos* (the law) is connected with the word *nomeus* (shepherd): the shepherd shares out, the law apportions. Then Zeus is called *Nomios* and *Nemeios* because he gives his sheep food. And, finally, the magistrate must be *philanthropos*, i.e., devoid of selfishness. He must be full of zeal and solicitude, like a shepherd.

Grube, the German editor of Archytas's *Fragments*, says that this proves a Hebrew influence unique in Greek literature. Other commentators, such as Delatte, say that the comparison between gods, magistrates and shepherds was common in Greece. It is therefore not to be dwelt upon.

I shall restrict myself to political literature. The results of the enquiry are clear: the political metaphor of the shepherd occurs neither in Isocrates, nor in Demosthenes, nor in Aristotle. This is rather surprising when one reflects that in his *Areopagiticus* Isocrates insists on the magistrates' duties; he stresses the need for them to be devoted and to show concern for young people. Yet not a word as to any shepherd.

By contrast, Plato often speaks of the shepherd–magistrate. He mentions the idea in *Critias*, *The Republic* and *Laws*. He thrashes it out in *The Statesman*. In the former the shepherd theme is rather subordinate. Sometimes, those happy days when mankind was governed directly by the gods and grazed on abundant pastures are evoked (*Critias*). Sometimes the magistrates' necessary virtue – as contrasted with Thrasymachos's vice – is what is insisted upon (*The Republic*). And sometimes the problem is to define the subordinate magistrates' role: indeed, they, just as the watchdogs, have to obey 'those at the top of the scale' (*Laws*).

But in *The Statesman* pastoral power is the central problem and it is treated at length. Can the city's decision-maker, can the commander, be defined as a sort of shepherd?

Plato's analysis is well known. To solve this question he uses the division method. A distinction is drawn between the man who conveys orders to inanimate things (e.g., the architect), and the man who gives orders to animals; between the man who gives orders to isolated animals (like a yoke of oxen) and he who gives orders to flocks; and he who gives orders to animal flocks, and he who commands human flocks. And there we have the political leader: a shepherd of men.

But this first division remains unsatisfactory. It has to be pushed further. The method opposing men to all the other animals isn't a good one. And so the dialogue starts all over again. A whole series of distinctions is established: between wild animals and tame ones; those that live in water, and those that live on land; those with horns, and those without; between cleft- and plain-hoofed animals; between those capable and incapable of cross-breeding. And the dialogue wanders astray with these never-ending subdivisions.

So, what do the initial development of the dialogue and its subsequent failure show? That the division method can prove nothing at all when it isn't managed correctly. It also shows that the idea of analysing political power as the relationship between a shepherd and his animals was probably rather a controversial one at the time. Indeed, it's the first assumption to cross the interlocutors' minds when seeking to discover the essence of the politician. Was it a commonplace at the time? Or was Plato rather discussing one of the Pythagorean themes? The absence of the shepherd metaphor in other contemporary political texts seems to tip the scale towards the second hypothesis. But we can probably leave the discussion open.

My personal enquiry bears upon how Plato impugns the theme in the rest of the dialogue. He does so first by means of methodological arguments and then by means of the celebrated myth of the world revolving round its spindle.

The methodological arguments are extremely interesting. Whether the king is a sort of shepherd or not can be told not by deciding which different species can form a flock but by analysing what the shepherd does.

What is characteristic of his task? First, the shepherd is alone at the head of his flock. Second, his job is to supply his cattle with food; to care for them when they are sick; to play them music to get them together, and guide them; to arrange their intercourse with a view to the finest offspring. So we do find the typical shepherd-metaphor themes of Oriental texts.

And what's the king's task in regard to all this? Like the shepherd, he is alone at the head of the city. But, for the rest who provides mankind with food? The king? No. The farmer, the baker do. Who looks after men when they are sick? The king? No. The physician. And who guides them with music? The gymnast – not the king. And so, many citizens could quite legitimately claim the title 'shepherd of men'. Just as the human flock's shepherd has many rivals, so has the politician. Consequently, if we want to find out what the politician really and essentially is, we must sift it out from 'the surrounding flood', thereby demonstrating in what ways he isn't a shepherd.

Plato therefore resorts to the myth of the world revolving round its axis in two successive and contrary motions. In a first phase, each animal species belonged to a flock led by a Genius-Shepherd. The human flock was led by the deity itself. It could lavishly avail itself of the fruits of the earth; it needed no abode; and after death, men came back to life. A crucial sentence adds: 'The deity being their shepherd, mankind needed no political constitution.'

In a second phase, the world turned in the opposite direction. The gods were no longer men's shepherds; they had to look after themselves. For they had been given fire. What would the politicians's role then be? Would he become the shepherd in the gods' stead? Not at all. His job was to weave a strong fabric for the city. Being a politician didn't mean feeding, nursing and breeding offspring, but binding: binding different virtues; binding contrary temperaments (either impetuous or moderate), using the 'shuttle' of popular opinion. The royal art of ruling consisted in gathering lives together 'into a community based upon concord and friendship', and so he wove 'the finest of fabrics'. The entire population, 'slaves and free men alike, were mantled in its folds'.

The *Statesman* therefore seems to be classical antiquity's most systematic reflection on the theme of the pastorate which was later to become so important in the Christian West. That we are discussing it seems to prove that a perhaps initially Oriental theme was important enough in Plato's day to deserve investigation, but we stress the fact that it was impugned.

Not impugned entirely, however. Plato did admit that the physician, the farmer, the gymnast, and the pedagogue acted as shepherds. But he refused to get them involved with the politician's activity. He said so explicitly: how would the politician ever find the time to come and sit by each person, feed him, give him concerts, and care for him when sick? Only a god in a Golden Age could ever act like that; or again, like a physician or pedagogue, be responsible for the lives and development of a few individuals. But, situated between the two – the gods and the swains – the men who hold political power are not to be shepherds. Their task doesn't consist in fostering the life of a group of individuals. It consists in forming and assuring the city's unity. In short, the political problem is that of the relation between the one and the many in the framework of the city and its citizens. The pastoral problem concerns the lives of individuals.

All this seems very remote, perhaps. The reason for my insisting on these ancient texts is that they show us how early this problem – or rather, this series of problems – arose. They span the entirety of Western history. They are still highly important for contemporary society. They deal with the relations between political power at work within the state as a legal framework of unity, and a power we can call 'pastoral', whose role is constantly to ensure, sustain and improve the lives of each and every one.

The well-known 'welfare state problem' does not bring to light only the needs or the new governmental techniques of today's world. It must be recognised for what it is: one of the extremely numerous reappearances of the tricky adjustment between poli- tical power wielded over legal subjects and pastoral power wielded over live individuals.

I have obviously no intention whatsoever of recounting the evolution of pastoral power throughout Christianity. The immense problems this would raise can easily be imagined: from doctrinal problems, such as Christ's denomination as 'the good shepherd', right up to institutional ones, such as parochial organisation, or the way pastoral responsibilities were shared between priests and bishops. All I want to do is bring to light two or three aspects I regard as important for the evolution of pastorship, i.e., the technology of power.

First of all, let us examine the theoretical elaboration of the theme in ancient Christian literature: Chrysostom, Cyprian, Ambrose, Jerome and, for monastic life, Cassian or Benedict. The Hebrew themes are considerably altered in at least four ways: 141

First, with regard to responsibility. We saw that the shepherd was to assume responsibility for the destiny of the whole flock and of each and every sheep. In the Christian conception the shepherd must render an account – not only of each sheep, but of all their actions, all the good or evil they are liable to do, all that happens to them.

Moreover, between each sheep and its shepherd Christianity conceives a complex exchange and circulation of sins and merits. The sheep's sin is also imputable to the shepherd. He'll have to render an account of it at the Last Judgement. Conversely, by helping his flock to find salvation, the shepherd will also find his own. But by saving his sheep, he lays himself open to getting lost; so if he wants to save himself, he must run the risk of losing himself for others. If he does get lost, it is the flock that will incur the greatest danger. But let's leave all these paradoxes aside. My aim was just to underline the force and complexity of the moral ties binding the shepherd to each member of his flock. And what I especially wanted to underline was that such ties not only concerned individuals' lives, but the details of their actions as well.

The second important alteration concerns the problem of obedience. In the Hebrew conception, God being a shepherd, the flock following him complies to his will, to his law. Christianity, on the other hand, conceived the shepherd–sheep relationship as one of individual and complete dependence. This is undoubtedly one of the points at which Christian pastorship radically diverged from Greek thought. If a Greek had to obey, he did so because it was the law, or the will of the city. If he did happen to follow the will of someone in particular (a physician, an orator, a pedagogue), then that person had rationally persuaded him to do so. And it had to be for a strictly determined aim: to be cured, to acquire a skill, to make the best choice.

In Christianity, the tie with the shepherd is an individual one. It is personal submission to him. His will is done, not because it is consistent with the law, and not just as far as it is consistent with it, but, principally, because it is his will. In Cassian's *Coenobitical Institutions* there are many edifying anecdotes in which the monk finds salvation by carrying out the absurdest of his superior's orders. Obedience is a virtue. This means that it is not, as for the Greeks, a provisional means to an end, but rather an end in itself. It is a permanent state; the sheep must permanently submit to their pastors: *subditi*. As St Benedict says, monks do not live according to their own free will; their wish is to be under the abbot's command: *ambulantes alieno judicio et imperio*. Greek Christianity named this state of obedience *apatheia*. The evolution of the word's meaning is significant. In Greek philosophy *apatheia* denotes the control that the individual, thanks to the exercise of reason, can exert over his passions. In Christian thought *pathos* is willpower exerted over oneself, for oneself. *Apatheia* delivers us from such wilfulness.

Third, Christian pastorship implies a peculiar type of knowledge between the pastor and each of his sheep. This knowledge is particular. It individualises. It isn't enough to know the state of the flock. That of each sheep must also be known. The theme existed long before there was Christian pastorship, but it was considerably amplified in three different ways: the shepherd must be informed as to the material needs of each member of the flock and provide for them when necessary. He must know what is going on, what each of them does – his public sins. Last and not least, he must know what goes on in the soul of each one, that is, his secret sins, his progress on the road to sainthood.

In order to ensure this individual knowledge, Christianity appropriated two essential instruments at work in the Hellenistic world: self-examination and the guidance of conscience. It took them over, but not without altering them considerably.

It is well known that self-examination was widespread among the Pythagoreans, the Stoics and the Epicureans as a means of daily taking stock of the good or evil performed in regard to one's duties. One's progress on the way to perfection, i.e., self-mastery and the domination of one's passions, could thus be measured. The guidance of conscience was also predominant in certain cultured circles, but as advice given – and sometimes paid for – in particularly difficult circumstances: in mourning, or when one was suffering a setback.

Christian pastorship closely associated these two practices. On one hand, conscience-guiding constituted a constant bind: the sheep didn't let itself be led only to come through any rough passage victoriously, it let itself be led every second. Being guided was a state and you were fatally lost if you tried to escape it. The ever-quoted phrase runs like this: he who suffers not guidance withers away like a dead leaf. As for self-examination, its aim was not to close self-awareness in upon itself but to enable it to open up entirely to its director – to unveil to him the depths of the soul.

There are a great many first-century ascetic and monastic texts concerning the link between guidance and self-examination that show how crucial these techniques were for Christianity and how complex they had already become. What I would like to emphasise is that they delineate the emergence of a very strange phenomenon in Graeco-Roman civilisation, that is, the organisation of a link between total obedience, knowledge of oneself and confession to someone else.

Fourth, there is another transformation – maybe the most important. All those Christian techniques of examination, confession, guidance, obedience, have an aim: to get individuals to work at their own 'mortification' in this world. Mortification is not death, of course, but it is a renunciation of this world and of oneself: a kind of everyday death. A death which is supposed to provide life in another world. This is not the first time we see the shepherd theme associated with death; but here it is other than in the Greek idea of political power. It is not a sacrifice for the city; Christian mortification is a kind of relation from oneself to oneself. It is a part, a constitutive part of the Christian self-identity.

We can say that Christian pastorship has introduced a game that neither the Greeks nor the Hebrews imagined. A strange game whose elements are life, death, truth, obedience, individuals, self-identity; a game which seems to have nothing to do with the game of the city surviving through the sacrifice of the citizens. Our societies proved to be really demonic since they happened to combine those two games – the city–citizen game and the shepherd–flock game – in what we call the modern states.

As you may notice, what I have been trying to do this evening is not to solve a problem but to suggest a way to approach a problem. This problem is similar to those I have been working on since my first book about insanity and mental illness. As I told you previously, the problem deals with the relations between experiences (like madness, illness, transgression of laws, sexuality, self-identity), knowledge (like psychiatry, medicine, criminology, sexology, psychology) and power (such as the power which is wielded in psychiatric and penal institutions, and in all other institutions which deal with individual control).

Our civilisation has developed the most complex system of knowledge, the most sophisticated structures of power: what has this kind of knowledge, this type of power made of us? In what way are those fundamental experiences of madness, suffering, death, crime, desire, individuality connected, even if we are not aware of it, with knowledge and power? I am sure I'll never get the answer; but that does not mean that we don't have to ask the question.

Lecture II

I have tried to show how primitive Christianity shaped the idea of a pastoral influence continuously exerting itself on individuals and through the demonstration of their particular truth. And I have tried to show how this idea of pastoral power was foreign to Greek thought despite a certain number of borrowings such as practical self-examination and the guidance of conscience.

I would like at this time, leaping across many centuries, to describe another episode which has been in itself particularly important in the history of this government of individuals by their own verity.

This instance concerns the formation of the state in the modern sense of the word. If I make this historical connection it is obviously not in order to suggest that the aspect of pastoral power disappeared during the ten great centuries of Christian Europe, Catholic and Roman, but it seems to me that this period, contrary to what one might expect, has not been that of the triumphant pastorate. And that is true for several reasons: some are of an economic nature – the pastorate of souls is an especially urban experience, difficult to reconcile with the poor and extensive rural economy at the beginning of the Middle Ages. The other reasons are of a cultural nature: the pastorate is a complicated technique which demands a certain level of culture, not only on the part of the pastor but also among his flock. Other reasons relate to the socio-political structure. Feudality developed between individuals a tissue of personal bonds of an altogether different type from the pastorate.

I do not wish to say that the idea of a pastoral government of men disappeared entirely in the medieval church. It has, indeed, remained, and one can even say that it has shown great vitality. Two series of facts tend to prove this. First, the reforms which had been made in the church itself, especially in the monastic orders – the different reforms operating successively inside existing monasteries – had the goal of restoring the rigour of pastoral order among the monks themselves. As for the newly created orders – Dominican and Franciscan – essentially they proposed to perform pastoral work among the faithful. The church tried ceaselessly during successive crises to regain its pastoral functions. But there is more. In the population itself one sees all through the Middle Ages the development of a long series of struggles whose object was pastoral power. Critics of the church which fails in its obligations reject its hierarchical structure, look for the more or less spontaneous forms of community in which the flock could find the shepherd it needed. This search for pastoral expression took on numerous aspects: at times extremely violent struggles as was the case for the Vaudois, sometimes peaceful quests as among the Frères de la Vie community. Sometimes it stirred very extensive movements such as the Hussites, sometimes it fermented limited groups like the Amis de Dieu de l'Oberland. It happened that these movements were close to heresy, as among the Beghards, at times stirring orthodox movements which dwelt within the bosom of the church (like that of the Italian Oratorians in the fifteenth century).

I raise all of this in a very allusive manner in order to emphasise that, if the pastorate was not instituted as an effective, practical government of men during the Middle Ages, it has been a permanent concern and a stake in constant struggles. There was across the entire period of the Middle Ages a yearning to arrange pastoral relations among men, and this aspiration affected both the mystical tide and the great millenarian dreams.

Of course, I don't intend to treat here the problem of how states are formed. Nor do I intend to go into the different economic, social and political processes from which they stem. Neither do I want to analyse the different institutions or mechanisms with which states equipped themselves in order to ensure their survival. I'd just like to give some fragmentary indications as to something midway between the state as a type of political organisation and its mechanisms, namely, the type of rationality implemented in the exercise of state power.

I mentioned this in my first lecture. Rather than wonder whether aberrant state power is due to excessive rationalism or irrationalism, I think it would be more appropriate to pin down the specific type of political rationality the state produced. After all, at least in this respect, political practices resemble scientific ones: it's not 'reason in general' that is implemented, but always a very specific type of rationality.

The striking thing is that the rationality of state power was reflective and perfectly aware of its specificity. It was not tucked away in spontaneous, blind practices. It was not brought to light by some retrospective analysis. It was formulated especially in two sets of doctrine: the *reason of state* and the *theory of police*. These two phrases soon acquired narrow and pejorative meanings, I know. But for the hundred and fifty or two hundred years during which modern states were formed, their meaning was much broader than now.

The doctrine of reason of state attempted to define how the principles and methods of state government differed, say, from the way God governed the world, the father his family, or a superior his community. The doctrine of the police defines the nature of the objects of the state's rational activity; it defines the nature of the aims it pursues and the general form of the instruments involved.

So, what I'd like to speak about today is the system of rationality. But first, there are two preliminaries. First, Meinecke having published a most important book on reason of state, I'll speak mainly of the policing theory. Second, Germany and Italy underwent the greatest difficulties in getting established as states, and they produced the greatest number of reflections on reason of state and the police. I'll often refer to the Italian and German texts.

Let's begin with *reason of state*. Here are a few definitions: *Botero* 'A perfect knowledge of the means through which states form, strengthen themselves, endure, and grow'. *Palazzo* (*Discourse on Government and True Reason of State*, 1606): 'A rule or art enabling us to discover how to establish peace and order within the Republic'. *Chemintz* (*De ratione status*, 1647): 'A certain political consideration required for all public matters, councils, and projects, whose only aim is the state's preservation, expansion, and felicity; to which end, the easiest and promptest means are to be employed'. Let me consider certain features these definitions have in common.

First, reason of state is regarded as an 'art', that is, a technique conforming to certain rules. These rules do not simply pertain to customs or traditions but to knowledge – rational knowledge. Nowadays the expression *reason of state* evokes 'arbitrariness' or 'violence'. But at the time, what people had in mind was a rationality specific to the art of governing states.

Second, from where does this specific art of government draw its rationale? The answer to this question provokes the scandal of nascent political thought. And yet it's very simple: the art of governing is rational, if reflection causes it to observe the nature of what is governed – here, the *state*.

Now, to state such a platitude is to break with a simultaneously Christian and judiciary tradition, a tradition which claimed that government was essentially just. It respected a whole system of laws: human laws; the law of nature; divine law.

There is a quite significant text by St Thomas, on these points. He recalls that 'art, in its field, must imitate what nature carries out in its own'; it is reasonable only under that condition. The king's government of his kingdom must imitate God's government of nature; or again, the soul's government of the body. The king must found cities just as God created the world; just as the soul gives form to the body. The king must also lead men towards their finality, just as God does for natural beings, or as the soul does, when directing the body. And what is man's finality? What's good for the body? No; he'd need only a physician, not a king. Wealth? No; a steward would suffice. Truth? Not even that; for only a teacher would be needed. Man needs someone capable of opening up the way to heavenly bliss through his conformity, here on earth, to what is *honestum*.

As we can see, the model for the art of government is that of God imposing his laws upon his creatures. St Thomas's model for rational government is not a political one, whereas what the sixteenth and seventeenth centuries seek under the denomination 'reason of state' are principles capable of guiding an actual government. They aren't concerned with nature and its laws in general. They're concerned with what the state is; what its exigencies are.

And so we can understand the religious scandal aroused by such a type of research.

It explains why reason of state was assimilated to atheism. In France, in particular, the expression generated in a political context was commonly associated with 'atheist'.

Third, reason of state is also opposed to another tradition. In *The Prince* Machiavelli's problem is to decide how a province or territory acquired through inheritance or by conquest can be held against its internal or external rivals. Machiavelli's entire analysis is aimed at defining what keeps up or reinforces the link between prince and state, whereas the problem posed by reason of state is that of the very existence and nature of the state itself. This is why the theoreticians of reason of state tried to stay aloof from Machiavelli; he had a bad reputation and they couldn't recognise their own problem in his. Conversely, those opposed to reason of state tried to impair this new art of governing, denouncing it as Machiavelli's legacy. However, despite these confused quarrels a century after *The Prince* had been written, *reason of state* marks the emergence of an extremely – albeit only partly – different type of rationality from Machiavelli's.

The aim of such an art of governing is precisely not to reinforce the power a prince can wield over his domain. Its aim is to reinforce the state itself. This is one of the most characteristic features of all the definitions that the sixteenth and seventeenth centuries put forward. Rational government is this, so to speak: given the nature of the state, it can hold down its enemies for an indeterminate length of time. It can do so only if it increases its own strength. And its enemies do likewise. The state whose only concern would be to hold out would most certainly come to disaster. This idea is a very important one. It is bound up with a new historical outlook. Indeed, it implies that states are realities which must [needs] hold out for an indefinite length of historical time – and in a disputed geographical area.

Finally, we can see that reason of state, understood as rational government able to increase the state's strength in accordance with itself presupposes the constitution of a certain type of knowledge. Government is possible only if the strength of the state is known; it can thus be sustained. The state's capacity, and the means to enlarge it, must be known. The strength and capacities of the other states must also be known. Indeed, the governed state must hold out against the others. Government therefore entails more than just implementing general principles of reason, wisdom and prudence. Knowledge is necessary; concrete, precise and measured knowledge as to the state's strength. The art of governing, characteristic of reason of state, is intimately bound up with the development of what was then called either political *statistics* or *arithmetic*; that is, the knowledge of different states' respective forces. Such knowledge was indispensable for correct government.

Briefly speaking, then: reason of state is not an art of government according to divine, natural or human laws. It doesn't have to respect the general order of the world. It's government in accordance with the state's strength. It's government whose aim is to increase this strength within an extensive and competitive framework.

So what the seventeenth- and eighteenth-century authors understand by 'the police' is very different from what we put under the term. It would be worth studying why these authors are mostly Italians and Germans, but whatever! What they understand by 'police' isn't an institution or mechanism functioning within the state but a governmental technology peculiar to the state; domains, techniques, targets where the state intervenes.

To be clear and simple, I will exemplify what I'm saying with a text which is both utopian and a project. It's one of the first utopia programmes for a policed state.

Turquet de Mayenne drew it up and presented it in 1611 to the Dutch States General. In his book *Science in the Government of Louis XIV* J. King draws attention to the importance of this strange work. Its title is *AristoDemocratic Monarchy*; that's enough to show what is important in the author's eyes: not so much choosing between these different types of constitution as their mixture in view to a vital end, namely the state. Turquet also calls it the City, the Republic, or yet again, the Police.

Here is the organisation Turquet proposes. Four grand officials rank beside the king. One is in charge of Justice; another, of the Army; the third, of the Exchequer, i.e., the king's taxes and revenues; the fourth is in charge of the *police*. It seems that this officer's role was to have been mainly a moral one. According to Turquet, he was to foster among the people 'modesty, charity, loyalty, industriousness, friendly co-operation, honesty'. We recognise the traditional idea that the subject's virtue ensures the kingdom's good management. But, when we come down to the details, the outlook is somewhat different.

Turquet suggests that in each province there should be boards keeping law and order. There should be two that see to people; the other two see to things. The first set of boards, the one pertaining to people, was to see to the positive, active, productive aspects of life. In other words it was concerned with education; determining each one's tastes and aptitudes; the choosing of occupations – useful ones: each person over the age of twenty-five had to be enrolled on a register noting his occupation. Those not usefully employed were regarded as the dregs of society.

The second ones were to see to the negative aspects of life: the poor (widows, orphans, the aged) requiring help; the unemployed; those whose activities required financial aid (no interest was to be charged); public health: diseases, epidemics; and accidents such as fire and flood.

One of these boards concerned with things was to specialise in commodities and manufactured goods. It was to indicate what was to be produced, and how; it was also to control markets and trading. The fourth board would see to the 'demesne', i.e., the territory, space: private property, legacies, donations, sales were to be controlled; manorial rights were to be reformed; roads, rivers, public buildings and forests would also be seen to.

In many features the text is akin to the political utopias which were so numerous at the time. But it is also contemporary with the great theoretical discussions on reason of state and the administrative organisation of monarchies. It is highly representative of what the epoch considered a traditionally governed state's tasks to be. What does this text demonstrate?

First, the 'police' appears as an administration heading the state, together with the judiciary, the army and the exchequer. True. Yet in fact, it embraces everything else. Turquet says so: 'It branches out into all of the people's conditions, everything they do or undertake. Its field comprises justice, finance, and the army.'

Second, the police includes everything. But from an extremely particular point of view. Men and things are envisioned as to their relationships: men's co-existence on a territory; their relationships as to property; what they produce; what is exchanged on the market. It also considers how they live, the diseases and accidents which can befall them. What the police sees to is a live, active, productive man. Turquet employs a remarkable expression: 'The police's true object is man.'

Third, such intervention in men's activities could well be qualified as totalitarian. What are the aims pursued? They fall into two categories. First, the police has to do with everything providing the city with adornment, form, and splendour. Splendour denotes not only the beauty of a state ordered to perfection; but also its strength, its vigour. The police therefore ensures and highlights the state's vigour. Second, the police's other purpose is to foster working and trading relations between men, as well as aid and mutual help. There again, the word Turquet uses is important: the police must ensure 'communication' among men, in the broad sense of the word. Otherwise, men wouldn't be able to live; or their lives would be precarious, poverty-stricken and perpetually threatened.

And here, we can make out what is, I think, an important idea. As a form of rational intervention wielding political power over men, the role of the police is to supply them with a little extra life; and by so doing, supply the state with a little extra strength. This is done by controlling 'communication', i.e., the common activities of individuals (work, production, exchange, accommodation).

You'll object: but that's only the utopia of some obscure author. You can hardly deduce any significant consequences from it! But I say: Turquet's book is but one example of a huge literature circulating in most European countries of the day. The fact that it is over-simple and yet very detailed brings out all the better the characteristics that could be recognised elsewhere. Above all, I'd say that such ideas were not stillborn. They spread all through the seventeenth and eighteenth centuries, either as applied policies (such as cameralism or mercantilism), or as subjects to be taught (the German *Polizeiwissenschaft*; don't let's forget that this was the title under which the science of administration was taught in Germany).

These are the two perspectives that I'd like not to study but at least to suggest. First I'll refer to a French administrative compendium, then to a German textbook.

First, every historian knows Delamare's *Compendium*. At the beginning of the eighteenth century this administrator undertook the compilation of the whole kingdom's police regulations. It's an infinite source of highly valuable information. The general conception of the police that such a quantity of rules and regulations could convey to an administrator like Delamare is what I'd like to emphasise.

Delamare says that the police must see to eleven things within the state: (1) religion; (2) morals; (3) health; (4) supplies; (5) roads, highways, town buildings; (6) public safety; (7) the liberal arts (roughly speaking, arts and science); (8) trade; (9) factories; (10) manservants and labourers; (11) the poor.

The same classification features in every treatise concerning the police. As in Turquet's utopia programme, apart from the army, justice properly speaking and direct taxes, the police apparently sees to everything. The same thing can be said differently: royal power had asserted itself against feudalism thanks to the support of an armed force and by developing a judicial system and establishing a tax system. These were the ways in which royal power was traditionally wielded. Now, 'the police' is the term covering the whole new field in which centralised political and   149 administrative power can intervene.

Now, what is the logic behind intervention in cultural rites, small-scale production techniques, intellectual life and the road network?

Delamare's answer seems a bit hesitant. Now he says, 'The police sees to everything pertaining to men's *happiness*'; now he says, 'The police sees to everything regulating "*society*" (social relations) carried on between men'. Now again, he says that the police sees to living. This is the definition I will dwell upon. It's the most original and it clarifies the other two; and Delamare himself dwells upon it. He makes the following remarks as to the police's eleven objects. The police deals with religion, not, of course, from the point of view of dogmatic truth, but from that of the moral quality of life. In seeing to health and supplies, it deals with the preservation of life: concerning trade, factories, workers, the poor and public order, it deals with the conveniences of life. In seeing to the theatre, literature, entertainment, its object is life's pleasures. In short, life is the object of the police: the indispensable, the useful and the superfluous. That people survive, live, and even do better than just that, is what the police has to ensure.

And so we link up with the other definitions Delamare proposes: 'The sole purpose of the police is to lead man to the utmost happiness to be enjoyed in this life.' Or again, the police cares for the good of the soul (thanks to religion and morality), the good of the body (food, health, clothing, housing), wealth (industry, trade, labour). Or again, the police sees to the benefits that can be derived only from living in society.

Now let us have a look at the German textbooks. They were used to teach the science of administration somewhat later on. It was taught in various universities, especially in Göttingen, and was extremely important for Continental Europe. Here it was that the Prussian, Austrian and Russian civil servants – those who were to carry out Joseph II's and Catherine the Great's reforms – were trained. Certain Frenchmen, especially in Napoleon's entourage, knew the teachings of *Polizeiwissenschaft* very well. What was to be found in these textbooks?

Hohenthal's *Liber de politia* featured the following items: the number of citizens; religion and morals; health; food; the safety of persons and of goods (particularly in reference to fires and floods); the administration of justice; citizens' conveniences and pleasures (how to obtain them, how to restrict them). Then comes a series of chapters about rivers, forests, mines, brine pits, housing, and finally several chapters on how to acquire goods either through farming, industry or trade.

In his *Précis for the Police* Willebrandt speaks successively of morals, trades and crafts, health, safety, and last of all of town building and planning. Considering the subjects at least, there isn't a great deal of difference from Delamare's.

But the most important of these texts is Von Justi's *Elements of Police*. The police's specific purpose is still defined as live individuals living in society. Nevertheless, the way Von Justi organises his book is somewhat different. He studies first what he calls the 'state's landed property', i.e., its territory. He considers it in two different aspects: how it is inhabited (town versus country), and then, who inhabit these territories (the number of people, their growth, health, mortality, immigration). Von Justi then analyses the 'goods and chattels', i.e., the commodities, manufactured goods and their circulation which involve problems pertaining to cost, credit and currency. Finally, the last part is devoted to the conduct of individuals: their morals, their occupational capabilities, their honesty and how they respect the Law.

In my opinion, Von Justi's work is a much more advanced demonstration of how the police problem was evolved than Delamare's 'introduction' to his compendium of statutes. There are four reasons for this.

First, Von Justi defines much more clearly what the central paradox of *police* is. The police, he says, is what enables the state to increase its power and exert its strength to the full. On the other hand, the police has to keep the citizens happy – happiness being understood as survival, life and improved living. He perfectly defines what I feel to be the aim of the modern art of government, or state rationality: namely, to develop those elements constitutive of individuals' lives in such a way that their development also fosters that of the strength of the state.

Von Justi then draws a distinction between this task, which he calls *Polizei*, as do his contemporaries, and *Politik, Die Politik. Die Politik* is basically a negative task. It consists in the state's fighting against its internal and external enemies. *Polizei*, however, is a positive task: it has to foster both citizens' lives *and* the state's strength.

And here is the important point: Von Justi insists much more than does Delamare on a notion which became increasingly important during the eighteenth century – population. Population was understood as a group of live individuals. Their characteristics were those of all the individuals belonging to the same species, living side by side. (They thus presented mortality and fecundity rates; they were subject to epidemics, overpopulation; they presented a certain type of territorial distribution.) True, Delamare did use the term 'life' to characterise the concern of the police, but the emphasis he gave it wasn't very pronounced. Proceeding through the eighteenth century, and especially in Germany, we see that what is defined as the object of the police is population, i.e., a group of beings living in a given area.

And last, one only has to read Von Justi to see that it is not only a utopia, as with Turquet, nor a compendium of systematically filed regulations. Von Justi claims to draw up a *Polizeiwissenschaft*. His book isn't simply a list of prescriptions. It's also a grid through which the state, i.e., territory, resources, population, towns etc., can be observed. Von Justi combines 'statistics' (the description of states) with the art of government. *Polizeiwissenschaft* is at once an art of government and a method for the analysis of a population living on a territory.

Such historical considerations must appear to be very remote; they must seem useless in regard to present-day concerns. I wouldn't go as far as Hermann Hesse, who says that only the 'constant reference to history, the past, and antiquity' is fecund. But experience has taught me that the history of various forms of rationality is sometimes more effective in unsettling our certitudes and dogmatism than is abstract criticism. For centuries, religion couldn't bear having its history told. Today, our schools of rationality balk at having their history written, which is no doubt significant.

What I've wanted to show is a direction for research. These are only the rudiments of something I've been working at for the last two years. It's the historical analysis of what we could call, using an obsolete term, the art of government. This study rests upon several basic assumptions. I'd sum them up like this:

First, power is not a substance. Neither is it a mysterious property whose origin must be delved into. Power is only a certain type of relation between individuals. Such relations are specific, that is, they have nothing to do with exchange, production, communication, even though they combine with them. The characteristic feature of power is that some men can more or less entirely determine other men's conduct – but never exhaustively or coercively. A man who is chained up and beaten is subject to force being exerted over him. Not power. But if he can be induced to speak, when his ultimate recourse could have been to hold his tongue, preferring death, then he has been caused to behave in a certain way. His freedom has been subjected to power. He has been submitted to government. If an individual can remain free, however little his freedom may be, power can subject him to government. There is no power without potential refusal or revolt.

Second, as for all relations among men, many factors determine power. Yet rationalisation is also constantly working away at it. There are specific forms to such rationalisation. It differs from the rationalisation peculiar to economic processes, or to production and communication techniques; it differs from that of scientific discourse. The government of men by men – whether they form small or large groups, whether it is power exerted by men over women, or by adults over children, or by one class over another, or by a bureaucracy over a population – involves a certain type of rationality. It doesn't involve instrumental violence.

Third, consequently, those who resist or rebel against a form of power cannot merely be content to denounce violence or criticise an institution. Nor is it enough to cast the blame on reason in general. What has to be questioned is the form of rationality at stake. The criticism of power wielded over the mentally sick or mad cannot be restricted to psychiatric institutions; nor can those questioning the power to punish be content with denouncing prisons as total institutions. The question is: how are such relations of power rationalised? Asking it is the only way to avoid other institutions, with the same objectives and the same effects, from taking their place.

Fourth, for several centuries, the state has been one of the most remarkable, one of the most redoubtable, forms of human government.

Very significantly, political criticism has reproached the state with being simultaneously a factor for individualisation and a totalitarian principle. Just to look at nascent state rationality, just to see what its first policing project was, makes it clear that, right from the start, the state is both individualising and totalitarian. Opposing the individual and his interests to it is just as hazardous as opposing it with the community and its requirements.

Political rationality has grown and imposed itself all throughout the history of Western societies. It first took its stand on the idea of pastoral power, then on that of reason of state. Its inevitable effects are both individualisation and totalisation. Liberation can come only from attacking not just one of these two effects but political rationality's very roots.

PART III

Christianity, sexuality and the self:
fragments of an unpublished volume

On the government of the living (1980)

Course summary at the Collège de France 1979–80. Originally published as 'Histoire des systèmes de pensée', *Annuaire du Collège de France*, vol. 80, 1980, pp. 449–52. It was republished as 'Du gouvernement des vivants', *Résumé des cours 1970–1982*, Julliard, Paris, 1989, pp. 123–9. Reprinted (with the footnotes) in Dits et écrits, vol. IV, Gallimard, Paris, 1994, pp. 125–9.

Translation by Richard Townsend

This year's course drew upon analyses made in preceding years bearing on the notion of 'government': this notion being understood in the wider sense of techniques and procedures designed to direct the behaviour of men. Government of children, government of souls or consciences, government of a household, of the state or of oneself. Inside this very general framework we have studied the problem of examining one's conscience and of confession.

Tomaso de Vio, on the subject of penitence, called the confession of sins an 'act of truth'.[1] Let us keep the phrase, with the meaning that Cajetan gave to it. The question posed is then this: How is it that within Western Christian culture the government of men requires, on the part of those who are led, in addition to acts of obedience and submission, 'acts of truth', which have this particular character that not only is the subject required to speak truthfully, but to speak truthfully about himself and his faults, his desires, the state of his soul etc.? How was a type of government of men formed where one is required not simply to obey, but to demonstrate in stating it, that which one is?

After a theoretical introduction on the notion of the 'regime of truth', most of the course was given over to the procedures of the examination of souls and of confession in early Christianity. Two concepts should be recognised, each one corresponding to a particular practice: *exomologesis* and *exagoreusis*. The study of *exomologesis* shows that this term is often applied in a very wide sense: it designates an act intended to show simultaneously a truth and the adherence of a subject to this truth; to carry out the exomologesis of one's belief is not simply to affirm that one believes but also the fact

[1] Father T. De Vio, *De confessione questiones in Opuscula*, F. Regnauly, Paris, 1530.

of this belief; it is to make the act of affirmation an object of affirmation, and thus to authenticate it either for oneself or before others. Exomologesis is an emphatic affirmation, whose emphasis bears above all on the fact that the subject ties himself to this affirmation and accepts the consequences of it.

Exomologesis as an 'act of faith' is indispensable to the Christian for whom these revealed and taught truths are not simply a matter of beliefs that he accepts but also obligations through which he commits himself – obligation to maintain his beliefs, to accept the authority that authenticates them, to make public profession of them if necessary, to live conforming to them, and so on. But another type of exomologesis is found very early: it is exomologesis of the sins. There, too, we have to make distinctions: to recognise that one has committed sins is an obligation imposed either on the catechumens who are wishing to be baptised or on Christians who may well have given into certain failings. To the latter the *Didascalia*[2] prescribes the carrying out of the exomologesis of their sins to the assembled group. Thus, this 'confession' does not seem to have taken on the form of a public and detailed statement of sins committed but, rather, a collective rite during which each one recognises himself a sinner before God. It is on the subject of serious faults and, in particular, idolatry, adultery and homicide, as well as at times of persecutions and apostasy, that exomologesis of faults takes on its specific character: it becomes a condition of being reintegrated and it is linked to a complex public ritual.

The history of penitential practices from the second to the fifth century shows that exomologesis did not have then the form of an analytical verbal confession of different faults together with their circumstances; and it did not grant remission from the simple fact of being completed in the canonical form to he who had been given the power to grant this remission. Penitence was a condition into which one entered after a ritual and which reached its conclusion (sometimes on the deathbed) after a second ceremony. Between these two moments, the penitent carried out exomologesis of his faults through his mortifications, through his acts of austerity and his way of life, his dressing and the obvious attitude of repentance – in a word, by a theatricality in which verbal expression did not have the main role, and where all analytical statement of one's faults and their specific nature seems to have been absent. It seems possible that before reconciliation there was some special ritual, and that this was given the special name of *exomologesis*. But even in that case it was still a question of a dramatic and synthetic expression through which the sinner recognised in front of all the fact of having sinned; he stated this recognition in a demonstration which at once linked him visibly to the state of sinner and prepared his deliverance. The verbalisation of the confession of sins in the canonical penitence would not be carried out systematically until much later, first of all with the practice of a tariff-linked penitence, then from the twelfth and thirteenth centuries, when it was organised into the sacrament of penitence.

---

[2] *Didascalia*: the teaching of the twelve apostles and other disciples, an ecclesiastical document of the third century. The Greek original has been lost. There survives a reworking of the six first books of the *Constitutions apostoliques. Didascalie, c'est-à-dire l'enseignement catholique des douze apôtres et des saints disciples de Notre sauveur*, trans. abbé F. Nau, Firmon Didot, Paris, 1902.

In monastic institutions the practice of confession took all sorts of other forms (which did not exclude recourse to forms of exomologesis in front of the assembled community when the monk had committed faults of a certain importance). To study these practices of confession in monastic life we need to make reference to a more detailed study of the monastic *Institutes* and *Conferences* of Cassian,[3] seen from the point of view of techniques of spiritual direction. Above all, three aspects were analysed: the mode of dependence with respect to the elder or the master, the way of conducting examination of one's own conscience, and the duty of saying everything on the movements of one's thoughts in a formulation that is intended to be exhaustive: the *exagoreusis*. On these three points considerable differences appear with the processes of the direction of conscience that one can find in ancient philosophy. Put simply, one may say that in the monastic institution the relationship to the master takes the form of unconditional and permanent obedience that bears upon all the aspects of life and, in principle, does not leave the novice any margin for initiative; if the value of this relationship depends on the quality of the master, it is no less true that by itself the form of obedience, whatever the object towards which it is directed, holds a positive value; finally, if obedience is indispensable for the novices, and the masters are normally the elders, the relationship of age is not in itself self-sufficient to justify the relationship – both because the ability to direct is charismatic and obedience should constitute in the form of humility a permanent relationship to oneself and to others.

The examination of conscience is also very different from that which is recommended in the philosophical schools of antiquity. Doubtless, like the latter it was made up of two main forms: the evening recollection of the day past and permanent vigilance towards oneself. It is this second form that is important in the monasticism described by Cassian. The procedures show clearly that it is not a question of determining what must be done in order not to commit a fault or even to recognise if one has not committed a fault in what one might have done. It is a question of seizing the movement of thoughts (*cogitatio* = *logismos*) of examining quite deeply in order to seize and decipher the origin from which it comes (from God, oneself or the Devil) and to carry out a sorting process (which Cassian describes using several metaphors, of which the most important is probably that of the moneychanger who checks his coins). It is the 'mobility of the soul' to which Cassian devotes one of the most interesting of his *Conferences* – he makes references to the words of the Abbot Serenus – which constitutes the domain of an examination of conscience in which we see clearly that its role was to make possible unity and permanence of contemplation.[4]

[3] J. Cassian, *Institutions cénobitiques* (*Institutes of the Cenobites*), trans. J. C. Guy, Éditions du Cerf, Paris, 1965, p. 109; *Conférences* (*Conferences*), trans. Dom Pichery, Éditions du Cerf, Paris, vol. 1, 1966, vol. 2, 1967, vol. 3, 1971. (For a translation of Cassian's work see *A Select Library of Nicene and Post-Nicene Fathers of the Christian Church*, second series. vol. XI, ed. P. Schaff and H. Wace, W. M. B. Eerdmans, Grand Rapids, Michigan, 1978, pp. 201–545.)

[4] J. Cassian, *Premiére conférence de abbé Serenus, De la mobilité de l'âme et des esprits du mal*, in *Conférences*, vol. 1, no. 42, pp. 242–77.

As for the confession prescribed by Cassian, this is not simply a listing of faults committed nor a global statement of the state of the soul; it should lean towards a permanent verbalising of all the movements of one's thoughts. This confession allows the director to give advice and to diagnose: Cassian thus reports examples of consultation; sometimes several elders take part in this and give their opinions. But verbalisation also includes intrinsic effects which are due to the simple fact that movements of the soul are transformed into statements addressed to another. In particular, the 'sorting-out', which is one of the objectives of the examination, is carried out through verbalisation thanks to the triple mechanism of the shame which makes one blush about formulating any kind of bad thought, of the material realisation, by means of the words uttered, of what is going on in the soul, and the incompatibility of the Devil (who seduces and deceives while hiding in the folds of consciousness) with the light that uncovers them. It is a question, therefore, of confession which is far-reaching, of a permanent exteriorisation of the words of the 'mysteries' of consciousness.

Unconditional obedience, uninterrupted examination and exhaustive confession form in this way a whole, with each element implying the other two; the verbal manifestation of the truth that is hidden deep inside oneself appears as an indispensable part of the government of men by each other, such as it was put into effect by the institutions of monasticism – and especially cenobite communities – from the fourth century. But we must underline that this expression does not have as its end the establishing of sovereign mastery of oneself by oneself; what is expected, on the contrary, is humility and mortification, detachment with respect to oneself and the establishing of a relationship with oneself which tends towards a destruction of the form of the self.

[A short list of those who delivered papers on nineteenth-century liberal thought during the year's seminar meetings follows the above course outline.]

CHAPTER THIRTEEN

About the beginning of the hermeneutics of the self (1980)

Two lectures delivered at Dartmouth College, Hanover, New Hampshire, USA, on 17 and 24 November 1980. The lectures were also given with slight amendments as the Howison Lectures at Berkeley, California, on 20–21 October 1980. The Dartmouth lectures were originally transcribed and edited by Thomas Keenan and later re-edited (with footnotes) by Mark Blasius with additional notes from the Howison lectures. This transcript has appeared only in English and was originally published in *Political Theory*, vol. 21, no. 2, May 1993, pp. 198–227.

Transcript by Thomas Keenan and Mark Blasius

Subjectivity and truth

In a work consecrated to the moral treatment of madness and published in 1840, a French psychiatrist, Leuret, tells of the manner in which he has treated one of his patients – treated and, as you can imagine, of course, cured. One morning Dr Leuret takes Mr A, his patient, into a shower room. He makes him recount in detail his delirium.

'Well, all that', says the doctor, 'is nothing but madness. Promise me not to believe in it any more.'

The patient hesitates, then promises.

'That's not enough,' replies the doctor. 'You have already made similar promises, and you haven't kept them.' And the doctor turns on a cold shower above the patient's head.

'Yes, yes! I am mad!' the patient cries.

The shower is turned off, and the interrogation is resumed.

'Yes, I recognise that I am mad,' the patient repeats, adding, 'I recognise, because you are forcing me to do so.'

Another shower. Another confession. The interrogation is taken up again.

'I assure you, however,' says the patient, 'that I have heard voices and seen enemies around me.'

Another shower.

'Well,' says Mr A., the patient 'I admit it. I am mad; all that was madness.'[1]

---

[1] See François Leuret, *Du traitement morale de la folie*, J. B. Baillière, Paris, 1840, and Foucault, *Maladie mentale et psychologie*, 3rd edition, PUF, Paris, 1966, pp. 85–6; *Mental Illness and Psychology*, trans. Alan Sheridan, Harper & Row, New York, 1976, p. 72 (also University of California Press, Berkeley, 1987).

To make someone suffering from mental illness recognise that he is mad is a very ancient procedure. Everybody in the old medicine, before the middle of the nineteenth century, everybody was convinced of the incompatibility between madness and recognition of madness. And in the works, for instance, of the seventeenth and of the eighteenth centuries, one finds many examples of what one might call truth-therapies. The mad would be cured if one managed to show them that their delirium is without any relation to reality.

But, as you see, the technique used by Leuret is altogether different. He is not trying to persuade his patient that his ideas are false or unreasonable. What happens in the head of Mr A is a matter of indifference for the doctor. Leuret wishes to obtain a precise act: the explicit affirmation, 'I am mad.' It is easy to recognise here the transposition within psychiatric therapy of procedures which have been used for a long time in judicial and religious institutions. To declare aloud and intelligibly the truth about oneself — I mean, to confess — has in the Western world been considered for a long time either as a condition for redemption for one's sins or as an essential item in the condemnation of the guilty. The bizarre therapy of Leuret may be read as an episode in the progressive culpabilisation of madness. But, I would wish, rather, to take it as a point of departure for a more general reflection on this practice of confession, and on the postulate, which is generally accepted in Western societies, that a man needs for his own salvation to know as exactly as possible who he is and also, which is something rather different, that he needs to tell it as explicitly as possible to some other people. The anecdote of Leuret is here only as an example of the strange and complex relationships developed in our societies between individuality, discourse, truth and coercion.

In order to justify the attention I am giving to what is seemingly so specialised a subject, let me take a step back for a moment. All that, after all, is for me only a means that I will use to take on a much more general theme — that is, the genealogy of the modern subject.

In the years that preceded the Second World War, and even more so after the Second World War, philosophy in France and, I think, in all Continental Europe, was dominated by the philosophy of the subject. I mean that philosophy set as its task par excellence the foundation of all knowledge and the principle of all signification as stemming from the meaningful subject. The importance given to this question of the meaningful subject was of course due to the impact of Husserl — only his *Cartesian Meditations* and the *Crisis* were generally known in France[2] — but the centrality of the subject was also tied to an institutional context. For the French university, since philosophy began with Descartes, it could advance only in a Cartesian manner. But we must also take into account the political conjuncture. Given the absurdity of wars, slaughters and despotism, it seemed then to be up to the individual subject to give meaning to his existential choices.

[2] Edmund Husserl, *Méditations Cartésiennes*, trans. by Gabrielle Peiffer and Emmanuel Lewis, Arman Colin, Paris, 1931; *Cartesian Meditations: An Introduction to Phenomenology*, trans. Dorian Cairns, Martinus Nijhoff, The Hague, 1973.

With the leisure and distance that came after the war, this emphasis on the philosophical subject no longer seemed so self-evident. Two hitherto-hidden theoretical paradoxes could no longer be avoided. The first one was that the philosophy of consciousness had failed to found a philosophy of knowledge, and especially scientific knowledge, and the second was that this philosophy of meaning paradoxically had failed to take into account the formative mechanisms of signification and the structure of systems of meaning. I am aware that another form of thought claimed then to have gone beyond the philosophy of the subject – this, of course, was Marxism. It goes without saying – and it goes indeed better if we say it – that neither materialism nor the theory of ideologies successfully constituted a theory of objectivity or of signification. Marxism put itself forward as a humanistic discourse that could replace the abstract subject with an appeal to the real man, to the concrete man. It should have been clear at the time that Marxism carried with it a fundamental theoretical and practical weakness: the humanistic discourse hid the political reality that the Marxists of this period none the less supported.

With the all-too-easy clarity of hindsight – what you call, I think, the 'Monday morning quarterback' – let me say that there were two possible paths that led beyond this philosophy of the subject. First, the theory of objective knowledge and, second, an analysis of systems of meaning, or semiology. The first of these was the path of logical positivism. The second was that of a certain school of linguistics, psychoanalysis and anthropology, all generally grouped under the rubric of structuralism.

These were not the directions I took. Let me announce once and for all that I am not a structuralist, and I confess with the appropriate chagrin that I am not an analytic philosopher – nobody is perfect. I have tried to explore another direction. I have tried to get out from the philosophy of the subject through a genealogy of this subject, by studying the constitution of the subject across history which has led us up to the modern concept of the self. This has not always been an easy task, since most historians prefer a history of social processes,[3] and most philosophers prefer a subject without history. This has prevented me neither from using the same material that certain social historians have used nor from recognising my theoretical debt to those philosophers who, like Nietzsche, have posed the question of the historicity of the subject.[4]

---

[3] 'where society plays the role of subject' [Howison].

[4] 'So much for the general project. Now a few words on methodology. For this kind of research, the history of science constitutes a privileged point of view. This might seem paradoxical. After all, the genealogy of the self does not take place within a field of scientific knowledge, as if we were nothing else than that which rational knowledge could tell us about ourselves. While the history of science is without doubt an important testing ground for the theory of knowledge, as well as for the analysis of meaningful systems, it is also fertile ground for studying the genealogy of subject. There are two reasons for this. All the practices by which the subject is defined and transformed are accompanied by the formation of certain types of knowledge, and in the West, for a variety of reasons, knowledge tends to be organised around forms and norms that are more or less scientific. There is also another reason maybe more fundamental and more specific to our societies. I mean the fact that one of the main moral obligations for any subject is to know oneself, to tell the truth about oneself, and to constitute oneself as an object knowledge both for other people and for oneself. The truth obligation for individuals and a scientific

Up to the present I have proceeded with this general project in two ways. I have dealt with the modern theoretical constitutions that were concerned with the subject in general. I have tried to analyse in a previous book theories of the subject as a speaking, living, working being.[5] I have also dealt with the more practical under-standing formed in those institutions like hospitals, asylums and prisons, where certain subjects became objects of knowledge and at the same time objects of domination.[6] And now, I wish to study those forms of understanding which the subject creates about himself. Those forms of self-understanding are important I think to analyse the modern experience of sexuality.[7]

But since I have started with this last type of project I have been obliged to change my mind on several important points. Let me introduce a kind of autocritique. It seems, according to some suggestions by Habermas, that one can distinguish three major types of techniques in human societies: the techniques which permit one to produce, to transform, to manipulate things; the techniques which permit one to use sign systems; and the techniques which permit one to determine the conduct of

---

organisation of knowledge; those are the two reasons why the history of knowledges constitutes a privileged point of view for the genealogy of the subject.

'Hence, it follows that I am not trying to do history of sciences in general, but only of those which sought to construct a scientific knowledge of the subject. Another consequence. I am not trying to measure the objective value of these sciences, nor to know if they can become universally valid. That is the task of an epistemological historian. Rather, I am working on a history of science that is, to some extent, regressive history that seeks to discover the discursive, the institutional and the social practices from which these sciences arose. This would be an archaeological history. Finally, the third consequence, this project seeks to discover the point at which these practices became coherent reflective techniques with definite goals, the point at which a particular discourse emerged from those techniques and came to be seen as true, the point at which they are linked with the obligation of searching for the truth and telling the truth. In sum, the aim of my project is to construct a genealogy of the subject. The method is an archaeology of knowledge, and the precise domain of the analysis is what I should call technologies. I mean the articulation of certain techniques and certain kinds of discourse about the subject.

'I would like to add one final word about the practical significance of this form of analysis. For Heidegger, it was through an increasing obsession with *techné* as the only way to arrive at an understanding of objects that the West lost touch with Being. Let's turn the question around and ask which techniques and practices form the Western concept of the subject, giving it its characteristic split of truth and error, freedom and constraint. I think that it is here where we will find the real possibility of constructing a history of what we have done and, at the same time, a diagnosis of what we are. This would be a theoretical analysis which has, at the same time, a political dimension. By this word 'political dimension' I mean an analysis that relates to what we are willing to accept in our world, to accept, to refuse, and to change, both in ourselves and in our circumstances. In sum, it is a question of searching for another kind of critical philosophy. Not a critical philosophy that seeks to determine the conditions and the limits of our possible knowledge of the object, but a critical philosophy that seeks the conditions and the indefinite possibilities of transforming the subject, of transforming ourselves.' [Howison]

[5] *Les mots et les choses*, Gallimard, Paris, 1966; *The Order of Things*, Routledge, London, 1989 (American edition: Pantheon, New York, 1970).

[6] *Naissance de la clinique*, Presses Universitaires de France, Paris, 1963, 1972; *The Birth of the Clinic*, trans. Alan Sheridan, Routledge, London, 1989, and *Surveiller et punir*, Gallimard, Paris, 1975; *Discipline and Punish*, trans. Alan Sheridan, Penguin, London, 1991 (American edition: Pantheon, New York, 1977).

[7] *La volonté de savoir*, Gallimard, Paris, 1976; *The History of Sexuality Volume One: An Introduction*, trans. Robert Hurley, Penguin, London, 1990 (American edition: Pantheon, New York, 1978); *L'usage des plaisirs*, Gallimard, Paris, 1984; *The Use of Pleasure*, trans. Robert Hurley, Penguin, London, 1992 (American edition: Pantheon, New York, 1985); *Le souci de soi*, Gallimard, Paris, 1984; *The Care of the Self*, trans. Robert Hurley, Penguin, London, 1990 (American edition: Pantheon, New York, 1986).

individuals, to impose certain wills on them and to submit them to certain ends or objectives. That is to say, there are techniques of production, techniques of signification and techniques of domination.[8]

Of course, if one wants to study the history of natural sciences, it is useful if not necessary to take into account techniques of production and semiotic techniques. But since my project was concerned with the knowledge of the subject, I thought that the techniques of domination were the most important, without any exclusion of the rest. But, analysing the experience of sexuality, I became more and more aware that there is in all societies, I think, in all societies whatever they are, another type of techniques: techniques which permit individuals to effect, by their own means, a certain number of operations on their own bodies, on their own souls, on their own thoughts, on their own conduct, and this in a manner so as to transform themselves, modify themselves, and to attain a certain state of perfection, of happiness, of purity, of supernatural power, and so on. Let's call this kind of techniques a techniques or technology of the self.[9]

I think that if one wants to analyse the genealogy of the subject in Western civilisation, one has to take into account not only techniques of domination but also techniques of the self. Let's say: one has to take into account the interaction between those two types of techniques – techniques of domination and techniques of the self. One has to take into account the points where the technologies of domination of individuals over one another have recourse to processes by which the individual acts upon himself. And conversely, one has to take into account the points where the techniques of the self are integrated into structures of coercion or domination. The contact point, where the individuals are driven[10] by others is tied to the way they conduct themselves,[11] is what we can call, I think, government.[12] Governing people, in the broad meaning of the word,[13] governing people is not a way to force people to do what the governor wants; it is always a versatile equilibrium, with complementarity and conflicts between techniques which assure coercion and processes through which the self is constructed or modified by oneself.

When I was studying asylums, prisons and so on, I insisted, I think, too much on the techniques of domination. What we can call discipline is something really important in these kinds of institutions, but it is only at one aspect of the art of governing people in our society. We must not understand the exercise of power as pure violence or strict coercion. Power consists in complex relations: these relations

---

[8] Jürgen Habermas, *Erkenntnis und Interesse*, Suhrkamp Verlag, Frankfurt am Main, 1968 and appendix in *Tecknik und Wissenschaft als 'Ideologie'*, Suhrkamp Verlag, Frankfurt am Main, 1968; *Knowledge and Human Interests*, trans. Jeremy Shapiro, Beacon, Boston, 1971, especially 'Appendix: knowledge and human interests, a general perspective', p. 313.

[9] *Technologies of the Self: A Seminar with Michel Foucault*, ed. L. H. Martin, H. Gutman and P. H. Hutton, Tavistock, London, 1988 (American edition: University of Massachusetts Press, Amherst, 1988).

[10] 'and known' [Howison].

[11] 'and know themselves' [Howison].

[12] *The Foucault Effect: Studies in Governmentality*, ed. G. Burchell, C. Gorden and P. Millar, Harvester Wheatsheaf, Hemel Hempstead, 1991.

[13] 'as they spoke of it in the sixteenth century, of governing children, or governing family, or governing souls' [Howison].

involve a set of rational techniques, and the efficiency of those techniques is due to a subtle integration of coercion-technologies and self-technologies. I think that we have to get rid of the more or less Freudian schema – you know it – the schema of interiorisation of the law by the self. Fortunately, from a theoretical point of view, and maybe unfortunately from a practical point of view, things are much more complicated than that. In short, having studied the field of government by taking as my point of departure techniques of domination, I would like in years to come to study government – especially in the field of sexuality – starting from the techniques of the self.[14]

Among those techniques of the self in this field of the self-technology, I think that the techniques oriented towards the discovery and the formulation of the truth concerning oneself are extremely important; and, if for the government of people in our societies everyone had not only to obey but also to produce and publish the truth about oneself, then examination of conscience and confession are among the most important of those procedures. Of course, there is a very long and very complex history, from the Delphic precept, *gnothi seauton* ('know yourself') to the strange therapeutics promoted by Leuret, about which I was speaking in the beginning of this lecture. There is a very long way from one to the other, and I don't want, of course, to give you even a survey this evening. I'd like only to underline a transformation of those practices, a transformation which took place at the beginning of the Christian era, of the Christian period, when the ancient obligation of knowing oneself became the monastic precept 'confess, to your spiritual guide, each of your thoughts'. This transformation is, I think, of some importance in the genealogy of modern subjectivity. With this transformation starts what we would call the hermeneutics of the self. This evening I'll try to outline the way confession and self-examination were conceived by pagan philosophers, and next week I'll try to show you what it became in the early Christianity.

It is well known that the main objective of the Greek schools of philosophy did not consist of the elaboration, the teaching, of theory. The goal of the Greek schools of philosophy was the transformation of the individual. The goal of the Greek philosophy was to give the individual the quality which would permit him to live differently, better, more happily, than other people. What place did the self-examination and the confession have in this? At first glance, in all the ancient philosophical practices, the obligation to tell the truth about oneself occupies a rather restrained place. And this for two reasons, both of which remain valid throughout the whole of Greek and Hellenistic antiquity. The first of those reasons is that the objective of philosophical training was to arm the individual with a certain number of precepts which permit him to conduct himself in all circumstances of life without his losing mastery of himself or without losing tranquillity of spirit, purity of body and soul. From this principle stems the importance of the master's discourse. The master's discourse has to talk, to explain, to persuade; he has to give the disciple a universal

---

[14] *Resumé de cours*, 1970–1982, Julliard, Paris, 1989, 133–66; 'Sexuality and solitude', in this volume.

code for all his life, so that the verbalisation takes place on the side of the master and not on the side of the disciple.

There is also another reason why the obligation to confess does not have a lot of importance in the direction of the antique conscience. The tie with the master was then circumstantial or, in any case, provisional. It was a relationship between two wills, which does not imply a complete or a definitive obedience. One solicits or one accepts the advice of a master or of a friend in order to endure an ordeal, a bereavement, an exile, or a reversal of fortune and so on. Or again, one places oneself under the direction of a master for a certain time of one's life so as one day to be able to behave autonomously and no longer have need of advice. Ancient direction tends towards the autonomy of the directed. In these conditions, one can understand that the necessity for exploring oneself in exhaustive depth does not present itself. It is not indispensable to say everything about oneself, to reveal one's least secrets, so that the master may exert complete power over one. The exhaustive and continual presentation of oneself under the eyes of an all-powerful director is not an essential feature in this technique of direction.

But, despite this general orientation which has so little emphasis on self-examination and on confession, one finds well before Christianity already elaborated techniques for discovering and formulating the truth about oneself. And their role, it would seem, became more and more important. The growing importance of these techniques is no doubt tied to the development of communal life in the philosophical school, as with the Pythagoreans or the Epicureans, and it is also tied to the value accorded to the medical model, in either the Epicurean or the Stoic schools.

Since it is not possible in so short a time even to give a sketch of this evolution of Greek and Hellenist civilisation, I'll take only two passages of a Roman philosopher, Seneca. They may be considered as rather good witnesses on the practice of self-examination and confession as it existed with the Stoics of the Imperial period at the time of the birth of Christianity. The first passage is to be found in the De ira of Seneca. Here is the passage:

What could be more beautiful than to conduct an inquest on one's day? What sleep better than that which follows this review of one's actions? How calm it is, deep and free, when the soul has received its portion of praise and blame, and has submitted itself to its own examination, to its own censure. Secretly, it makes the trial of its own conduct. I exercise this authority over myself, and each day I will myself as witness before myself. When my light is lowered and my wife at last is silent, I reason with myself and take the measure of my acts and of my words. I hide nothing from myself, I spare myself nothing. Why, in effect, should I fear anything at all from amongst my errors whilst I can say: 'Be vigilant in not beginning it again; today I will forgive you. In a certain discussion you spoke too aggressively or you did not correct the person you were reproaching, you offended him.'[15]

There is something paradoxical in seeing the Stoics, such as Seneca and also Sextus, Epictetus, Marcus Aurelius, and so on, according so much importance to the examination of conscience while, according to the terms of their doctrine, all faults were

[15] Seneca, 'On anger', Moral Essays, Volume 1, trans. John W. Basore, Leob Classical Library, Harvard University Press, Cambridge, Massachusetts, 1958, pp. 340–1.

supposed equal. It should not therefore be necessary to interrogate themselves on each one of them.

But, let's look at this text a little more closely. First of all, Seneca employs a vocabulary which at first glance appears, above all, judicial. He uses expressions like *cognoscere de moribus suis*, and *me causam dico* — all that is typical judicial vocabulary. It seems, therefore, that the subject is, with regard to himself, both the judge and the accused. In this examination of conscience it seems that the subject divides itself in two and organises a judicial scene, where it plays both roles at once. Seneca is like an accused confessing his crime to the judge, and the judge is Seneca himself. But, if we look more closely, we see that the vocabulary used by Seneca is much more administrative than judicial. It is the vocabulary of the direction of goods or territory. Seneca says, for instance, that he is *speculator sui*, that he inspects himself, that he examines with himself the past day, *totum diem meum scrutor*; or that he takes the measure of things said and done; he uses the word *remetior*. With regard to himself, he is not a judge who has to punish; he is, rather, an administrator who, once the work has been done or the year's business finished, does the accounts, takes stock of things, and sees if everything has been done correctly. Seneca is a permanent administrator of himself, more than a judge of his own past.[16]

The examples of the faults committed by Seneca and with which he reproaches himself are significant from this point of view. He reproaches himself for having criticised someone and instead of correcting him has hurt him; or again, he says that he has discussed with people who were in any case incapable of understanding him. These faults, as he says himself, are not really faults; they are mistakes. And why mistakes? Either because he did not have in his mind the aims which the sage should set himself or because he had not applied in the correct manner the rules of conduct to be deduced from them. The faults are mistakes in that sense that they are bad adjustments between aims and means. Significant is also the fact that Seneca does not recall those faults in order to punish himself; he has as a goal only to memorise exactly the rules which he had to apply. This memorisation has for an object a reactivation of fundamental philosophical principles and the readjustment of their application. In the Christian confession the penitent has to memorise the law in order to discover his own sins, but in this Stoic exercise the sage has to memorise acts in order to reactivate the fundamental rules.

One can therefore characterise this examination in a few words. First, this examination, it's not at all a question of discovering the truth hidden in the subject. It is rather a question of recalling the truth forgotten by the subject. Second, what the subject forgets is not himself, nor his nature, nor his origin, nor a supernatural affinity. What the subject forgets is what he ought to have done, that is, a collection of rules of conduct that he had learned. Third, the recollection of errors committed during the day serves to measure the distance which separates what has been done from what should have been done. And fourth, the subject who practices this examination on himself is not the operating ground for a process more or less obscure which has to be deciphered. He is the point where rules of conduct come together and register themselves in the form of memories. He is at the same time the point of departure for actions more or less in conformity with these rules. He constitutes, the subject constitutes, the point of intersection between a set of memories which must be brought into the present and acts which have to be regulated.

This evening examination has its logical place among a set of other Stoic exercises:[17] continual reading, for instance, of the manual of precepts (that's for the present); the examination of the evils which could happen in life, the well-known *premeditatio malorum* (that was for the possible); the enumeration each morning of the tasks to be accomplished during the day (that was for the future); and, finally, the evening examination of conscience (so much for the past). As you see, the self in all those exercises is not considered as a field of subjective data which have to be interpreted. It submits itself to the trial of possible or real action.

After this examination of conscience, which constitutes a kind of confession to one's self, I would like to speak about the confession to others: I mean to say the exposé of one's soul which one makes to someone, who may be a friend, an adviser, a guide. This was a practice not very developed in philosophical life, but it had been developed in some philosophical schools, for instance among the Epicurean schools, and it was also a very well known medical practice. The medical literature is rich in such examples of confession or exposé of the self. For instance, the treatise of Galen *On the Passions of the Soul*[18] quotes an example like that; or Plutarch, in the *De profectibus in virtute* writes, 'There are many sick people who accept medicine and others who refuse them; the man who hides the shame of soul, his desire, his unpleasantness, his avarice, his concupiscence, has little chance of making progress. Indeed, to speak one's evil reveals one['s] nastiness; to recognise it instead of taking pleasure in hiding it. All this is a sign of progress.'[19]

Another text of Seneca might also serve us as an example here of what was confession in the late antiquity. It is in the beginning of *De tranquillitate animi*.[20] Serenus, a young friend of Seneca, comes to ask him for advice. It is very explicitly a medical consultation on his own state of soul. 'Why,' says Serenus, 'should I not confess to you the truth, as to a doctor? ... I do not feel altogether ill but nor do I feel entirely in good health.' Serenus feels himself in a state of malaise, rather as he says, like on a boat which does not advance but is tossed about by the rolling of the ship. And he fears staying at sea in this condition, in view of firm land and of the virtues which remain inaccessible. In order to escape this state, Serenus therefore decides to consult Seneca and to confess his state to Seneca. He says that he wants *verum fateri*, to tell the truth, to Seneca.[21]

---

[17] 'all of them being a way to incorporate in a constant attitude a code of actions and reactions, whatever situation may occur' [Howison].

[18] Galen, 'On the diagnosis and cure of the soul's passions' in *On the Passions and Errors of the Soul*, trans. Paul W. Harkins, Ohio State University Press, Columbus, Ohio, 1963.

[19] Plutarch, 'How a man may become aware of his progress in virtue' in *Moralia Volume 1*, trans. Frank Cole Babbitt, Leob Classical Library, Putman, New York, 1927, pp. 400–57, especially pp. 436–57.

[20] Seneca, 'On tranquillity of mind' in *Moral Essays, Volume 2*, trans. John W. Basore, Loeb Classical Library, Harvard University Press, Cambridge, Massachussets, 1935, pp. 202–82, especially pp. 202–13.

[21] 'But, through this confession, through this description of his own state, he asks Seneca to tell him the truth about his own state. Seneca is at the same time confessing the truth and lacking in truth.' [Howison]

Now what is this truth, what is this *verum*, that he wants to confess? Does he confess faults, secret thoughts, shameful desires and things like that? Not at all. The text of Serenus appears as an accumulation of relatively unimportant, at least for us unimportant, details; for instance, Serenus confesses to Seneca that he uses the earthenware inherited from his father, that he gets easily carried away when he makes public speeches, and so on and so on. But, it is easy, beneath this apparent disorder, to recognise three distinct domains for this confession: the domain of riches, the domain of political life and the domain of glory; to acquire riches, to participate in the affairs of the city, to gain public opinion. These are – these were – the three types of activity possible for a free man, the three commonplace moral questions that are asked by the major philosophical schools of the period. The framework of the exposé of Serenus is not therefore defined by the real course of his existence; it is not defined by his real experiences, nor by a theory of the soul or of its elements, but only by a classification of the different types of activity which one can exercise and the ends which one can pursue. In each one of these fields Serenus reveals his attitude by enumerating that which pleases him and that which displeases him. The expression 'it pleases me' (*placet me*) is the leading thread in his analysis. It pleases him to do favours for his friends. It pleases him to eat simply, and to have not other than that which he has inherited, but the spectacle of luxury in others pleases him. He takes pleasure also in inflating his oratorical style with the hope that posterity will retain his words. In thus exposing what pleases him, Serenus is not seeking to reveal what are his profound desires. His pleasures are not the means of revealing what Christians later call *concupiscensia*. For him it is a question of his own state and of adding something to the knowledge of the moral precepts. This addition to what is already known is a force, the force which would be able to transform pure knowledge and simple consciousness in a real way of living. And that is what Seneca tries to do when he uses a set of persuasive arguments, demonstrations, examples, in order not to discover a still unknown truth inside and in the depth of Serenus's soul but in order to explain, if I may say, to which extent truth in general is true. Seneca's discourse has for an objective not to add to some theoretical principle a force of coercion coming from elsewhere but to transform them in a victorious force. Seneca has to give a place to truth as a force.

Hence, I think, several consequences. First, in this game between Serenus's confession and Seneca's consultation, truth, as you see, is not defined by a correspondence to reality but as a force inherent to principles and which has to be developed in a discourse. Second, this truth is not something which is hidden behind or under the consciousness in the deepest and most obscure part of the soul. It is something which is before the individual as a point of attraction, a kind of magnetic force which attracts him towards a goal. Third, this truth is obtained not by an analytical exploration of what is supposed to be real in the individual but by rhetorical explanation of what is good for anyone who wants to approach the life of a sage. Fourth, the confession is not oriented toward an individualisation of Serenus by the discovery of some personal characteristics but towards the constitution of a self which could be at the same time and without any discontinuity subject of knowledge and subject of will. Fifth,[22] we can see that such a practice of confession and consultation remains within the framework of what the Greeks for a long time called the gnomé. The term gnomé designates the unity of will and knowledge; it designates also a brief piece of discourse through which truth appeared with all its force and encrusts itself in the soul of people.[23] Then, we could say that even as late as the first century AD the type of subject which is proposed as a model and as a target in the Greek, or in the Hellenistic or Roman, philosophy is a gnomic self, where force of the truth is one with the form of the will.

In this model of the gnomic self we found several constitutive elements: the necessity of telling truth about oneself, the role of the master and the master's discourse, the long way that leads finally to the emergence of the self. All those elements we find also in the Christian technologies of the self, but with a very different organisation. I should say, in sum, and I'll conclude there, that as far as we followed the practices of self-examination and confession in the Hellenistic or Roman philosophy, you see that the self is not something that has to be discovered or deciphered as a very obscure text. You see that the task is not to put in the light what would be the most obscure part of our selves. The self has, on the contrary, not to be discovered but to be constituted, to be constituted through the force of truth. This force lies in[24] the rhetorical quality of the master's discourse, and this rhetorical quality depends for a part on the exposé of the disciple, who has to explain how far he is in his way of living from the true principles that he knows.[25] And I think that this organisation of the self as a target, the organisation of what I call the gnomic self, as the objective, the aim, towards which the confession and the self-examination is oriented, is something deeply different to what we meet in the Christian technologies of the self. In the Christian technologies of the self, the problem is to discover what is hidden inside the self; the self is like a text or like a book that we have to decipher, and not something

[22] 'If the role of confession and consultation is to give place to truth as a force, it is easy to understand that self-examination has nearly the same role. We have seen that, if Seneca recalls every evening his mistakes, it is to memorise the moral precepts of the conduct, and memory is nothing else than the force of the truth when it is permanently present and active in the soul. A permanent memory in the individual and in his inner discourse, a persuasive rhetorics in the master's advice – those are the aspects of truth considered as a force. Then we may conclude that self-examination and confession may be in ancient philosophy considered as truth-game, and important truth-game, but the objective of this truth-game is not to discover a secret reality inside the individual. The objective of this truth-game is to make of the individual a place where truth can appear and act as a real force through the presence of memory and the efficiency of discourse.' [Howison]

[23] 'In the earliest form of Greek philosophy, poets and divine men told the truth to ordinary mortals through this kind of gnomé. Gnomai were very short, very imperative, and so deeply illuminated by the poetical light that it was impossible to forget them and to avoid their power. I think you can see that self-examination, confession, as you find them, for instance, in Seneca, but also in Marcus Aurelius, Epictetus, and so on, even as late as the first century AD, self-examination and confession were still a kind of development of the gnomé.' [Howison]

[24] 'the mnemonic aptitude of the individual and' [Howison].

[25] 'These depend in part on arts of memory and acts of persuasion. So, technologies of the self in the ancient world are linked not with an art of interpretation, but with arts such as mnemotechnics and rhetoric. Self-observation, self-interpretation, self-hermeneutics won't intervene in the technologies of the self before Christianity.' [Howison]

which has to be constructed by the superposition, the superimposition, of the will and the truth. This organisation, this Christian organisation, so different from the pagan one, is something which is I think quite decisive for the genealogy of the modern self, and that's the point I'll try to explain next week when we meet again. Thank you.

Christianity and confession

The theme of this lecture is the same as the theme of last week's lecture.[26] The theme is: how was formed in our societies what I would like to call the interpretative analysis of the self; or, how was formed the hermeneutics of the self in the modern, or at least in the Christian and the modern, societies? In spite of the fact that we can find very early in the Greek, in the Hellenistic, in the Latin cultures, techniques such as self-examination and confession, I think that there are very large differences between the Latin and Greek – the Classical – techniques of the self and the techniques developed in Christianity. And I'll try to show this evening that the modern hermeneutics of the self is rooted much more in those Christian techniques than in the Classical ones. The gnothi seauton is, I think, much less influential in our societies, in our culture, than it is supposed to be.

As everybody knows, Christianity is a confession. That means that Christianity belongs to a very special type of religion, the religions which impose on those who practise them obligation[s] of truth. Such obligations in Christianity are numerous; for instance, a Christian has the obligation to hold as true a set of propositions which constitutes a dogma; or, he has the obligation to hold certain books as a permanent source of truth; or,[27] he has the obligation to accept the decisions of certain authorities in matters of truth.[28]

But Christianity requires another form of truth obligation quite different from those I just mentioned. Everyone, every Christian, has the duty to know who he is,

---

[26] [At the beginning of the second Howison lecture, Foucault said the following:] 'Several persons asked me to give a short résumé of what I said last night. I will try to do it as if it were a good television series. So, what happened in the first episode? Very few important things. I have tried to explain why I was interest in the practice of self-examination and confession. Those two practices seem to me to be good witnesses for a major problem, which is the genealogy of the modern self. This genealogy has been my obsession for years because it is one of the possible ways to get rid of a traditional philosophy of the subject. I would like to outline this genealogy from the point of view of techniques, what I call techniques of the self. Among these techniques of the self, the most important, in modern societies, is, I think, that which deals with the interpretative analysis of the subject, with the hermeneutics of the self. How was the hermeneutics of the self formed? This is the theme of the two lectures. Yesterday night I spoke about Greek and Roman techniques of the self, or at least about two of these techniques, confession and self-examination. It is a fact that we meet confession and self-examination very often in the late Hellenistic and Roman philosophies. Are they the archetypes of Christian confession and self-examination? Are they the early forms of the modern hermeneutics of the self? I have tried to show that they are quite different from that. Their aim is not, I think, to decipher a hidden truth in the depth of the individual. Their aim is something else. It is to give force to truth in the individual. Their aim is to constitute the self as the ideal unity of the will and the truth. Well, now let us turn toward Christianity as the cradle of Western hermeneutics of the self.'

[27] 'at least in the Catholic branch of Christianity' [Howison].

[28] 'obligations not only to believe in certain things but also to show that one believes in them. Every Christian is obliged to manifest his faith.' [Howison]

what is happening in him. He has to know the faults he may have committed: he has to know the temptations to which he is exposed. And, moreover, everyone in Christianity is obliged to say these things to other people, to tell these things to other people, and hence, to bear witness against himself.

A few remarks. These two ensembles of obligations, those regarding the faith, the book, the dogma, and the obligations regarding the self, the soul, the heart, are linked together. A Christian is always supposed to be supported by the light of faith if he wants to explore himself, and, conversely, access to the truth of the faith cannot be conceived of without the purification of the soul. As Augustine said, in a Latin formula I'm sure you'll understand, *qui facit veritatem venit ad lucem*. That means: *facite veritatem*, 'to make truth inside oneself', and *venire ad lucem*, 'to get access to the light'. Well, to make truth inside of oneself, and to get access to the light of God, and so on, those two processes are strongly connected in the Christian experience. But those two relationships to truth, you can find them equally connected, as you know, in Buddhism, and they were also connected in all the Gnostic movements of the first centuries. But there, either in Buddhism or in the Gnostic movements, those two relationships to truth were connected in such a way that they were almost identified. To discover the truth inside oneself, to decipher the real nature and the authentic origin of the soul, was considered by the Gnosticists as one thing with coming through to the light.[29]

On the contrary, one of the main characteristics of orthodox Christianity, one of the main differences between Christianity and Buddhism, or between Christianity and Gnosticism, one of the main reasons for the mistrust of Christianity towards mystics, and one of the most constant historical features of Christianity, is that those two systems of obligation, of truth obligation – the one concerned with access to light and the one concerned with the making of truth, the discovering of truth inside oneself – those two systems of obligation have always maintained a relative autonomy. Even after Luther, even in Protestantism, the secrets of the soul and the mysteries of the faith, the self and the book, are not in Christianity enlightened by exactly the same type of light. They demand different methods and put into operation particular techniques.

Let's put aside the long history of their complex and often conflictual relations before and after the Reformation. I'd like this evening to focus attention on the second of those two systems of obligation. I'd like to focus on the obligation imposed on every Christian to manifest the truth about himself. When one speaks of confession and self-examination in Christianity, one of course has in mind the sacrament of penance and the canonic confession of sins. But these are rather late innovations in Christianity. Christians of the first centuries knew completely different forms for the showing forth of the truth about themselves, and you'll find these obligations of manifesting

[29] 'If the gnomic self of the Greek philosophers, of which I spoke yesterday evening, had to be built as an identification between the force of the truth and the form of the will, we could say that there is a gnostic self. This is the gnostic self that we can find described in Thomas Evangilium or the Manichean texts. This gnostic self has to be discovered inside the individual, but as a part, as a forgotten sparkle of the primitive light.' [Howison]

the truth about oneself in two different institutions – in penitential rites and monastic life. And I would like first to examine the penitential rites and the obligations of truth, the truth obligations which are related, which are connected with those penitential rites. I will not enter, of course, into the discussions which have taken place and which continue until now as to the progressive development of these rites. I would like only to underline one fundamental fact: in the first centuries of Christianity, penance was not an act. Penance, in the first centuries of Christianity, penance is a status, which presents several characteristics. The function of this status is to avoid the definitive expulsion from the church of a Christian who has committed one or several serious sins. As penitent, this Christian is excluded from many of the ceremonies and collective rites, but he does not cease to be a Christian, and by means of this status he can obtain his reintegration. And this status is therefore a long-term affair. This status affects most aspects of his life – fasting obligations, rules about clothing, interdictions on sexual relations – and the individual is marked to such an extent by this status that even after his reconciliation, after his reintegration in the community, he will still suffer from a certain number of prohibitions (for instance, he will not be able to become a priest). So penance is not an act corresponding to a sin; it is a status, a general status in the existence.

Now, among the elements of this status, the obligation to manifest the truth is fundamental. I don't say that enunciation of sins is fundamental; I employ a much more imprecise and obscure expression. I say that manifestation of the truth is necessary and is deeply connected with this status of penance. In fact, to designate the truth games or the truth obligations inherent to penitents, the Greek fathers used a word, a very specific word (and very enigmatic also): the word *exomologesis*. This word was so specific that even Latin writers, Latin fathers, often used the Greek word without even translating it.[30]

What does this term *exomologesis* mean? In a very general sense, the word refers to the recognition of an act, but more precisely, in the penitential rite, what was the *exomologesis*? Well, at the end of the penitential procedure, at the end and not at the beginning, at the end of the penitential procedure, when the moment of the reintegration came, an episode took place which the texts regularly call *exomologesis*. Some descriptions are very early and some very late, but they are quite identical. Tertullian, for instance, at the end of the second century, describes the ceremony in the following manner. He wrote, 'The penitent wears a hair shirt and ashes. He is wretchedly dressed. He is taken by the hand and led into the church. He prostrates himself before the widows and the priest. He hangs on the skirts of their garments. He kisses their knees.'[31] And much later after this, in the beginning of the fifth century, Jerome described in the same way the penitence of Fabiola. Fabiola was a woman, a well-known Roman noblewoman, who had married a second time before the death of her first husband, which was something quite bad, and she then was obliged to do

---

[30] *Technologies of the Self*, pp. 39–43.

[31] Tertullian, 'On repentance' in *The Ante-Nicene Fathers*, ed. A. Roberts and J. Donaldson, Eerdmans, Grand Rapids, Michigan, no date, reprinted 1979, pp. 657–68, especially 'Exomologesis', chapters 9–12, pp. 664–6.

penance. And Jerome describes thus this penance: 'during the days which preceded Easter', which was the moment of the reconciliation:

during the days which preceded Easter, Fabiola was to be found among the ranks of the penitents. The bishop, the priests, and the people wept with her. Her hair dishevelled, her face pale, her hands dirty, her head covered in ashes, she chastened her naked breast and the face with which she had seduced her second husband. She revealed to all her wound, and Rome, in tears, contemplated the scars on her emaciated body.[32]

No doubt Jerome and Tertullian were liable to be rather carried away by such things; however, in Ambrose and in others one finds indications which show clearly the existence of an episode of dramatic self-revelation at the moment of the reconciliation of the penitent. That was, specifically, the *exomologesis*.

But the term of *exomologesis* does not apply only to this final episode. Frequently the word *exomologesis* is used to designate everything that the penitent does to obtain his reconciliation during the time in which he retains the status of penitent. The acts by which he punishes himself must be indissociable from the acts by which he reveals himself. The punishment of oneself and the voluntary expression of oneself are bound together.

A correspondent of Cyprian in the middle of the third century writes, for instance, that those who wish to do penance must, I quote, 'prove their suffering, show their shame, make visible their humility, and exhibit their modesty'.[33] And, in the *Paraenesis*, Pacian says that the true penance is not accomplished in a nominal fashion but finds its instruments in sackcloth, ashes, fasting, affliction and the participation of a great number of people in prayers. In a few words, penance in the first Christian centuries is a way of life acted out at all times out of an obligation to show oneself. And that is, exactly, *exomologesis*.[34]

As you see, this *exomologesis* did not obey to a judicial principle of correlation, of exact correlation, adjusting the punishment to the crime. *Exomologesis* obeyed a law of dramatic emphasis and of maximum theatricality. And neither did this *exomologesis* obey a truth principle of correspondence between verbal enunciation and reality. As you see, no description in this *exomologesis* is of a penance; no confession, no verbal enumeration of sins, no analysis of the sins, but somatic expressions and symbolic expressions. Fabiola did not confess her fault, telling to somebody what she has done, but she put under everybody's eyes the flesh, the body, which has committed the sin. And, paradoxically, the *exomologesis* is this time to rub out the sin, restitute the previous

[32] Jerome, 'Letter LXXVII, to Oceanus', in *The Principal Works of St Jerome*, trans. W. H. Freemantle, vol. 6 in *A Selected Library of Nicene and Post-Nicene Fathers*, Christian Literature Co., New York, 1893, pp. 157–62, especially 159–60.

[33] Cyprian, 'Letter XXXVI, from the priests and deacons abiding in Rome to Pope Cyprian', in *Saint Cyprian: Letters (1–8)*, 90–4 at 93, trans. Sister Rose Bernard Donna, CSJ, vol. 51 in *The Fathers of the Church*, Catholic University of America Press, Washington, DC, 1964.

[34] 'This form, attested to from the end of the second century, will subsist for an extremely long time in Christianity, since one finds its after-effects in the orders of penitents so important in the fifteenth and sixteenth century. One can see that the procedure for showing forth the truth are multiple and complex in it. Certain acts of *exomologesis* take place in private but most are addressed to the public.' [Howison]

purity acquired by baptism, and this by showing the sinner as he [sic] is in his reality – dirty, defiled, sullied.[35]

Tertullian has a word to translate the Greek word *exomologesis*; he said it was *publicatio sui*, the Christian had to publish himself.[36] Publish oneself, that means that he has two things to do. One has to show oneself as a sinner; that means, as somebody who, choosing the path of the sin, preferred filthiness to purity, earth and dust to heaven, spiritual poverty to the treasures of faith. In a word, he has to show himself as somebody who preferred spiritual death to earthen life. And that was the reason why *exomologesis* was a kind of representation of death. It was the theatrical representation of the sinner as dead or as dying. But this *exomologesis* was also a way for the sinner to express his will to get free from this world, to get rid of his own body, to destroy his own flesh and get access to a new spiritual life. It is the theatrical representation of the sinner as willing his own death as a sinner. It is the dramatic manifestation of the renunciation to oneself.

To justify this *exomologesis* and this renunciation to oneself in manifesting the truth about oneself, Christian fathers had recourse to several models. The well-known medical model was very often used in pagan philosophy: one has to show one's wounds to the physicians if one wants to be healed. They also used the judicial model: one always appeases the court when spontaneously confessing the faults.[37] But the most important model to justify the necessity of *exomologesis* is the model of martyrdom. The martyr is he who prefers to face death rather than to abandon his faith.[38] The sinner abandons the faith in order to keep the life of here below; he will be reinstated only if in his turn he exposes himself voluntarily to a sort of martyrdom to which all will be witnesses, and which is penance, or penance as *exomologesis*.[39] Such a demonstration does not therefore have as its function the establishment of the personal identity. Rather, such a demonstration serves to mark this dramatic demonstration of what one is: the refusal of the self, the breaking off from one's self.

One recalls what was the objective of Stoic technology: it was to superimpose, as I tried to explain to you last week, the subject of knowledge and the subject of will by means of the perpetual rememorising of the rules. The formula which is at the heart of *exomologesis* is, in contrary, *ego non sum ego*. The *exomologesis* seeks, in opposition to the Stoic techniques, to superimpose by an act of violent rupture the truth about oneself

---

[35] 'The greater part of the acts which constitute penance has the role not of telling the truth about the sin; it has the role of showing the true being of the sinner, or the true sinful being of the subject. The Tertullian expression, *publicatio sui*, is not a way to say the sinner has to explain his sins. The expression means he has to produce himself as a sinner in his reality of sinner. And now the question is why the showing forth of the sinner should be efficient to efface the sins.' [Howison]

[36] 'On repentance', chapter 10.

[37] 'The day of judgement, the Devil himself will stand up to accuse the sinner. If the sinner has already anticipated him by accusing himself, the enemy will be obliged to remain quiet.' [Howison]

[38] 'It must not be forgotten that the practice and the theory of penitence were elaborated to great extent around the problem of the relapsed ... The relapsed abandons the faith in order to keep the life of here below.' [Howison]

[39] 'In brief, penance in so far as it is a reproduction of martyrdom is an affirmation of change – of rupture with one's self, with one's past *metanoia*, of a rupture with the world, and with all previous life.' [Howison]

and the renunciation of oneself. In the ostentatious gestures of maceration, self-revelation in *exomologesis* is, at the same time, self-destruction.

If we turn to the confession in monastic institutions, it is of course quite different from this *exomologesis*. In the Christian institutions of the first centuries another form of confession is to be found, very different from this one. It is the organised confession in the monastic communities. In a certain way, this confession is close to the exercise practiced in the pagan schools of philosophy. There is nothing astonishing in this, since the monastic life presented itself as the true form of philosophical life, and the monastery was presented as the school of philosophy. There is an obvious transfer of several technologies of the self in Christian spirituality from practices of pagan philosophy.

Concerning this continuity I'll quote only one witness, John Chrysostom, who describes an examination of conscience which has exactly the same form, the same shape, the same administrative character, as that described by Seneca in the *De ira* and which I spoke about last week. John Chrysostom says, and you'll recognise exactly (well, nearly) the same words as in Seneca. Chrysostom writes:

It is in the morning that we must take account of our expenses, then it is in the evening, after our meal, when we have gone to bed and no one troubles us and disquiets us, that we must ask ourselves to render account of our conduct to ourselves. Let us examine what is to our advantage and what is prejudicial. Let us cease spending inappropriately and try to set aside useful funds in the place of harmful expenses, prayers in place of indiscreet words.[40]

You'll recognise exactly the same administrative self-examination you could find last week with Seneca. But these kinds of ancient practices were modified under the influence of two fundamental elements of Christian spirituality: the principle of obedience and the principle of contemplation. First, the principle of obedience – we have seen that in the ancient schools of philosophy the relationship between the master and the disciple was, if I may say, instrumental and provisory. The obedience of the disciple was founded on the capacity of the master to lead him to a happy and autonomous life. For a long series of reasons that I haven't time to discuss here, obedience has very different features in the monastic life and above all, of course, in the cenobite communities. Obedience in the monastic institutions must bear on all the aspects of life; there is an adage, very well known in the monastic literature, which says, 'everything that one does not do on order of one's director, or everything that one does without his permission, constitutes a theft'. Therefore, obedience is a permanent relationship, and even when the monk is old, even when he became, in his turn, a master, even then he has to keep the spirit of obedience as a permanent sacrifice of his own will.

Another feature distinguishes monastic discipline from the philosophical life. In the monastic life the supreme good is not the mastership of oneself; the supreme

[40] See especially St John Chrysostom, 'Homily XLII', on Matthew 12:33, in *St Chrysostom: Homilies on the Gospel of St Matthew*, ed. Phillip Schaff, vol. 10 in *A Select Library of the Nicene and Post-Nicene Fathers*, Eerdmans, Grand Rapids, Michigan, reprinted 1975, p. 271.

good in the monastic life is the contemplation of God. The obligation of the monk is continuously to turn his thoughts to that single point which is God, and his obligation is also to make sure that his heart, his soul and the eye of his soul is pure enough to see God and to receive light from him.

Placed under this principle of obedience, and oriented towards the objective of contemplation, you understand that the technology of the self which develops in Christian monasticism presents peculiar characteristics. John Cassian's *Institutiones* and *Collationes* give a rather systematic and clear exposé of self-examination and of the confession as they were practised among the Palestinian and Egyptian monks.[41] And I'll follow several of the indications you can find in those two books, which were written in the beginning of the fifth century. First, about the self-examination, the first point about the self-examination in the monastic life is that the self-examination in this kind of Christian exercise is much more concerned with thoughts than with actions. Since he has to turn his thought continuously towards God, you understand very well that the monk has to take in hand not the course of his actions, as the Stoic philosopher; he has to take in hand the course of his thoughts. Not only the passions which might make vacillate the firmness of his conduct; he has to take in hand the images which present themselves to the spirit, the thoughts which come to interfere with contemplation, the diverse suggestions which turn the attention of the spirit away from its object, that means away from God. So much so that the primary material for scrutiny and for the examination of the self is an area anterior to actions, of course, anterior to will also, even an area anterior to the desires – a much more tenacious material than the material the Stoic philosopher had to examine in himself. The monk has to examine a material which the Greek fathers call (almost always pejoratively) the *logismoi*, that is in Latin, *cogitationes*, the nearly imperceptible movements of the thoughts, the permanent mobility of soul.[42] That's the material which the monk has to examine continuously in order to maintain the eye of his spirit always directed towards the unique point which is God. But, when the monk scrutinises his own thoughts, what is he concerned with? Not of course with the relation between the idea and the reality. He is not concerned with this truth relation which makes an idea wrong or true. He is not interested in the relationship between his mind and the external world. What he is concerned with is the nature, the quality, the substance of his thoughts.

We must, I think, pause for a moment on this important point. In order to make comprehensible what this permanent examination consists in, Cassian uses three comparisons. He uses first the comparison of the mill. Thought, says Cassian, thought is like a millstone which grinds the grains. The grains are of course the ideas which present themselves continuously in the mind. And in the comparison of the millstone, it is up to the miller to sort out among the grains those which are bad and those

---

[41] John Cassian, *De institutiones coenobiorum* and *Collationes patrum*, ed. Phillip Schaff, in vol. 11 of *A Selected Library of Nicene and Post-Nicene Fathers*, Eerdmans, Grand Rapids, Michigan, reprinted 1973.

[42] 'This is the soul that Cassian described with two Greek words [indecipherable]. It means that the soul is always moving and moving in all directions.' [Howison]

which can be admitted to the millstone because they are good. Cassian has recourse also to the comparison of the officer who has the soldiers file past him and makes them pass to the right or to the left, allotting to each his task according to his capacities. And lastly, and that I think is the most important, the most interesting, Cassian says that one must be with respect to oneself like a moneychanger to whom one presents coins, and whose task consists in examining them, verifying their authenticity, so as to accept those which are authentic while rejecting those which are not. Cassian develops this comparison at length. When a moneychanger examines a coin, says Cassian, the moneychanger looks at the effigy the money bears, he considers the metal of which it is made, to know what it is and if it is pure. The moneychanger seeks to know the workshop from which it comes, and he weighs it in his hand in order to know if it has been filed down or ill-used. In the same way, says Cassian, one must verify the quality of one's thoughts, one must know if they really bear the effigy of God; that is to say, if they really permit us to contemplate him, if their surface brilliance does not hide the impurity of a bad thought, What is their origin? Do they come from God, or from the workshop of the demon? Finally, even if they are of good quality and origin, have they not been whittled away and rusted by evil sentiments?

I think that this form of examination is at the same time new and historically important. Perhaps I have insisted a little too much with regard to the Stoics on the fact that their examination, the Stoic examination, was concerned with acts and rules. One must recognise, however, the importance of the question of truth with the Stoic, but the question was presented in terms of true or false opinions favourable to forming good or bad actions. For Cassian, the problem is not to know if there is a conformity between the idea and the order of external things; it is a question of examining the thought in itself. Does it really show its true origin, is it as pure as it seems, have not foreign elements insidiously mixed themselves with it? Altogether, the question is not 'Am I wrong to think such a thing?' but 'Have I not been deceived by the thought which has come to me?' Is the thought which comes to me, and independently of the truth as to the things it represents, is there not an illusion about myself on my part? For instance, the idea comes to me that fasting is a good thing. The idea is certainly true, but maybe this idea has been suggested not by God but by Satan in order to put me in competition with other monks, and then bad feelings about the other ones can be mixed to the project of fasting more than I do. So, the idea is true in regard to the external world, or in regard to the rules, but the idea is impure since from its origin it is rooted in bad sentiments. And we have to decipher our thoughts as subjective data which have to be interpreted, which have to be scrutinised, in their roots and in their origins.

It is impossible not to be struck by the similarity of this general theme, and the similarity of this image of the moneychanger and several texts of Freud about censorship. One could say that Freudian censorship is both the same thing and the reverse of Cassian's changer; both the Cassian changer and the Freudian censorship have to control the access to consciousness – they have to let some representations in and to reject the others. But Cassian's changer has for a function to decipher what is false or illusory in what presents itself to consciousness and then to let in only what is authentic. For that purpose the Cassian moneychanger uses a specific aptitude that the Latin fathers called *discretio*.[43] The Freudian censorship is, compared to the Cassian changer, both more perverse and more naive. The Freudian censorship rejects that what presents itself as it is, and the Freudian censorship accepts that what is sufficiently disguised. Cassian's changer is a truth-operator through *discretio*; Freudian censorship is a falsehood-operator through symbolisation. But I don't want to go further in such a parallel; it's only an indication, but I think that the relations between Freudian practice and the Christian techniques of spirituality could be, if seriously done, a very interesting field of research.[44]

But we have to go further, for the problem is how is it possible to perform, as Cassian wishes, how is it possible to perform continuously this necessary self-examination, this necessary self-control of the tiniest movements in the thoughts? How is it possible to perform this necessary hermeneutics of our own thoughts? The answer given by Cassian and his inspirators is both obvious and surprising. The answer given by Cassian is, well, you interpret your thoughts by telling them to the master or to your spiritual father. You interpret your thoughts by confessing not of course your acts, not confessing your faults, but confessing continuously the movement you can notice in your thought. Why is this confession able to assume this hermeneutical role? One reason comes to the mind: in exposing the movements of his heart, the disciple permits his *seigneur* to know those movements and, thanks to his greater experience, to his greater wisdom, the *seigneur*, the spiritual father, can better understand what's happening. His seniority permits him to distinguish between truth and illusion in the soul of the person he directs.

But that is not the principal reason that Cassian invokes to explain the necessity of confession. There is for Cassian a specific virtue of verification in this act of verbalisation. Among all the examples that Cassian quotes there is one which is particularly enlightening on this point. Cassian quotes the following anecdote: a young monk, Serapion, incapable of enduring the obligatory fast, stole every evening a loaf of bread.

---

[43] 'and the Greek fathers called *diacrisis*' [Howison].

[44] 'What I would like to insist upon this evening is something else, or at least, something indirectly related to that. There is something really important in the way Cassian poses the problem of truth about the thought. First of all, thoughts (not desires, not passions, not attitudes, not acts) appear in Cassian's work and in all the spirituality it represents as a field of subjective data which have to be considered and analysed as an object. And I think that is the first time in history that thoughts are considered as possible objects for an analysis. Second, thoughts have to be analysed not in relation to their object, according to objective experience, or according to logical rules, they have to be suspected since they can be secretly altered, disguised in their own substance, Third, what man needs if he does not want to be victim of his own thoughts is a perpetual hermeneutics interpretation, a perpetual work of hermeneutics. The function of this hermeneutics is to discover the reality hidden inside the thought. Fourth, this reality which is able to hide in my thoughts is a power, a power which is not of another nature than my soul, as is, for instance, the body. The power which hides inside my thoughts, this power is of the same nature of my thoughts and of my soul. It is the Devil. It is the presence of somebody else in me. This constitution of the thoughts as a field of subjective data needing an interpretative analysis in order to discover the power of the other in me is, that is, I think, if we compare it to the Stoic technologies of the self, a quite new manner to organise the relationships between truth and subjectivity. I think that hermeneutics of the self begins there.' [Howison]

But of course he did not dare to confess it to his spiritual director, and one day this spiritual director, who no doubt guessed all, gives a public sermon on the necessity of being truthful. Convinced by this sermon, the young Serapion takes out from under his robe the bread that he has stolen and shows it to everyone. Then he prostrates himself and confesses the secret of his daily meal, and then, not at the moment when he showed the bread he has stolen, but at the very moment when he confesses, verbally confesses, the secret of his daily meal, at this very moment of the confession, a light seems to tear itself away from his body and cross the room, in spreading a disgusting smell of sulphur.

One sees that in this anecdote the decisive element is not that the master knows the truth. It is not even that the young monk reveals his act and restores the object of his theft. It is the confession, the verbal act of confession, which comes last and which makes appear, in a certain sense, by its own mechanics, the truth, the reality of what has happened. The verbal act of confession is the proof, is the manifestation, of truth. Why? I think it is because what marks the difference between good and evil thoughts, following Cassian, is that the evil ones cannot be referred to without difficulty. If one blushes in recounting them, if one seeks to hide one's own thoughts, if even quite simply one hesitates to tell one's thoughts, that is the proof that those thoughts are not good as they may appear. Evil inhabits them. Thus verbalisation constitutes a way of sorting out thoughts which present themselves. One can test their value according to whether they resist verbalisation or not. Cassian gives the reason of this resistance: Satan as principle of evil is incompatible with the light, and he resists when confession drags him from the dark caverns of the conscience into the light of explicit discourse. I quote Cassian: 'A bad thought brought into the light of day immediately loses its veneer. The terrible serpent that this confession has forced out of its subterranean lair, to throw it out into the light and make its shame a public spectacle, is quick to beat a retreat.'[45] Does that mean that it would be sufficient for the monk to tell his thoughts aloud even when alone? Of course not. The presence of somebody, even if he does not speak, even if it is a silent presence, this presence is requested for this kind of confession, because the *abbé*, or the brother, or the spiritual father, who listens at this confession is the image of God. And the verbalisation of thoughts is a way to put under the eyes of God all the ideas, images, suggestions, as they come to consciousness, and under this divine light they show necessarily what they are.

From this, we can see, first, that verbalisation in itself has an interpretative function. Verbalisation contains in itself a power of *discretio*.[46] Second, this verbalisation is not a kind of retrospection about past acts. Verbalisation, Cassian imposes to monks, this verbalisation has to be a permanent activity, as contemporaneous as possible of the stream of thoughts. Third, this verbalisation must go as deep as possible in the depth of the thoughts. These, whatever they are, have an inapparent origin, obscure roots, secret parts, and the role of verbalisation is to excavate these origins and those

---

[45] John Cassian, *Second Conference of Abbot Moses*, chapter 11, 312–13 at 312, in vol. 11 of *A Selected Library of Nicene and Post-Nicene Fathers of the Christian Church*, ed. Phillip Schaft and Henry Wace, Eerdmans, Grand Rapids, Michigan, 1955.

[46] 'a power of *diacrisis*, of differences' [Howison].

secret parts. Fourth, as verbalisation brings to the external light the deep movement of the thought, it leads also and by the same process the human soul from the reign of Satan to the law of God. That means that verbalisation is a way for the conversion[47] (for the *metanoia*, said the Greek fathers), for the conversion to develop itself and to take effect. Since under the reign of Satan the human being was attached to himself, verbalisation as a movement toward God is a renunciation to Satan, and a renunciation to oneself. Verbalisation is a self-sacrifice. To this permanent, exhaustive and sacrificial verbalisation of the thoughts which was obligatory for the monks in the monastic institution, to this permanent verbalisation of the thoughts the Greek fathers gave the name of *exagoreusis*.[48]

Thus, as you see, in the Christianity of the first centuries the obligation to tell the truth about oneself was to take two major forms, the *exomologesis* and the *exagoreusis*, and as you see they are very different from one another. On the one hand, the *exomologesis* is a dramatic expression by the penitent of his status of sinner, and this in a kind of public manifestation. On the other hand, in the *exagoreusis* we have an analytical and continuous verbalisation of the thoughts, and in this relation of complete obedience to the will of the spiritual father. But it must be remarked that this verbalisation, as I just told you, is also a way of renouncing self and no longer wishing to be the subject of the will. Thus the rule of confession in *exagoreusis*, this rule of permanent verbalisation, finds its parallel in the model of martyrdom which haunts *exomologesis*. The ascetic maceration exercised on the body and the rule of permanent verbalisation applied to the thoughts, the obligation to macerate the body and the obligation of verbalising the thoughts – those things are deeply and closely related. They are supposed to have the same goals and the same effect. So much that one can isolate as the common element to both practices the following principle: the revelation of the truth about oneself cannot, in those two early Christian experiences, the revelation of the truth about oneselves cannot be dissociated from the obligation to renounce oneselves. We have to sacrifice the self in order to discover the truth about ourselves, and we have to discover the truth about ourselves in order to sacrifice ourselves. Truth and sacrifice, the truth about ourselves and the sacrifice of ourselves, are deeply and closely connected. And we have to understand this sacrifice not only as a radical change in the way of life but as the consequence of a formula like this: you will become the subject of the manifestation of truth when and only when you disappear or you destroy yourself as a real body or as a real existence.

Let's stop here. I have been both too long and much too schematic. I would like you to consider what I have said only as a point of departure, one of those small origins that Nietzsche liked to discover at the beginning of great things. The great things that those monastic practices announced are numerous. I will mention, just before I finish, a few of them. First, as you see, the apparition of a new kind of self, or at least a new kind of relationship to our selves. You remember what I told you last week: the Greek technology, or the philosophical techniques, of the self tended to produce a self

---

[47] 'for the rupture of the self' [Howison].
[48] *Technologies of the Self*, pp. 43–9.

which could be, which should be, the permanent superposition in the form of memory of the subject of knowledge and the subject of the will.[49]

I think that in Christianity we see the development of a much more complex technology of the self. This technology of the self maintains the difference between knowledge of being, knowledge of word, knowledge of nature and knowledge of the self, and this knowledge of the self takes shape in the constitution of thought as a field of subjective data which are to be interpreted. And the role of interpreter is assumed by the work of a continuous verbalisation of the most imperceptible movements of the thought – that's the reason we could say that the Christian self which is correlated to this technique is a gnosiologic self.

And the second point which seems to me important is this: you may notice in early Christianity an oscillation between the truth-technology of the self oriented towards the manifestation of the sinner, the manifestation of the being – what we would call the ontological temptation of Christianity, and that is the *exomologesis* – and another truth-technology oriented towards the discursive and permanent analysis of the thought – that is the *exagoreusis*, and we could see there the epistemological temptation of Christianity. And, as you know, after a lot of conflicts and fluctuation, the second form of technology, this epistemological technology of the self, or this technology of the self oriented towards the permanent verbalisation and discovery of the most imperceptible movements of our self, this form became victorious after centuries and centuries, and it is nowadays dominating.

Even in these hermeneutical techniques derived from the *exagoreusis* the production of truth could not be met, you remember, without a very strict condition: hermeneutics of the self implies the sacrifice of the self. And that is, I think, the deep contradiction, or, if you want, the great richness, of Christian technologies of the self: no truth about the self without a sacrifice of the self.[50] I think that one of the great problems of Western culture has been to find the possibility of founding the hermeneutics of the self not, as was the case in early Christianity, on the sacrifice of the self but, on the contrary, on a positive, on the theoretical and practical, emergence of the self. That was the aim of judicial institutions, that was the aim also of medical and psychiatric practices, that was the aim of political and philosophical theory – to constitute the ground of the subjectivity as the root of a positive self, what we could call the permanent anthropologism of Western thought. And I think that this anthropologism is linked to the deep desire to substitute the positive figure of man for the sacrifice which for Christianity was the condition for the opening of the self as a field of indefinite interpretation.[51] During the last two centuries the problem has

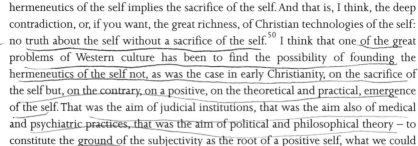

[49] 'what I call the gnomic self. In the beginning of the lecture, I indicated that the Gnostic movements were a question of constituting an ontological unity, the knowledge of the soul and the knowledge of the being. Then, what could be called the gnostic self could be constituted in Christianity.' [Howison]

[50] 'The centrality of the confession of sins in Christianity finds an explanation here. The verbalisation of the confession of sins is institutionalised as a discursive truth-game, which is a sacrifice of the subject.' [Howison]

[51] 'In addition, we can say that one of the problems of Western culture was: how could we save the hermeneutics of the self and get rid of the necessary sacrifice of the self which was linked to this hermeneutics since the beginning of Christianity.' [Howison]

been: what could be the positive foundation for the technologies of the self that we have been developing during centuries and centuries? But the moment, maybe, is coming for us to ask: do we need, really, this hermeneutics of the self?[52] Maybe the problem of the self is not to discover what it is in its positivity, maybe the problem is not to discover a positive self or the positive foundation of the self. Maybe our problem is now to discover that the self is nothing else than the historical correlation of the technology built in our history. Maybe the problem is to change those technologies.[53] And in this case, one of the main political problems would be nowadays, in the strict sense of the word, the politics of ourselves.

I thank you very much.

[52] 'which we have inherited from the first centuries of Christianity? Do we need a positive man who serves as the foundation of this hermeneutics of the self?' [Howison]

[53] 'or maybe to get rid of those technologies, and then, to get rid of the sacrifice which is linked to those technologies' [Howison].

181

CHAPTER FOURTEEN

Sexuality and solitude (1980)

Extract from the James Lecture, at the Institute for the Humanities, New York University, 20 November 1980. The lecture included contributions from the sociologist and novelist Richard Sennett, which are not included in this extract. It was originally published in full in the *London Review of Books*, vol. III, no. 9, 21 May – 5 June 1981, pp. 3, 5 and 6. The text was translated into French, with additional source references and corrections, by F. Durand-Bogaett, and published as 'Sexualité et solitude' in *Dits et écrits*, vol. 4, Gallimard, Paris, 1994, pp. 168–78. A slightly different version of the James lecture appeared in *On Signs*, ed. Marshall Blonsky, Basil Blackwell, Oxford, 1985, pp. 365–72.[1] I have included the significant differences to the *On Signs* version in brackets or in footnotes.

The lecture begins with the story, published in 1840, of the French psychiatrist Dr. Leuret[2] and his patient which formed the introduction of Foucault's Dartmouth lecture. (See 'About the beginning of the hermeneutics of the self' in this volume.) Foucault continued the James Lecture with a slightly abbreviated discussion of the philosophy of the subject, Habermas and the technologies of the self found at the beginning of the Dartmouth lectures, and then developed the following discussion of Christianity.

Now, what about truth as a duty in our Christian societies? As everybody knows, Christianity is a confession. This means that Christianity belongs to a very special type of religion – those which impose obligations of truth on those who practise them. Such obligations in Christianity are numerous. For instance, there is the obligation to hold as truth a set of propositions which constitute dogma, the obligation to hold certain books as a permanent source of truth, obligations to accept the decisions of certain authorities in matters of truth. But Christianity requires another form of truth obligation. Everyone in Christianity has the duty to explore who he is, what is happening within himself, the faults he may have committed, the temptations to which he is exposed. Moreover, everyone is obliged to tell these things to other

---

[1] The *London Review of Books* (LRB) version is the original transcript of the lecture and the *On Signs* version is a written text of the lecture supplied by The New York Institute for the Humanities/Richard Sennett and Patrick Merla to Marshall Blonsky. (I am grateful to Richard Sennett for confirming this detail and for permission to note the differences between the texts.)

[2] In the original English publications of the James Lecture this was printed inaccurately as 'Louren'. In the *Dits et écrits* edition this is amended with the following reference: F. Leuret, *Du traitement moral de la folie*, Baillière, Paris, 1840, pp. 197–8. The Dartmouth Lectures have the correct version of the name.

people, and hence to bear witness against himself.

These two ensembles of obligation – those regarding the faith, the book, the dogma and those regarding the self, the soul and the heart – are linked together. A Christian needs the light of faith when he wants to explore himself. Conversely, his access to the truth cannot be conceived of without the purification of the soul. [Maybe you will object that you can find the same two obligations in Buddhism.] The Buddhist also has to go to the light and discover the truth about himself. But the relation between these two obligations is quite different in Buddhism and in Christianity. In Buddhism it is the same type of enlightenment which leads you to discover what you are and what is the truth. In this simultaneous enlightenment of yourself and the truth, you discover [in Buddhism] that your self was only an illusion. [In Christianity, these two types of truth obligation, the one concerned with access to light and the one concerned with discovering truth inside oneself, have always kept a relative autonomy even after Luther and Protestantism.]

I would like to underline that the Christian discovery of the self does not reveal the self as an illusion. It gives place to a task which cannot be anything else but undefined. This task has two objectives. First, there is the task of clearing up all the illusions, temptations and seductions which can occur in the mind, and discovering the reality of what is going on within ourselves. Second, one has to get free from any attachment to this self, not because the self is an illusion, but because the self is much too real. The more we discover the truth about ourselves, the more we have to renounce ourselves; and the more we want to renounce ourselves the more we need to bring to light the reality of ourselves. That is what we could call the spiral of truth formulation and reality renouncement which is at the heart of the Christian techniques of the self.

Recently, Professor Peter Brown stated to me that what we have to understand is why it is that sexuality became, in Christian cultures, the seismograph of our subjectivity.[3] It is a fact, a mysterious fact, that [in] this indefinite spiral of truth and reality in the self sexuality has been of major importance since the first centuries of our era. It has become more and more important. Why is there such a fundamental connection between sexuality, subjectivity and truth obligation? This is the point at which I met Richard Sennett's work.[4]

Our point of departure in the seminar has been a passage of St François de Sales. Here is the text in a translation made in the beginning of the seventeenth century:

I will tell you a point of the elephant's honesty. An elephant never changes his mate. He loves her tenderly. With her he couples not, but from three years to three years. And that only for five days, and so secretly that he is never seen in the act. But the sixth day, he shows himself abroad again, and the first thing he does is to go directly to some river and wash his body, not willing to return to his troupe of companions till he be purified. Be not these goodly and honest qualities in a beast by which he teaches married folk not to be given too much to sensual and carnal pleasures?[5]

[3] See P. Brown, *The Body in Society*, Columbia University Press, New York, 1988.

[4] See Richard Sennett's section of 'Sexuality and solitude' in the LRB, vol. III, no. 9, 21 May–5 June 1981, pp. 3, 5 and 6.

[5] In *Dits et écrits* the following reference is given: François de Sales, *Introduction à la vie dévote* [1604], Pierre Rigaud, Lyon, 1609; Bluzet-Guimier, Dôle, 1888, book 3, chap. xxxix, pp. 431–2. For an English translation see Francis de Sales, *Introduction to the Devout Life*, Anthony Clarke, Wheathampstead, 1990, p. 197.

Everybody may recognise here the pattern of decent sexual behaviour: monogamy, faithfulness and procreation as the main, or maybe the single, justification of sexual acts – sexual acts which remain, even in such conditions, intrinsically impure. Most of us are inclined, I think, to attribute this pattern either to Christianity or to modern Christian society as it developed under the influence of capitalist or so-called bourgeois morality. But what struck me when I started studying this pattern is the fact that one can find it also in Latin and even Hellenistic literature. One finds the same ideas, the same words and eventually the same reference to the elephant. It is a fact that the pagan philosophers in the first centuries before and after the death of Christ proposed a sexual ethics which was partly new but which was very similar to the alleged Christian ethics. In our seminar it was very convincingly stressed that this philosophical pattern of sexual behaviour, this elephant pattern, was not at that time the only one to be known and put into practice.[6] It was in competition with several others. But this pattern soon became predominant, because it was related to a social transformation involving the disintegration of city-states, the development of the imperial bureaucracy and the increasing influence of the provincial middle class.

During this period we may witness all evolution towards the nuclear family, a real monogamy, faithfulness between married people and distress about sexual acts. The philosophical campaign in favour of the elephant pattern was both an effect and an adjunct of this transformation. If these assumptions are correct, we have to concede that Christianity did not invent this code of sexual behaviour. Christianity accepted it, reinforced it and gave to it a much larger and more widespread strength than it had before. But the so-called Christian morality is nothing more than a piece of pagan ethics inserted into Christianity. Shall we say then that Christianity did not change the state of things? [The thesis I propose is that] early Christians introduced important changes, if not in the sexual code itself, at least in the relationships everyone has to his own sexual activity. Christianity proposed a new type of experience of oneself as a sexual being.

To make things clearer, I shall compare two texts. One was written by Artemidorus, a pagan philosopher of the third century, and the other is the well-known fourteenth book of the *City of God* by Augustine. Artemidorus wrote a book about the interpretation of dreams in the third century after the death of Christ, but he was a pagan. Three chapters of this book are devoted to sexual dreams. What is the meaning, or, more precisely, what is the prognostic value, of a sexual dream? It is significant that Artemidorus interpreted dreams in a way contrary to Freud, and gives all interpretation of sexual dreams in terms of economics, social relations, success and reverses in political activity and everyday life. For instance, if you dream that you have sex with your mother, that means that you will succeed as a magistrate, since your mother is obviously the symbol of your city or country.

It is also significant that the social value of the dream does not depend on the nature of the sexual act, but mainly on the social status of the partners. For instance, for Artemidorus it is not important in your dream whether you had sex with a girl or

[6] This appears to correct the *On Signs* text, which only stated without qualification: 'this philosophical pattern, this elephant pattern, was at the time the only one to exist'. *On Signs*, p. 369.

with a boy. The problem is to know whether the partner was rich or poor, young or old, slave or free, married or not. Of course, Artemidorus takes into account the question of the sexual act, but he sees it only from the point of view of the male. The only act he knows or recognises as sexual is penetration. Penetration is for him not only a sexual act but also part of the social role of a man in a city. I would say that for Artemidorus sexuality is relational, and that sexual relations cannot be dissociated from social relations.

Now let's turn to Augustine's text, whose meaning is the point at which we want to arrive in our analysis. In *The City of God*, and later on in the *Contra Julian*, Augustine gives a rather horrifying description of the sexual act. He sees the sexual act as a kind of spasm. All the body, says Augustine, is shaken by terrible jerks. One entirely loses control of oneself. 'This sexual act takes such a complete and passionate possession of the whole man, both physically and emotionally, that what results is the keenest of all pleasures on the level of sensations, and at the crisis of excitement it practically paralyses all power of deliberate thought.'[7] It is worthwhile to note that this description is not all invention of Augustine: you can find the same in the medical and pagan literature of the previous century. Moreover Augustine's text is almost an exact transcription of a passage written by a [well-known] pagan philosopher, Cicero in the *Hortensius*.[8]

The surprising point is not that Augustine would give such a classical description of the sexual act, but the fact that, having made such a horrible description, he then admits that sexual relations could have taken place in Paradise before the Fall. This is all the more remarkable since Augustine is one of the first Christian Fathers to admit this possibility. Of course, sex in Paradise could not have the epileptic form which we unfortunately know now. Before the Fall, Adam's body, every part of it, was perfectly obedient to the soul and the will. If Adam wanted to procreate in Paradise, he could do it in the same way and with the same control as he could, for instance, sow seeds in the earth. He was not involuntarily excited. Every part of his body was like the fingers, which one can control in all their gestures. Sex was a kind of hand gently sowing the seed. But what happened with the Fall? Adam rose up against God with the first sin. Adam tried to escape God's will and to acquire a will of his own, ignoring the fact that

[7] This is not given in quotation in the *On Signs* text and may be an attempt either to paraphrase Augustine or to reflect a distorted rendition of the original text as it was translated from Latin and/or French into English for the lecture. In the English translation of Augustine's *City of God* we read: 'This lust assumes power not only over the whole body, and not only from the outside, but also internally; it disturbs the whole man, when the mental emotion combines and mingles with the physical delights. So intense is the pleasure that when it reaches its climax there is an almost total extinction of mental alertness; the intellectual sentries, as it were, are overwhelmed.' *City of God*, trans. David Knowles, Penguin, London, 1972, p. 577.

[8] This title is given inaccurately in both the *LRB* and the *On Signs* texts as 'Otensius' but corrected in the French translation in *Dits et écrits*. The *Hortensius* survives only in fragments but in its complete form was influential in Augustine's conversion to Christainity (see Augustine, *Confessions*, trans. R. S. Pine-Coffin, book 3, sec. 4, Penguin, London, 1961, pp. 58–9). It is therefore not surprising that Foucault recognises close parallels between Augustine and Cicero. As Paul Mackendrick points out: 'Augustine was thunderstruck by the *Hortensius*, and he came to see, not only that Cicero's rhetoric led to his philosophy, but that his philosophy led to something which, for Augustine, was infinitely greater.' P. MacKendrick, *The Philosophical Books of Cicero*, Duckworth, London, 1989, p. 113. Cf. MacKendrick's outline of the *Hortensius*, pp. 109–11. (I am grateful to my colleague Scott Matthews for the reference to MacKendrick's work.)

185

the existence of his own will depended entirely on the will of God. As a punishment of this revolt and as a consequence of this will to will independently from God, Adam lost control of himself. He wanted to acquire an autonomous will, and lost the ontological support for that will. That then became mixed in an indissociable way with involuntary movements, and this weakening of Adam's will had a disastrous effect. His body, and parts of his body, stopped obeying his commands, revolted against him, and the sexual parts of his body were the first to rise up in this disobedience. The famous gesture of Adam covering his genitals with a fig leaf is, according to Augustine, due not to the simple fact that Adam was ashamed of their presence but to the fact that his sexual organs were moving by themselves without his consent. Sex in erection is the image of man revolted against God. The arrogance of sex is the punishment and consequence of the arrogance of man. His uncontrolled sex is exactly the same as what he himself has been towards God – a rebel.

Why have I insisted so much on what may be nothing more than one of those exegetic fantasies of which Christian literature has been so prodigal? I think this text bears witness to the new type of relationship which Christianity established between sex and subjectivity. Augustine's conception is still dominated by the theme and form of male sexuality. But the main question is not, as it was in Artemidorus, the problem of penetration: it is the problem of erection. As a result, it is not the problem of a relationship to other people, but the problem of the relationship of oneself to oneself, or, more precisely, the relationship between one's will and involuntary assertions.

The principle of autonomous movements of sexual organs is called libido by Augustine. The problem of libido, of its strength, origin and effect, thus becomes the main issue of one's will. It is not in external obstacle to the will. It is a part, an internal component, of the will. And it is not the manifestation of petty desires. Libido is the result of one's will when it goes beyond the limits God originally set for it. As a consequence, the means of the spiritual struggle against libido do not consist, as with Plato, in turning our eyes upwards and memorising the reality we have previously known and forgotten. The struggle consists, on the contrary, in turning our eyes continuously downwards or inwards in order to decipher, among the movements of the soul, which ones come from the libido. The task is at first indefinite, since libido and will can never be substantially dissociated from one another. And this task is not only an issue of mastership but also a question of the diagnosis of truth and illusion. It requires a permanent hermeneutics of oneself.

In such a perspective, sexual ethics imply very strict truth obligations. These do not consist only in learning the rules of a moral sexual behaviour but also in constantly scrutinising ourselves as libidinal beings. Shall we say that after Augustine we experience our sex in the head? Let us say at least that in Augustine's analysis we witness a real libidinisation of sex. Augustine's moral theology is, to a certain extent, a systematisation of a lot of previous speculation, but it is also an ensemble of spiritual techniques. [The techniques were mainly developed in the ascetic milieu and monastic institutions, and those relayed by the Augustinian theory of libido had, I think, a huge influence on Western technologies of the self. I shall be very brief about those spiritual techniques.]

When one reads the ascetic and monastic literature of the fourth and fifth centuries, one cannot but be struck by the fact that these techniques are not directly concerned with the effective control of sexual behaviour. There is very little mention of homosexual relations, in spite of the fact that most ascetics lived in permanent and numerous communities. The techniques were mainly concerned with the stream of thoughts flowing into consciousness, disturbing, by their multiplicity, the necessary unity of contemplation, and secretly conveying images or suggestions from Satan. The monk's task was not the philosopher's task: to acquire mastership over oneself by the definite victory of the will. It was perpetually to control one's thoughts, examining them to see if they were pure, whether something dangerous was not hiding in or behind them, if they were not conveying something other than what primarily appeared, if they were not a form of illusion and seduction. Such data have always to be considered with suspicion; they need to be scrutinised and tested.

According to Cassian, for instance, one has to be towards oneself as a money changer who has to try the coins he receives. Real purity is not acquired when one can lie down with a young and beautiful boy without even touching him, as Socrates did with Alcibiades. A monk was really chaste when no impure image occurred in his mind, even during the night, even during dreams. The criterion of purity does not consist in keeping control of oneself even in the presence of the most desirable people: it consists in discovering the truth in myself and defeating the illusions in myself, in cutting out the images and thoughts my mind continuously produces.[9] Hence the axis of the spiritual struggle against impurity.

The main question of sexual ethics has moved from relations to people, and from the penetration model to the relation to oneself and to the erection problem: I mean the set of internal movements which develop from the first and nearly imperceptible thought to the final but still solitary pollution [, through those ascetic techniques, as through the Augustinian theology]. However different and eventually contradictory they were, a common effect was elicited. Sexuality, subjectivity and truth were strongly linked together. This, I think, is the religious framework in which the masturbation problem – which was nearly ignored or at least neglected by the Greeks, who considered that masturbation was a thing for slaves and for satyrs, but not for free citizens – appeared as one of the main issues of sexual life.[10]

[9] In the On Signs text 'myself' is written 'oneself' and reads: 'it consists in discovering the truth in oneself and defeating the illusions in oneself, in cutting out the images and thoughts one's mind produces continuously'. On Signs, p. 372.

[10] In the On Signs text the last phrase reads: 'in our society is one of the main issues of sexual life'. On Signs, p. 372.

CHAPTER FIFTEEN

The battle for chastity (1982)

Originally published as 'Le combat de la chasteté', *Communications*, no. 35: *Sexualités occidentales*, ed. Philippe Ariès and André Bejin, May 1982, pp. 15–25. It was originally presented as an extract from the forthcoming third volume of the *History of Sexuality* but is almost certainly part of the unpublished fourth volume, *Les aveux de la chair (Confessions of the Flesh)*. This translation originally appeared in *Western Sexuality*, ed. Ariès and Bejin, Oxford, Basil Blackwell, 1985.

Translated by Anthony Forster

The battle for chastity is discussed in detail by Cassian in the sixth chapter of the *Institutiones*, 'Concerning the spirit of fornication', and in several of his *Conferences*: the fourth on 'the lusts of the flesh and of the spirit', the fifth on 'the eight principal vices', the twelfth on 'chastity' and the twenty-second on 'night visions'. It ranks second in a list of eight battles,[1] in the shape of a fight against the spirit of fornication. As for fornication itself it is subdivided into three categories.[2] On the face of it a very unjuridical list if one compares it with the catalogue of sins that are to be found when the medieval church organises the sacrament of penance on the lines of a penal code. But Cassian's specifications obviously have a different meaning.

Let us first examine the place of fornication among the other sinful tendencies. Cassian arranges his eight sins in a particular order. He sets up pairs of vices that seem linked in some specifically close way:[3] pride and vainglory, sloth and accidie, avarice and wrath. Fornication is coupled with greed, for several reasons. They are two 'natural' vices, innate and hence very difficult to cure. They are also the two vices that involve the participation of the body, not only in their growth but also in achieving their object; and finally they also have a direct causal connection – over-indulgence in food and drink fuels the urge to commit fornication.[4] In addition, the spirit of fornication occupies a position of peculiar importance among the other vices, either

---

[1] The seven others are greed, avarice, wrath, sloth, accidie, vainglory and pride.

[2] See below, note 17.

[3] *Conferences*, V, 10. [For this and the other texts see *A Selected Library of Nicene and Post-Nicene Fathers*, ed. Phillip Schaff, vol. II, Eerdmans, Grand Rapids, Michigan, 1973.]

[4] *Institutions*, V and *Conferences*, V.

because it is closely bound with greed or simply by its very nature.

First the causal chain. Cassian emphasises the fact that the vices do not exist in isolation, even though an individual may be particularly affected by one vice or another.[5] There is a causal link that binds them all together. It begins with greed, which arises in the body and inflames the spirit of fornication: these two engender avarice, understood as an attachment to worldly wealth, which in turn leads to rivalries, quarrelling and wrath. The result is despondency and sorrow, provoking the sin of accidie and total disgust with monastic life. Such a progression implies that one will never be able to conquer a vice unless one can conquer the one on which it leans: 'The defeat of the first weakens the one that depends on it; victory over the former leads to the collapse of the latter without further effort.' Like the others, the greed–fornication pair, like 'a huge tree whose shadow stretches afar', has to be uprooted. Hence the importance for the ascetic of fasting as a way of conquering greed and suppressing fornication. Therein lies the basis of the practice of asceticism, for it is the first link in the causal chain.

The spirit of fornication is seen as being in an odd relationship to the last vices on the list, and especially pride. In fact, for Cassian, pride and vainglory do not form part of the causal chain of other vices. Far from being generated by them they result from victory over them:[6] 'carnal pride', i.e. flaunting one's fasts, one's chastity, one's poverty etc. before other people, and 'spiritual pride', which makes one think that one's progress is all due to one's own merits.[7] One vice that springs from the defeat of another means a fall that is that much greater. And fornication, the most disgraceful of all the vices, the one that is most shameful, is the consequence of pride – a chastisement, but also a temptation, the proof that God sends to the presumptuous mortal to remind him that he is always threatened by the weakness of the flesh if the grace of God does not come to his help. 'Because someone has for long exulted in the pureness of his heart and his body, it naturally follows ... that in the back of his mind he rather prides himself on it ... so it is a good thing for the Lord to desert him, for his own good. The pureness which has been making him so self-assured begins to worry him, and in the midst of his spiritual well-being he finds himself faltering.'[8] When the soul has only itself to combat, the wheel comes full circle, the battle begins again and the prickings of the flesh are felt anew, showing the inevitable continuance of the struggle and the threat of a perpetual recurrence.

Finally, fornication has, as compared with other vices, an ontological particularity which gives it a special ascetic importance. Like greed it is rooted in the body, and impossible to beat without chastisement. While wrath or despondency can be fought only in the mind, fornication cannot be eradicated without 'mortifying the flesh, by vigils, fasts and back-breaking labour'.[9] This still does not exclude the battle the mind

---

[5] Conferences, V, 13–14.

[6] Conferences, V, 10.

[7] Institutions, XII, 2.

[8] Conferences, XII, 6. For examples of lapses into pride and presumptuousness, see Conferences, II, 13; and especially Institutions, XII, 20 and 21, where offences against humility are punished by the most humiliating temptatio, that of a desire contra usum naturae.

[9] Conferences, V, 4.

has to wage against itself, since fornication may be born of thoughts, images and memories. 'When the Devil, with subtle cunning, has insinuated into our hearts the memory of a woman, beginning with our mother, our sisters, or certain pious women, we should as quickly as possible expel these memories for fear that, if we linger on them too long, the tempter may seize the opportunity to lead us unwittingly to think about other women.'[10] Nevertheless there is one fundamental difference between fornication and greed. The fight against the latter has to be carried on with a certain restraint, since one cannot give up all food: 'The requirements of life have to be provided for ... for fear lest the body, deprived through our own error, may lose the strength to carry out the necessary spiritual exercises.'[11] This natural propensity for eating has to be kept at arm's length, treated unemotionally, but not abolished. It has its own legitimacy; to repudiate it totally, that is to say to the point of death, would be to burden one's soul with a crime. On the other hand there are no holds barred in the fight against the spirit of fornication; everything that can direct our steps to it must be eradicated and no call of nature can be allowed to justify the satisfaction of a need in his domain. This is an appetite whose suppression does not lead to our bodily death, and it has to be totally eradicated. Of the eight sins fornication is the only one which is at once innate, natural, physical in origin and needing to be as totally destroyed as the vices of the soul, such as avarice and pride. There has to be severe mortification therefore, which lets us live in our bodies while releasing us from the flesh. 'Depart from this flesh while living in the body.'[12] It is into this region beyond nature, but in our earthly lives, that the fight against fornication leads us. It 'drags us from the slough of the earth'. It causes us to live in this world a life which is not of this world. Because this mortification is the harshest, it promises the most to us in this world below: 'rooted in the flesh', it offers 'the citizenship which the saints have the promise of possessing once they are delivered from the corruption of the flesh'.[13]

Thus one sees how fornication, although just one of the elements in the table of vices, has its own special position, heading the causal chain, and is the sin chiefly responsible for backsliding and spiritual turmoil, at one of the most difficult and decisive points in the struggle for an ascetic life.

In his fifth *Conference* Cassian divides fornication into three varieties. The first consists of the 'joining together of the two sexes' (*commixtio sexus utriusque*); the second takes place 'without contact with the woman' (*absque femineo tactu*) – the damnable sin of Onan; the third is 'conceived in the mind and the thoughts'.[14] Almost the same distinction is repeated in the twelfth *Conference*: 'carnal conjunction' (*carnalis commixtio*), which Cassian calls *fornicatio* in its restricted sense; next uncleanness, *immunditia*, which takes place without contact with a woman, while one is either sleeping or awake, and which is due to 'the negligence of an unwatchful mind'; finally there is libido, which develops in 'the dark corners of the soul' without 'physical passion' (*sine passione*

[10] *Institutions*, VI, 13.
[11] *Institutions*, V, 8.
[12] *Institutions*, VI, 6.
[13] *Institutions*, VI, 6.
[14] *Conferences*, V, 11.

corporis).[15] These distinctions are important, for they alone help one to understand what Cassian meant by the general term *fornicatio*, to which he gives no definition elsewhere. But they are particularly important for the way he uses these three categories – in a way that differs so much from what one finds in earlier texts.

There already existed a traditional trilogy of the sins of the flesh: adultery, fornication (meaning sexual relations outside marriage) and 'the corruption of children'. At least these are the three categories to be found in the *Didache*: 'Thou shalt not commit adultery; thou shalt not commit fornication; thou shalt not seduce young boys.'[16] And these are what we find in the 'Epistle of St Barnabas': 'Do not commit fornication or adultery; do not corrupt the young.'[17] We often find later that only the first two precepts are imposed, fornication covering all sexual offences, and adultery covering those which infringe the marriage vows.[18] But in any case these were habitually accompanied by precepts about covetousness in thought or sight or anything that might lead one to commit a forbidden sexual act: 'Refrain from covetousness, for it leads to fornication; abstain from obscene talk and brazen looks, for all this sort of thing leads to adultery.'[19]

Cassian's analysis has two special features: one is that he does not deal separately with adultery but places it with fornication in its limited sense, and the other is that he devotes attention mostly to the other two categories. Nowhere in the various texts in which he speaks of the battle for chastity does he refer to actual sexual relations. Nowhere are the various sins set out dependent on actual sexual relations – the partner with whom it was committed, his or her age or possible degree of consanguinity. Not one of the categories that in the Middle Ages were to be built up into a great code of sins is to be found here. Doubtless Cassian, who was addressing an audience of monks who had taken vows to renounce all sexual relations, felt he could skip these preliminaries. One notices, however, that on one very important aspect of celibacy, where Basil of Caesarea and Chrysostom had given explicit advice,[20] Cassian does make discreet allusion: 'Let no one, especially when among young folk, remain alone with another, even for a short time, or withdraw with him or take him by the hand.'[21] He carries on his discussion as if he is interested only in his last two categories (about what goes on without sexual relationship or physical passion), as if he was passing over fornication as a physical union of two individuals and devoting

---

[15] *Conferences*, XII, 2.

[16] *Didache*, II, 2.

[17] *Epistle of St Barnabas*, XIX, 4. Earlier on, dealing with forbidden foods, the same text interprets the ban on eating hyena flesh as forbidding adultery, of hare as forbidding the seduction of children, of weasel as forbidding oral sex.

[18] For instance St Augustine, *Sermon*, 56.

[19] *Didache*, III, 3.

[20] Basil of Caesarea, *Exhortation to Renounce the World*, 5. 'Eschew all dealing, all relations with young men of your own age. Avoid them as you would fire. Many, alas, are those who through mixing with them, have been consigned by the Enemy to burn eternally in hell-fire.' Cf. the precautions laid down in *The Great Precepts* (34) and *The Short Precepts* (220). See also John Crysostom, *Adversus oppugnatores vitae monasticae*.

[21] *Institutions*, II, 15. Those who infringe this rule commit a grave offence and are under suspicion (*conjurationis pravique consilii*). Are these words hinting at amorous behaviour, or are they simply aimed at the danger of members of the same community showing particular favour to one another? Similar recommendations are to be found in *Institutions*, IV, 16.

serious attention only to behaviour which up till then had been severely censured only when leading up to real sexual acts.

But even though Cassian's analysis ignores physical sex, and its sphere of action is quite solitary and secluded, his reasoning is not purely negative. The whole essence of the fight for chastity is that it aims at a target which has nothing to do with actions or relationships; it concerns a different reality to that of a sexual connection between two individuals. A passage in the twelfth Conference reveals the nature of this reality. In it Cassian describes the six stages that mark the advance towards chastity. The object of the description is not to define chastity itself, but to pick out the negative signs by which one can trace progress towards it – the various signs of impurity which disappear one by one – and so get an idea of what one has to contend with in the fight for chastity.

First sign of progress: when the monk awakes he is not 'smitten by a carnal impulse' – impugnatione carnali non eliditur, i.e. the mind is no longer troubled by physical reactions over which the will has no control.

Second stage: if 'voluptuous thoughts' (voluptariae cogitationes) should arise in the monk's mind, he does not let it dwell on them. He can stop thinking about things that have arisen in his mind involuntarily and in spite of himself.[22]

Third stage: when a glimpse of the world outside can no longer arouse lustful feelings, and one can look upon a woman without any feeling of desire.

Fourth stage: one no longer on one's waking hours feels any, even the most innocent, movement of the flesh. Does Cassian mean that there is no movement of the flesh, and that therefore one has total control over one's own body? Probably not, since elsewhere he often insists on the persistence of involuntary bodily movements. The term he uses, perferre, signifies no doubt that such movements are not capable of affecting the mind, which thus does not suffer from them.

Fifth stage: 'If the subject of a discourse or the logical consequence of a reading involves the idea of human procreation, the mind does not allow itself to be touched by the remotest thought of sexual pleasure, but contemplates the act in a mood of calmness and purity, as a simple function, a necessary adjunct to the prolongation of the human race, and departs no more affected by the recollection of it than if it had been thinking about brickmaking or some other trade.'

Finally, the last stage is reached when our sleep is not troubled by the vision of a seductive woman. Even though we may not think it a sin to be subject to such illusions, it is however a sign that some lustful feeling still lurks in the depths of our being.[23]

Amid all this description of the different symptoms of fornication, gradually fading out as one approaches the state of chastity, there is no mention of relationships with others, no acts, not even any intention of committing one. In fact there is no fornication in the strict sense of the word. This microcosm of the solitary life lacks the two major elements on which are centred the sexual ethics not only of the philosophers of the ancient world, but also of a Christian like Clement of Alexandria (at

---

[22] The word used by Cassian for dwelling on such thoughts is immorari. Later, delectatio morosa has an important place in the medieval sexual ethic.

[23] Conferences, XII, 7.

least in Epistle II of his *Pedagogus*), namely the sexual union of two individuals (*sunousia*) and the pleasure of the act (*aphrodisia*). Cassian is interested in the movements of the body and the mind, images, feelings, memories, faces in dreams, the spontaneous movements of thoughts, the consenting (or refusing) will, waking and sleeping. Now two opposing poles appear, not, one has to realise, those of mind versus body. They are, first, the involuntary pole, which consists either of physical movements or of feelings evoked by memories and images that survive from the past and ferment in the mind, besieging and enticing the will, and, second, the pole of the will itself, which accepts or repels, averts its eyes or allows itself to be ensnared, holds back or consents. On the one side then bodily and mental reflexes that bypass the mind and, becoming infected with impurity, may proceed to corruption, and on the other side an internal play of thoughts. Here we find the two kinds of 'fornication' as broadly defined by Cassian, to which he confines the whole of his analysis, leaving aside the question of physical sex. His theme is *immunditia*, something which catches the mind, waking or sleeping, off its guard and can lead to pollution, without any contact with another; and the *libido*, which develops in the dark comers of the mind. In this connection Cassian reminds us that *libido* has the same origin as *libet* (it pleases).[24]

The spiritual battle and the advance towards chastity, whose six stages are described by Cassian, can thus be seen as a task of dissociation. We are now far away from the rationing of pleasure and its strict limitation to permissible actions; far away too from the idea of as drastic a separation as possible between mind and body. But what does concern us is a never-ending struggle over the movements of our thoughts (whether they extend or reflect those of our body, or whether they motivate them), over its simplest manifestations, over the factors that can activate it. The aim is that the subject should never be affected in his effort by the obscurest or the most seemingly 'unwilled' presence of will. The six stages that lead to chastity represent steps towards the disinvolvement of the will. The first step is to exclude its involvement in bodily reactions; then exclude it from the imagination (not to linger on what crops up in one's mind); then exclude it from the action of the senses (cease to be conscious of bodily movements); then exclude it from figurative involvement (cease to think of things as possible objects of desire); and finally from oneiric involvement (the desires that may be stirred by images that appear, albeit spontaneously, in dreams). This sort of involvement, of which the wilful act or the explicit will to commit an act are the most visible form, Cassian calls *concupiscence*. This is the enemy in the spiritual battle, and this is the effort of dissociation and disinvolvement that has to be made.

Here is the reason why, all through this battle against the spirit of fornication and for chastity, the sole fundamental problem is that of pollution – whether as something that is subservient to the will and a possible form of self-indulgence or as something happening spontaneously and involuntarily in sleep or dreams. So important is this that Cassian makes the absence of erotic dreams and nocturnal pollution a sign that one has reached the pinnacle of chastity. He often returns to this topic: 'The proof that one has achieved this state of purity will be that no apparition will beguile us when resting or stretched out in sleep',[25] or again 'This is the sum of integrity and the final proof: that we are not visited by voluptuous thoughts during sleep and that we should be unaware of the pollutions to which we are subjected by nature.'[26] The whole of the twenty-second *Conference* is devoted to the question of 'nocturnal pollutions' and 'the necessity of using all our strength to be delivered from them'. And on various occasions Cassian calls to mind holy characters like Serenus, who had attained such a high degree of virtue that they were never troubled by inconveniences of this kind.[27]

Obviously, in a rule of life where renunciation of all sexual relations was absolutely basic, it was quite logical that this topic should assume such importance. One is reminded of the importance, in groups inspired by Pythagorean ideas, accorded to the phenomena of sleep and dreams for what they reveal about the quality of existence, and to the self-purification that was supposed to guarantee its serenity. Above all one must realise that nocturnal pollution raised problems where ritual purity was concerned, and it was precisely these problems which prompted the twenty-second *Conference*: can one draw near to the 'holy altars' and partake of the bread and wine when one has suffered nocturnal defilement?[28] But even if all these reasons can explain such preoccupations among the theoreticians of monastic life, they cannot account for the absolutely central position occupied by the question of voluntary or involuntary pollution in the whole discussion of the battle for chastity. Pollution was not simply the object of a stricter ban than anything else, or harder to control. It was a yardstick of concupiscence in that it helped to decide – in the light of what formed its background, initiated it and finally unleashed it – the part played by the will in forming these images, feelings and memories in the mind. The monk concentrates his whole energy on never letting his will be involved in this reaction, which goes from the body to the mind and from the mind to the body, and over which the will may have a hold, either to encourage it or halt it through mental activity. The first five stages of the advance towards chastity constitute increasingly subtle disengagements of the will from the increasingly restricted reactions that may bring on this pollution.

There remains the final stage, attainable by holiness: absence of 'absolutely' involuntary pollutions during sleep. Again Cassian points out that these pollutions are not necessarily all involuntary. Over-eating and impure thoughts during the day all show that one is willing, if not intending, to have them. He makes a distinction between the type of dream that accompanies them and the degree of impurity of the images. Anyone who is taken by surprise would be wrong to blame his body or sleep: 'It is a sign of the corruption that festers within, and not just a product of the night. Buried in the depth of the soul, the corruption has come to the surface during sleep, revealing the hidden fever of passions with which we have become infected by glutting ourselves all day long on unhealthy emotions.'[29] Finally there is the pollution that is totally involuntary, devoid of the pleasure that implies consent, without even

---

[25] *Institutions*, VI, 10.

[26] *Institutions*, VI, 20.

[27] *Conferences*, VII, 1. XII, 7. Other allusions to this theme in *Institutions*, II, 13.

[28] *Conferences*, XXII, 5.

[29] *Institutions*, VI, 11.

the slightest trace of a dream image. Doubtless this is the goal attainable by the ascetic who has practised with sufficient rigour; the pollution is only a 'residue', in which the person concerned plays no part. 'We have to repress the reactions of our minds and the emotions of our bodies until the flesh can satisfy the demands of nature without giving rise to any pleasurable feelings, getting rid of the excess of our bodily humours without any unhealthy urges and without having to plunge back into the battle for our chastity.'[30] Since this is a supra-natural phenomenon, only a supra-natural power can give us this freedom, spiritual grace. This is why non-pollution is the sign of holiness, the stamp of the highest chastity possible, a blessing one may hope for but not attain.

For his part man must do no less than keep ceaseless watch over his thoughts and bodily movements day and night – during the night for the benefit of the day and during the day in thinking of the approaching night. 'As purity and vigilance during the day dispose one to be chaste during the night, so too nocturnal vigilance replenishes the strength of the heart to observe chastity during the day.'[31] This vigilance means exerting the sort of 'discrimination' that lies at the heart of the self-analysis developed in active spirituality. The work of the miller sorting out his grain, the centurion picking his troops, the money changer who weighs coins before accepting or refusing them – this is how the monk must unceasingly treat his own thoughts, so as to identify those that may bring temptation. Such an effort will allow him to sort out his thoughts according to their origin, to distinguish them by their quality and to separate the objects they represent from the pleasure they can evoke. This is an endless task of analysis that one has to apply to oneself and, by the duty of confession, to our relations with others.[32] Neither the idea of the inseparability of chastity and 'fornication' affirmed by Cassian, nor the way in which he analyses them, nor the different elements that, according to him, inhere in them, nor the connections he establishes between them – pollution, libido, concupiscence – can be understood without reference to the techniques of self-analysis which characterise monastic life and the spiritual battle that is fought across it.

Do we find that, between Tertullian and Cassian, prohibitions have been intensified, an even greater importance attached to absolute continence, and the sexual act increasingly stigmatised? Whatever the answer, this is not the way the question should be framed. The organisation of monasticism and the dimorphism that developed between monastic and secular life brought about important changes in the problem of sexual renunciation. They brought with them the development of very complex techniques of self-analysis. So, in the very manner in which sex was renounced there appeared a rule of life and a mode of analysis which, in spite of obvious continuities,

---

[30] Institutions, VI, 22.

[31] Institutions, VI, 23.

[32] Cf. in the twenty-second *Conferences* (6) the case of a consultation over a monk, who each time he was going to communion suffered a nocturnal visitation and dared not participate in the holy mysteries. The 'spiritual physicians' after an interrogation and discussions diagnosed that it was the Devil who sent these visitations so as to prevent the monk from attending the desired communion. To abstain was to fall into the Devil's trap; to communicate in spite of everything was to defeat him. Once this decision had been taken the Devil appeared no more.

showed important differences with the past. With Tertullian the state of virginity implied the external and internal posture of one who has renounced the world and has adopted the rules governing appearance, behaviour and general conduct that this renunciation involves. In the mystique of virginity which developed after the thirteenth century the rigour of this renunciation (in line with the theme, already found in Tertullian, of union with Christ) transforms the negative aspect of continence into the promise of spiritual marriage. With Cassian, who describes rather than innovates, there occurs a sort of double action, a withdrawal that also reveals hidden depths within.

This has nothing to do with the internalisation of a whole list of forbidden things, merely substituting the prohibition of the intention for that of the act itself. It is rather the opening up of an area (whose importance has already been stressed by the writings of Gregory of Nyssa and, especially, of Basil of Ancyra) which is that of thought, operating erratically and spontaneously, with its images, memories and perceptions, with movements and impressions transmitted from the body to the mind and the mind to the body. This has nothing to do with a code of permitted or forbidden actions, but is a whole technique for analysing and diagnosing thought, its origins, its qualities, its dangers, its potential for temptation and all the dark forces that can lurk behind the mask it may assume. Given the objective of expelling for good everything impure or conducive to impurity, this can be achieved only by eternal vigilance, a suspiciousness directed every moment against one's thought, an endless self-questioning to flush out any secret fornication lurking in the inmost recesses of the mind.

In this chastity-oriented asceticism one can see a process of 'subjectivisation' which has nothing to do with a sexual ethic based on physical self-control. But two things stand out. This subjectivisation is linked with a process of self-knowledge which makes the obligation to seek and state the truth about oneself an indispensable and permanent condition of this asceticism; and, if there is subjectivisation, it also involves an indeterminate objectivisation of the self by the self-indeterminate in the sense that one must be forever extending as far as possible the range of one's thoughts, however insignificant and innocent they may appear to be. Moreover, this subjectivisation, in its quest for the truth about oneself, functions through complex relations with others, and in many ways. One has to rid oneself of the power of the Other, the Enemy, who hides behind seeming likenesses of oneself, and eternal warfare has to be waged against this Other, which one cannot win without the help of the Almighty, who is mightier than he. Finally, confession to others, submission to their advice and permanent obedience to one's superiors are essential in this battle.

These new fashions in monastic sexual mores, the build-up of a new relationship between the subject and the truth and the establishment of complex relations of obedience to the other self all form part of a whole whose coherence is well illustrated in Cassian's text. No new point of departure is involved. Going back in time before Christianity, one may find many of these elements in embryonic form and sometimes fully shaped in ancient philosophy – Stoic or Neo-Platonic, for instance. Moreover Cassian himself presents in a systematic way (how far he makes his own contribution is another question which need not concern us here) a sum of experience which he asserts to be that of Eastern monasticism. In any case, study of a text of this kind shows that it hardly makes sense to talk about a 'Christian sexual ethic', still less about a 'Judaeo-Christian' one. So far as consideration of sexual behaviour was concerned, some fairly involved thinking went on between the Hellenistic period and St Augustine. Certain important events stand out such as the guidelines for conscience laid down by the Stoics and the Cynics, the organisation of monasticism and many others. On the other hand the coming of Christianity, considered as a massive rupture with earlier moralities and the dominant introduction of a quite different one, is barely noticeable. As P. Brown says, in speaking of Christianity as part of our reading of the giant mass of antiquity, the topography of the parting of the waters is hard to pin down.

'I am not what I am' – Foucault, Christian asceticism and a 'way out' of sexuality

Mark Vernon

On 11 October 1979 Michel Foucault was in Palo Alto, California, to deliver the Tanner Lectures on Human Values at Stanford University. One of the discussions he had during that day survives on tape and records Foucault enjoying a rich intellectual exchange with his interlocutors.[1] During the conversation he recalled an encounter that happened to him earlier in the afternoon. The encounter struck him very deeply, particularly in the light of his own questioning of the construction of sexuality.

Foucault explained how he had been talking to a group of students following a seminar; several of them had lingered until finally he was left with one and they walked out across the campus. After some minutes the student, clearly unsettled by the prolonged attention of the master, turned and asked him why he remained with him. He wanted to know if it was for homosexual reasons. Foucault was surprised. The young man was certainly beautiful, as well as bright, but sex for the student had raised itself early and uncomfortably. It seemed impossible to appreciate this fortuitous meeting simply for itself without posing the anxious question of whether or not they would go to bed together. Foucault saw the incident as a symbol of the alienation caused by sexuality.

In his introductory essay, Jeremy Carrette speculates as to whether Foucault's *History of Sexuality* represents a long struggle to overcome the oppression of Christianity in the emergent regimes of sexuality. In this postscript I want to reflect on how the 'Christian' fragments of Foucault's work may provide a way of reimagining Foucault's personal and academic project by relating them to the contemporary problematic of gayness amongst men.[2] In short, what I want to argue is that the phenomenon of male homosexuality is indeed, as Foucault put it, an historic occasion to re-open affective possibilities for human relationships, though precisely not as a call for gay men to 'come out', nor as another exposé of the strategies of homophobia, rather it is an

---

[1] 'Discussion at Stanford': 11 October 1979, C9*, Foucault Archive, Paris.

[2] I am here addressing male homosexuality but this is not to say that what is explored is not applicable to female homosexuality or other sexual relationships. As Foucault commented: 'One would have to speak about the different pressures experienced by men and women who are coming out or are trying to make a life for themselves as homosexual' (Foucault [1982], 'Sexual choice, sexual act' in *Foucault Live: Collected Interviews, 1961–1984*, 2nd edition, ed. S. Lotringer, Semiotext(e), New York, [1989], 1996, p. 325). It is also important to recognise that Foucault's work on Christianity is concerned principally with male monastic experience.

attempt to explore an attitude that is awakened to a 'way out' of certain construals of sexuality. What I am seeking to develop is an ethos of creative renunciation, which Foucault derived from certain Christian practices, and a spirituality of relationships in which to locate these ideas. My goal is to follow just one trajectory from the richness of Foucault's work on Christianity in order to unfold some new elements for the study of homosexuality and contribute to the reinvigoration of the neglected and sentimentalised theme of friendship.

If we have to speculate after his death, or rather struggle with his legacy, his 'force of flight' as Bernauer described it, then we are in a predicament not unknown to those who knew Foucault during his life. Foucault was frequently elusive, both in his personal life and in his academic work, to say nothing of the connection between the two. When it came to his sexuality, Foucault's refusal to 'come out' even provoked outrage, though it was widely known that he had homosexual relationships, notably with Daniel Defert, his partner of some twenty-five years. David Macey, one of Foucault's biographers, notes that some of the most vicious personal remarks are found in the context of sustained criticism of Foucault's alleged privileging of discourse over lived experience and it was the similar charge of hypocrisy that led others to public outbursts of anger too.[3]

Foucault's own reticence about being 'gay identified' was not for reasons of fear or self-loathing. There is no doubt that in his earlier life he had to struggle with the implications of his sexual desire. In the 1960s and 1970s France could be a dangerous place for men who pursued a lifestyle that included homosexual relationships, symbolised most powerfully in the famous Miguet amendment (1960) which committed the government to 'combating' homosexuality. But there are also signs that Foucault was reconciled to his sexuality from a relatively young age, as were his family and friends. He, for example, admitted on a number of occasions that choosing to study the normalising power of psychiatry and sexuality had its roots in his own life and experience.[4] So why did he not just 'come out', be done with it and put everyone's mind at rest? Was Foucault being not so much personally reserved as deliberately obscurantist?

Foucault's reticence is actually a resistance to what he called the 'austere monarchy of sex'. In the first volume of The History of Sexuality, illuminatingly subtitled in the French edition La volontè de savoir (The Will to Know), he had explored the idea that the exercise of power through sexuality was increasing under an apparent freedom – the guise of liberation from the so-called repressive Victorians. 'For a long time, the story goes, we supported a Victorian regime, and we continue to be dominated by it even today.'[5] The real problem was actually an expansion of control, in the form of a pursuit of a privileged knowledge of people focused on their sexuality. Foucault gave a

[3] D. Macey, The Lives of Michel Foucault, Vintage, New York, 1995, p. 477 (British edition: Hutchison, London, 1993).

[4] Or, as Foucault put it, 'to become someone else that you were not at the beginning'. Cited in Macey, The Lives of Michel Foucault, p. xiv.

[5] Foucault [1976], The History of Sexuality, Volume One: An Introduction, Penguin, London, 1990, p. 3 (American edition: Pantheon, New York, 1978).

graphic account of the effect of this development in the life of the nineteenth-century hermaphrodite Herculine Barbin.[6] Up to the age of twenty Barbin lived as a woman with a respected place as a teacher in her village but committed suicide following the intervention of the French courts in 1860 which changed her gender status to that of a man.

The reach of this disciplinary regime of sexuality, and the difficulty of addressing it, is demonstrated in both the attitude of Foucault's fiercest critics and the anxiety of the beautiful Californian student with which we began. It is also embedded in the ideology of various gay movements, where the story of the repression of sexuality continues accompanied by the imperative to liberate one's sexuality. Even in the more sophisticated gay discourses that acknowledge the constructed nature of sexuality we still find the command to 'come out', or indeed be 'outed'. Peter Tatchell, the driving force behind the British activist group Outrage, for example, employs a logic which says that it is by overexposing men as gay, wherever they may be found, that the discourse of homosexuality can be exhausted and the ultimate emancipation, the eradication of the homosexual, be achieved.[7] But the demand to 'come out' produces apprehension not only in those who might be accused of being undercover homosexuals but also in those whose life is overtly gay. By way of illustration, Foucault tells of another meeting with a beautiful Californian youth, this time in Europe in 1983, which was again very striking to him.[8] As he told his interlocutors on this occasion, he remembered it well, not only because this was a wonderful young man and incredibly beautiful but because he told Foucault that he had a compulsive sexual problem. He did not know when to stop having sex and why he should stop. The young man felt he had to stop but did not know what he could do! Here again, the connection between the experience of sex and liberation is problematic even for those who 'come out'.

Foucault's challenge to the various manifestations of this predicament is subtle and often misunderstood. It can however be summed up succinctly. The aim should be not to liberate one's sexuality but to be liberated from sexuality. Or to put it differently, the point is not to 'come out', but to find a 'way out' of sexuality. Foucault is not against liberation or sex. What he challenges is the discourses which shape, control and determine our pleasures.

In his essay 'What is Enlightenment?' Foucault picks up on Kant's persistent question. He notes that Kant understands *Aufklärung* in a negative way, as an *Ausgang*. 'Kant indicates right away that the "way out" that characterises Enlightenment is a process that releases us from the status of "immaturity".'[9] Kant's formalist conception of immaturity, the subjugation of reason, is different from that of the Nietzschean

[6] Foucault, *Herculine Barbin, Being the Recently Discovered Memoirs of a Nineteenth-century Hermaphrodite*, trans. R. McDougall, Pantheon, New York, 1980.

[7] P. Tatchell, 'It's just a phase: why homosexuality is doomed', in M. Simpson, *Anti-gay*, Cassell, London, 1996, p. 35.

[8] 'Discussion with Michel Foucault': 15 April 1983, C27*, Foucault Archive, Paris.

[9] Foucault [1984], 'What is Enlightenment?' in *The Foucault Reader*, ed. P. Rabinow, Penguin, London and New York, 1991, p. 34.

Foucault, but this is not to say that Enlightenment has little real interest for Foucault. Indeed, Christopher Norris concludes that it is pivotal to Foucault's work. 'There was no question more central to the evolving project of Foucault's life and work than the one taken up in Kant's inaugural essay on the theme "What is Enlightenment?".'[10] The mistake is in failing to understand Foucault's perception of Enlightenment correctly, as a 'way out' of certain categories and forms of knowledge, including sexuality.

Foucault interprets Kant's question as stemming from a recognition that a point of departure has been reached. It gives 'the outline of what one might call the attitude of modernity'.[11] This attitude, which is close to the Greek term *ethos* explored in Foucault's later works, is 'a mode of relating to contemporary reality; a voluntary choice made by certain people; in the end, a way of thinking and feeling; a way, too, of acting and behaving that at one and the same time marks a relation of belonging and presents itself as a task'.[12] This attitude relates fundamentally to what Bernauer and Mahon called Foucault's 'politics of ourselves'.[13] It presents an ethical framework for the relationship of oneself to one's self, where the possessive pronoun indicates that complex of social and cultural factors which constitute identity.

Foucault continues his revision of the traditional conception of the Enlightenment project by further elaborating the idea of a 'way out'. He describes it as 'an indispensable asceticism ... to take oneself as an object of complex and difficult elaboration'.[14] Such a task, as Foucault's work on Christianity makes clear, required treating the self as an 'obscure text' needing to be worked upon.[15] The struggle is to overcome the 'blackmail' of the Enlightenment, the way in which it has constructed inescapable domains of analysis, notably sexuality. Modern man, therefore, must exercise his ascetic attitude as a permanent critique of himself. It is in this resistance that release might be found, since modern man 'is not the man who goes off to discover himself, his secrets and his hidden truth; he is the man who tries to invent himself. This modernity does not "liberate man in his own being"; it compels him to face the task of producing himself.'[16] Indeed, it is clear from later suggestions that in relation to sexuality Foucault believes the development of an aesthetical ethics such as this may be the only alternative to the choice of either repression or liberation as traditionally conceived.[17] More is required than a 'gesture of rejection ... to move beyond the outside–inside alternative; we have to be at the frontiers'.[18] Foucault diagnoses the problem as precisely one of a lack of new ethics or even the principles from which to elaborate it.

[10] C. Norris, '"What is enlightenment?": Kant and Foucault' in *The Cambridge Companion to Michel Foucault*, ed. G. Cutting, Cambridge University Press, Cambridge, 1994, p. 194.
[11] Foucault [1984], 'What is Enlightenment?', p. 38.
[12] Foucault [1984], 'What is Enlightenment?', p. 39.
[13] J. Bernauer and M. Mahon, 'The ethics of Michel Foucault' in *The Cambridge Companion to Foucault*, p. 147.
[14] Foucault [1984], 'What is Enlightenment?', p. 41.
[15] J. Bernauer, *Michel Foucault's Force of Flight: Toward an Ethics for Thought*, Humanities Press, Atlantic Highlands, New Jersey, 1990, p. 164.
[16] Foucault [1984], 'What is Enlightenment?', p. 42.
[17] 'Entretien de Berkeley sur l'esthétique de l'existence': D250 (11)*, 26 April 1983, Foucault Archive, Paris.
[18] Foucault [1984], 'What is Enlightenment?', p. 45.

At the end of his essay on the Enlightenment, Foucault notes that the philosophical attitude of a 'way out' must be applied to a wide range of issues. It was undoubtedly such an attitude that led Foucault to Christianity. In what was perhaps a surprising shift Foucault turned to the texts of the early church as a 'way out' of sexuality.

Foucault's theological approach to the problem of sexuality was informed by his study of certain Patristic writers, notably Augustine and Cassian. This work suggests a 'way out' of the discourse of sexuality by exploring their hermeneutics of the self, beginning with an intriguing alliance between Foucault and Augustine concerning sexual desire. For Augustine the loss of control of parts of the body, notably in involuntary response to sexual desire, is the supreme reminder to man of his disobedience in the garden of Eden. 'Sex in erection is the image of man revolted against God. The sexual parts of his body were the first to rise up in this disobedience.'[19] The title of his great work of praise to God, Confessions, simultaneously connotes the necessary response of the Christian to the rising phallus, that is penitence. Ironically then, it is over this confessional response to sexual desire that Foucault locates his interest in Augustine, since for both their ethic required a constant suspicion of the sexual self.[20]

Foucault's analysis of what he regarded as the paradoxical practice of Christian confession is central in this respect. 'Everyone in Christianity has to explore who he is, what is happening within himself, the faults he may have committed, the temptations to which he is exposed. Moreover everyone is obliged to tell these things to other people, and hence bear witness against himself.'[21] It is in this simultaneous process of truth-telling and renunciation that the Christian can attain to the perfection that is in Christ. 'That is what we could call the spiral of truth formation and reality renouncement which is at the heart of Christian techniques of the self.'[22]

At the heart of Foucault's understanding of the Christian hermeneutic of the self is a loss which makes for transformation. He who loses his life gains it, or as Bernauer pointed out: 'All truth about the self is tied to the sacrifice of that same self and the Christian experience of subjectivity declares itself most clearly in the sounds of a rupture with oneself, of an admission that "I am not who I am".'[23] 'I am not who I am' is not only the historical declaration of the neophyte emerging from the waters of death in baptism to new life, but is the core text of a contemporary Foucauldian ethic. But the Christian calling leads along the narrow path and, as Foucault realised, confession could also become an oppressive regime which makes individuals subject to authority.[24] Truth formation is replaced by the imposition of a 'truth' which rather than renouncing reality fixes on the essentialist question of what one is. In discourses about sexuality in modernity, Foucault called this reification of identities 'scientia

---

[19] Foucault, 'Sexuality and solitude' in this volume, p.186.

[20] The point of contact between contemporary philosophy and the Christian suspicion of the self has recently been explored by Alistair MacIntyre in the 1998 John Coffin Memorial Lecture at the University of London, entitled, 'What has Christianity to say to the moral philosopher?'

[21] 'Sexuality and solitude', pp.182–3.

[22] 'Sexuality and solitude', p.183.

[23] Bernauer, Michel Foucault's Force of Flight, p. 165.

[24] See Foucault, 'Sexuality and power', trans. R. A. Lynch, in this volume, pp.115–30.

sexualis', as opposed to the creative 'ars erotica'.[25] Self-renunciation becomes self-abasement, as Nietzsche understood Christianity, so that the creation of the new self degenerates into the command to identify with a predetermined self. This is not a 'way out', but a 'coming out' – saying, 'I am what I am' – a tyranny in the guise of a freedom. When it comes to liberation from sexuality, those familiar with the famous call of Albert in *La cage aux folles* will spot the dissonance; or as Mark Simpson, who puts the humour back into the hermeneutics of suspicion, provocatively stated in his work *Anti-gay*:

The truth shall still set ye free. When one comes out, and ceases to be a private homosexual and becomes instead a public gay, the burden of deceit and false consciousness is thrown off, the sex police are vanquished and the out person demonstrates new-found whistle-blowing pride in sexuality instead of shame. It is a confessional narrative of sinner and saved. When a man comes out as gay he is coming out as what he was meant to be all along – he has found his true self, his existential soul, and rejected the sin/guilt of the previous, inauthentic, closeted self that thought baggy clothes were quite comfortable really.[26]

This reduction of confession to control, whether in religion as prohibitions or in culture as stereotypes, was recognised by Foucault as an important concern for another Christian father, the desert monastic Cassian. Foucault notes a great richness for the hermeneutic of the self in Cassian's relentless concern for the practice of confession in his monk's ascetic lifestyle,[27] revealed in Foucault's analysis of three interrelated practices.

First, Cassian desexualises the quest for chastity. For Cassian the issue for the solitary monk is not a matter of overcoming the temptation of sex acts with another person nor even the matter of sex acts conceived alone; Cassian has his sights set on a more profound eradication than the fantasies of onanism. Only when the monk does not even experience involuntary thoughts does he know he is blessed by God and only God. The monk might be able to control his thoughts but it is God that brings about the transformation which removes these thoughts entirely. In this respect the route to sanctification which Cassian charts attends not to the comparatively trivial matter of concupiscence but to the far greater task of embodying a spirituality of self-analysis. The result is that the struggle against carnal passions is characterised as essentially non-sexual. 'The work of the miller sorting out his grain, the centurion picking his troops, the moneychanger who weighs coins before accepting or refusing them – this is how the monk must unceasingly treat his own thoughts, so as to identify those that may bring temptation.'[28]

Desexualisation is therefore the ethical ideal and appears as such intermittently throughout the Christian tradition amidst the more common imposition of sexual codes. It is arguably inaugurated, though not invented, by the writer of John's Gospel

---

[25] Foucault [1976], *The History of Sexuality, Volume One: An Introduction*, p. 58.

[26] M. Simpson, 'Gay dream believer: inside the gay underwear cult' in *Anti-gay*, ed. M. Simpson, Cassell, London, 1996, p. 5.

[27] Foucault preferred the term *askesis* since he believed that 'asceticism' carries connotations of an imposed discipline rather than a liberative practice.

[28] Foucault, 'The battle for chastity' in this volume, p. 195.

in the story of the woman caught in adultery and Jesus's reply to her accusers that the one who is without sin should cast the first stone. In the story the accusers' confidence that they are not as her, a sexual sinner, is disturbed. To the reader of the Biblical text the story intimates that a new ethic is at work in some sense opposed to the policing of sex.

Foucault, in his own context, noted that ignoring the desexualising imperative risks missing the real potential of this ethic.

One of the concessions one makes to others is not to present homosexuality as a kind of immediate pleasure, of two young men meeting in the street, seducing each other with a look, grabbing each other's arses and getting each other off in a quarter of an hour. There you have a kind of neat image of homosexuality without any possibility of creating unease ... I think that's what makes homosexuality 'disturbing': the homosexual mode of life, much more so than the sexual act itself. Imagining a sexual act that doesn't conform to law or nature is not what disturbs people. But that individuals are beginning to love one another – there's the problem.[29]

The disturbance here is caused by friendship not sexuality.

A second important characteristic of Cassian's asceticism for Foucault focuses on the process by which the monk's will is rendered a neutral player in the battle for chastity. 'The first five stages of the advance towards chastity constitute increasingly subtle disengagements of the will from the increasingly restricted reactions that may bring on this pollution.'[30] This distinguishes Cassian's method because it seeks to move beyond the 'internalisation of a whole list of forbidden things, merely substituting the prohibition of the intention for that of the act itself'.

In the context of Foucault's work, we can see how the effort to disengage the will in Cassian is parallel to uncoupling thought about the self from forms that are derivative of the discourse of sexuality. In common with Cassian, Foucault wants to liberate the problem of pleasure from the matter of its control. To achieve this he draws a distinction between pleasure and desire: desire is already pathologised so that a declaration of one's desires is tantamount to declaring one's classification according to the science of sex.[31] Pleasure on the other hand remains undifferentiated, imposing no intrinsic limitations upon the self. The use of pleasure, as opposed to the delineation of desire, as we shall see, is crucial to the development of a Foucauldian 'way out'.

The third characteristic relates to the end to which Cassian leads the monk – deification, the putting on of a new person. This is nothing less than a genuine transformation of the self 'expelling for good everything impure or conducive to impurity'.[32] Cassian sought a community of holiness in which, through an eternal warfare waged against the Other, the power of the Enemy, who hides behind the seeming likenesses of oneself, is vanquished for ever.

It is here that the problem of 'gay culture' can be brought alongside this analysis of Christian practices. Macey notes that desexualisation was part of Foucault's vision of a 'gay culture'. He recalls that Foucault looked forward to 'a culture which invents ways

[29] Foucault [1981], 'Friendship as a way of life', in Foucault, Foucault Live, p. 309.
[30] 'The battle for chastity'. p. 194.
[31] 'Discussion with Michel Foucault': 26 April 1983, D250(9)*, Foucault Archive, Paris.
[32] 'The battle for chastity', p. 196.

of relating, types of existence, types of exchanges between individuals that are really new and are neither the same as, not superimposed on, existing cultural forms'.[33] This project is nothing to do with the liberation of an essence or the assertion of an identity. The emergence of an industry around the production of gay novels, gay painting, let alone gay philosophy, is no less than the perpetuation of the rule of sex, hiding behind seeming likenesses of oneself. Under this regime the discipline of suspicion is rejected in favour of the vacuous celebration of gayness in a perpetual cycle of 'coming out'. The creative potential of an ascetic 'way out' is reduced to the deadly dreariness of declaring a nature.

So how might 'the Enemy' be vanquished for ever? In comments on the great aesthete Oscar Wilde, Foucault recognised that such an effort had to work with strategies that were realistic. He notes how Wilde, and Gide, interiorised the notion of sexuality saying 'we are homosexual' in order that the crime of sodomy against them might be reduced to the lesser matter of a pathology. But Foucault is also careful to point out that they deploy this ideology only in order to engage in their own struggle which necessitates starting from the position to which they have been brought by others. A strategy does not succeed if it does not take account of the real situation; though it also must not be fixed at this point but constantly be ready for exits from the oppressive regimes. It was in this respect that Foucault pointed to two possibilities that he believed presented themselves as 'ways out' of sexuality: sadomasochism (S/M) and friendship – a neglected theme of Christianity.[34]

Foucault's discussion of S/M practices have been taken by some, notably James Miller, and turned into a hermeneutical lens through which the whole of Foucault's life, and more particularly his death, might be viewed. Carrette provides a detailed refutation of Miller's misguided association of S/M with mysticism, though it is worth noting why Foucault talked about S/M at all. It is important for the same reasons that friendship is important – it offered the possibility of reconceiving a 'way out' of sexuality. The theme of S/M in gay sexuality has already been usefully explored by David Halperin in his work Saint Foucault. He locates S/M within the realisation that Foucault understands sexuality 'as a device whose operation can be analyzed rather than as a thing whose nature can be known, by treating sexuality as the instrument and effect of a series of discursive and political strategies'.[35] S/M is a practice that attempts to desexualise, or at least 'degenitalise' sex by inventing new forms not focused on traditional constructions of pleasure. S/M in this sense is about experi-

[33] Macey, The Lives of Michel Foucault, p. 367.

[34] I am grateful to John Inge, who has drawn my attention to two of the classic expositions of friendship in the Christian tradition. The first is found in the writings of Ambrose who, given Foucault's study of the Greeks, interestingly drew on the work of Cicero, itself derivative of Aristotle; and, the second, in Aelred of Rievaulx, who in Spiritual Friendship wrote: 'Thus, from that holy love with which he embraces his friend, [the monk] rises to that by which he embraces Christ' (Spiritual Friendship, Cistercian Publications, Kalamazoo, Michigan, 1977, p. 45). Foucault also picks up the centrality of friendship in the Christian tradition in his work on Augustine. Augustine recalls the pain of the death of a very dear friend in his Confessions (Penguin, London, 1961, p. 75), though Foucault also notes that Augustine was troubled by his feelings for this man due to Augustine's own problem with desire ('Discussion with Michel Foucault': 15 April 1983, Tape C27*, Foucault Archive, Paris).

[35] D. Halperin, Saint Foucault: Towards a Gay Hagiography, Oxford University Press, Oxford, 1995, p. 121.

menting with relational dynamics that constantly change, notably over and against predetermined, stereotypical roles. S/M is not about the liberation of desire but about the creation of new pleasures, a polymorphous perversity whose aim is to break free of the scientific knowledge of the way to do sex. It can be viewed as an aesthetic of existence if an exotic one at that – although as has been pointed out it can easily hide the wider political dynamics of power.

It is, however, significant that Halperin's work does not develop any of Foucault's reflections on Christian texts, and this fact provides us with a point of departure. On the one hand, following Foucault's work on Cassian, the question that needs to be addressed is whether S/M is a practice that is able to expel for good the dominant discourse, no matter how sophisticated its strategic reversals, or whether the demand to constantly 'queer things up' is not a perpetuation of the cycle of 'coming out' as opposed to the genuine possibility of a 'way out' of sexuality. More generally we might now redirect Halperin's own question to ask not what have 'straight-liberal critics' missed in Foucault but what have gay activists missed in Foucault and why? The answer to these questions is to be found in Foucault's work on Christianity and the development of modes of friendship, a less sexy subject, but then that is in a way the point.

There are a number of points in Foucault's later work where he indicates the importance of friendship to his ethics of the self – the theme that pervades the second and third volumes of the *History of Sexuality*. However, Foucault addresses the question more directly in his 1981 interview 'Friendship as a way of life'.[36] In this article the contemporary phenomenon of male homosexuality is situated by Foucault within the larger quest for affective male friendships. He urges the predominantly homosexual readership to stop obstinately holding on to essentialist constructions of their sexuality and to use it instead to discover other potentialities, notably those set within rich patterns of friendship. 'Perhaps it would be better to ask oneself, "What relations, through homosexuality, can be established, invented, multiplied and modulated?" The development towards which the problem of homosexuality tends is the one of friendship.'

Homosexuality is not therefore so much a form of desire but desirable because of the relationships it might make possible. Men feel uneasy about homosexuality precisely because of an amorphous desire 'to be naked among men', that is to relate to each other without the clothing of 'institutional relations, family, profession and obligatory camaraderie'.[37] Foucault is not resorting to the old sexual discourse to uncover questionable motives in supposedly oppressed men; as he indicates: 'It's not to say: "Ah, there you have homosexuality!" I detest that kind of reasoning.' The correlation of homosexuality and this male longing is far more complex than an essentialist sexual identity. The point is developed by Michael Vasey in his book *Strangers and Friends*,[38] which he summarises as follows: 'The gay identity … emerges not only as

---

[36] *Foucault Live*, p. 308. This interview first appeared in the French magazine *Gai Pied*. It appears here in an edited form with its arguments helpfully tightened up.

[37] *Foucault Live*, p. 308.

[38] M. Vasey, *Strangers and Friends: New Exploration of Homosexuality and the Bible*, Hodder & Stoughton, London, 1995.

the way in which certain imaginatively non-conforming individuals negotiate (or are pigeonholed) by society *but also as the bearer of certain broader human intuitions that are being suppressed in the wider culture.*[39] For Foucault, in another desexualising move, the point of entering into a friendship is not to enjoy it sexually – that will happen if so desired. The challenge in this sense is to suspend the question of sex as the defining characteristic of relationships. 'We must escape and help others escape the two ready-made formulas of the pure sexual encounter and the lovers' fusion of identities.'[40]

Friendship is strategically important because it opens up new spaces for affection, tenderness, fidelity, camaraderie and companionship and so reveals the emotional emptiness of the tyranny of sexuality. Foucault illustrates how male homosexuality can be treated as an opportunity, an historic occasion to form new ways of being together. In this respect Foucault highlights the importance of relationships between men of significantly different ages. The advantage of such relationships is the heady freedom to chart new ways of relating precisely because what is normative is denied them. 'They face each other without terms of convenient words, with nothing to assure them about the meaning of the movement that carries them towards each other. They have to invent it, from A to Z, a relationship which is still formless, which is friendship.'[41] In this way friendship is politicised and might create a 'way out' through an offensive of affection. 'Institutional codes can't validate these relations with multiple intensities, variable colours, imperceptible movements and changing forms. These relations short-circuit it and introduce love where there's supposed to be only law, rule or habit.'[42]

In Foucault's interview on friendship the argument turns back on the reader when Foucault warns against 'coming out' becoming a programme that codifies relationships and prohibits inventiveness. Instead of 'coming out' Foucault suggests the term 'showing oneself' which, after the reading of the Christian texts, must be implicitly coupled to the act of renunciation, speaking of oneself only in order to find a 'way out' of one's self, the exact opposite of conformity to a predetermined way of being.[43] The trouble is that, in the rejection of asceticism because of its traditionally negative associations against pleasure, the crux of renunciation has been lost. The question is, as Foucault states, 'Can that be our problem today? We've rid ourselves of asceticism.'[44]

The Enlightenment attitude of an ethical 'way out' perhaps most fruitfully exists within a spirituality of friendship – that is, a mode of being which transforms the self through the power of the imagination.[45] Describing the ethic of friendship as a spirituality draws together both Foucault's theological analysis and the dynamic of

---

[39] M. Vasey, 'Travelling together?' in *The Way Forward?*, ed. T. Bradshaw, Hodder & Stoughton, London, 1997, p. 66 (Italics my own).

[40] *Foucault Live*, p. 310.

[41] *Foucault Live*, p. 309.

[42] *Foucault Live*, p. 309.

[43] Foucault, 'Friendship as a way of life', p. 312. For the relation of 'showing oneself' and Christianity see Foucault, 'About the beginning of the hermeneutics of the self' in this volume, pp. 171–2; 173.

[44] *Foucault Live*, p. 310.

[45] This in some way rescues Foucault's early work on the imagination and the body discussed by Carrette in his introductory essay above.

transcendence which is suggested by his conception of relationships attained by creativity, even inspiration.[46] The ascetic imperative is to give up for good the safe confinement of the sexual self, in order that affective friendship might, as Oliver O'Donovan put it, liberate 'the energies evoked by sexual imagery for transference to the higher cultural, moral and spiritual goods, commuting the yearnings of the body into the heroism of the soul and the visionary rapture of the spirit'.[47] It is not enough simply to reverse discourses, to overcome rulers with their own rules, to pervert them and invert their meaning, as Foucault had previously advised.[48] What is sought is a 'way out' that invents, not discovers, 'a manner of being that is still improbable.'[49]

The 'post-Christian' Foucault assembled here by Carrette from the fragments of the last years of his life and work presents Foucault scholarship with a new set of challenges. I have attempted to sketch only one possible outline in the attempt to open a new dialogue with this forgotten dimension of Foucault's work. The late Foucault highlights the grip upon men of the dominant modes of sexuality that have such a powerful and constraining hold on the imagination. Even for gay men when the comforts of 'coming out' have been renounced, a huge struggle remains in the attempt to move beyond this threshold towards a new ethos. 'To be "gay"', as Foucault states, 'is not to identify with the psychological traits and the visible marks of the homosexual, but to try and to define and develop a way of life.'[50] His work on early Christian literature presents a new call to seize the historic occasion of male homosexuality and work at a spirituality of friendship.

Foucault leaves the task of finding a 'way out' not only to this constituency but to all who experience the tyranny of sexuality and the pressure to 'come out'. 'I do not know whether we will ever achieve mature adulthood', Foucault ponders at the end of his essay on Enlightenment.[51] But who knows what freedoms may emerge from the practice of such an ethic which, nurtured in the possibilities of erotic transcendence and liberated from sexuality, loves and allows others to love?

---

[46] 'Love', as Wilde said, 'is fed by the imagination, by which we become wiser than we know, better than we feel, nobler than we are' (Wilde, De Profundis, Penguin, London, 1976, p. 126).

[47] O. O'Donovan, 'Homosexuality in the church: can there be a fruitful debate?' in The Way Forward?, ed. T. Bradshaw, Hodder & Stoughton, London, 1997, p. 35.

[48] Foucault [1971], 'Nietzsche, genealogy, history' in Language, Counter-memory, Practice, ed. Donald F. Bouchard, Cornell University Press, Ithaca, 1980, p. 151.

[49] Foucault Live, p. 310.

[50] Foucault Live, p. 310.

[51] Foucault [1984], 'What is Enlightenment?', p. 4.

James Bernauer SJ is Professor of Philosophy at Boston College, Massachusetts, USA. He has written numerous articles on Foucault and is the author of *Michel Foucault's Force of Flight: Towards an Ethics for Thought* (Humanities Press, New Jersey, 1990).

Mark Blasius is Professor of Political Science at the City University of New York (La Guardia and Graduate School), USA. He has written and edited numerous pieces on gay and lesbian politics and is the author of *Gay and Lesbian Politics: Sexuality and the Emergence of a New Ethic* (Temple University Press, Philadelphia, 1994).

Donald F. Bouchard and Sherry Simon translated the texts for *Language, Counter-Memory and Practice* (Cornell University Press, Ithaca, New York, 1977). I am grateful to Cornell University Press for use of their work.

Lucille Cairns is Lecturer in French at the University of Stirling, UK. She is the author of *Marie Cardinal: Motherhood and Creativity* (Glasgow University, 1992) and *Privileged Pariahdom: Homosexuality in the Novels of Dominique Fernandez* (Peter Lang, 1996). She is currently preparing a book on lesbianism in post-1968 French literature.

Jeremy R. Carrette is Lecturer in Religious Studies at the University of Stirling, UK. He teaches in the areas of the psychology of religion and critical theory and religion. He is also author of *Foucault and Religion* (Routledge, London and New York, 2000).

Elizabeth Ezra teaches cultural studies in the French department at the University of Stirling, UK; she is the author of a book on French colonial culture and a study of the films of Georges Méliès.

Anthony Forster translated the 'The battle of chastity', which originally appeared in *Western Sexuality* (Basil Blackwell, Oxford, 1985). I am grateful to Basil Blackwell for permission to use his work.

Thomas Keenan teaches literary and political theory, and media studies, in the Comparative Literature Department at SUNY Binghamton, USA. He is the author of *Fables of Responsibility* (Stanford University Press, Stanford, 1997).

Richard A. Lynch is a doctoral candidate in philosophy at Boston College, Massachusetts, USA. His dissertation is on Foucauldian ethics.

Stephen Sartarelli is Visiting Professor of Italian, in the Division of Languages and Literature, Bard College, Annandale-on-Hudson, New York State, USA. He jointly translated, with Sophie Hawkes, Pierre Klossowski's *The Baphomet* (Eridanos Press, Hygienne, Colorado, 1988).

Richard Townsend lives and works in Dorset, England. He previously taught in France for many years. He plays the melodion in his spare time.

Mark Vernon is a freelance journalist based in London. He writes on a range of subjects, including gay issues. He used to be a priest in the Church of England and carried out research into Foucault, Christianity and gay identity at Durham University.

Note: 'n' after a page reference indicates a note number on that page.

Sprenger, J. 51–2
standpoint theory 12
Strenski, I. 4 n10
structuralism 89, 91, 93, 160
   see also post–structuralism
subjectivity 133, 158–63, 165, 169
   n26, 177 n44, 196
   see also philosophy
surrealism 20, 31, 72–3

Tatchell, P. 201
Teresa of Avila 112
Tertullian 2, 43, 45, 171–2, 173,
   173 n35, 195–6
theology 1–7, 15, 19–21, 30, 32, 37
   see also negative theology
Thomas Aquinas, St 146
Townsend, R. 25 n120, 50, 106, 154
transgression 19, 22, 27–9, 34, 50, 56,
   57–71, 73, 82, 83, 144
truth 64, 133, 158, 161 n4, 164, 165,
   167, 168, 168 n22, 169, 170,

172, 173, 176, 177 n44, 178,
179, 180, 180 n50, 196, 203
Turner, B. 3 n10
Turquet de Mayenne, L. 148–9

Vasey, M. 207
Vernon, M. 12, 199
Veyne, P. 120–1
Vio, T. de 154
Voeltzel, T. 15, 39, 106–9

Welch, S. 3 n10
Wier, J. 51
Wilde, O. 206
Willbrandt, J. P. 150
witch 50–4

Yount, M. 4 n10

Zen xi, 15, 39, 40, 110–14
   see also Buddhism